Law of Adverse Possession

An Anglo-Nigerian Perspective

By

Prof. Imran Smith, PhD.

Law of Adverse Possession: An Anglo-Nigerian Perspective

By Prof. Imran Smith, PhD.

This book first published 2022

Ethics International Press Ltd, UK

British Library Cataloguing in Publication Data

A catalogue record for this book is available from the British Library

Print Book ISBN: 978-1-871891-43-0

eBook ISBN: 978-1-871891-44-7

CONTENT

PREFACE

This book engages a comprehensive discourse of the Law of Adverse Possession from the Anglo-Nigerian perspective. Whilst the pre-colonial geographical entity which later became known as Nigeria had both the customary and Islamic systems of land tenure in place before the British rule, the ensuing colonial administration facilitated the reception of English law which introduced the English land tenure system including the doctrine of adverse possession into Nigeria, subject to local circumstances and local legislation.

Consequently, a plural system of land tenure emerged with an attempt by the Land Use Act enacted in 1978 to consolidate them and streamline the system of landholding in the country. This historical background informed this comparative study of the application of the doctrine of adverse possession in its pristine form under English law (applicable in England and Wales), and its application in Nigeria - a country driven by a plural legal system.

Amongst other areas of engagement, the book discusses the theoretical foundation and analyses the rationale underlying the application of the doctrine of adverse possession under Anglo-Nigerian Law. It also delves into a robust doctrinal analysis of the application of the doctrine in both jurisdictions including the impact of the global human rights regime and the criminalisation policy of the State on the doctrine. This book would, therefore, appeal to both the English and Nigerian readers including students, academics, professionals and researchers.

This book offers a different approach to the application of the doctrine in many respects: First, in terms of engaging a comparative study of the application of the doctrine in England and Wales on the one hand, and Nigeria on the other hand, it is the first of its kind. Second, it goes beyond a mere doctrinal study of the subject as it is the case with existing literature, and focuses also on the application of the doctrine within the peculiar legal and social contexts of the two jurisdictions. Third, it takes a global view of minor interests in property against the backdrop of individual and common property rights to housing, and the expected role of the State in harmonising various property rights. Fourth, unlike the existing literature on the subject, it challenges the State perception of property right in the contemporary world and faults the punitive and retributive stance of the state in criminalising adverse possession in certain instances. Finally, it identifies lapses in the application and enforcement of interests under the doctrine in both jurisdictions and proffers enduring solutions.

It is therefore a book meant for students/researchers in the field; a hand book for legal practitioners in finding the law; a useful guide for the court in the dispensation of justice; and a pilot for the State in managing property relations-all in one.

Imran Oluwole Smith, SAN
Professor of Law, University of Lagos-Nigeria,
Professorial Research Associate, SOAS, University of London.

TABLE OF CASES

A

B

C

D

E

F

G

H

I

J

K

L

M

N

O

P

R

S

T

U

W

Y

Z

TABLE OF STATUTES

ENGLISH LOCAL STATUTES (APPLICABLE IN ENGLAND AND WALES)

LEGISLATION IN CIVIL LAW COUNTRIES

OTHER FOREIGN CONSTITUTION/STATUTE

COLONY OF LAGOS

FEDERAL STATUTES

REGIONAL LAWS

NORTHERN NIGERIA

WESTERN NIGERIA

STATE LAWS IN NIGERIA

ANAMBRA STATE

KANO STATE

KATSINA STATE

LAGOS STATE

NIGER STATE

INTERNATIONAL CONVENTIONS

LIST OF ABBREVIATIONS

A.C.	Appeal Cases (Third Series)
A.C.H.P.R.	African Charter on Human and People's Rights
All E.R.	All England Reports
All N.L.R.	All Nigerian Law Reports
App. Cas	Appeal Cases (Second Series)
A.U.	African Union
Bing N.C.	Bingham's New Cases
Bos. & P.	Bosanquet and Puller's Reports
C.A.	Court of Appeal
Ch.	Chapter
Ch.	Chancery Reports
Ch.	D Chancery Division
Chi.L.Rev.	Chicago Law Review
Civ.	Civil Division
C.J.	Chief Justice
C.J.N.	Chief Justice of Nigeria
C.L.R.	Commercial Law Reports
CLR	Commonwealth Law Reports
Cowp.	Cowper's Reports
D.E.T.R.	Department of the Environment, Transport, and the Region
D.L.R.	Dominion Law Reports
Dru.& War.	Drury & Warren's Report

Ed.	Edition or Edited
E.C.H.R.	European Convention on Human Rights
ECtHR	European Court of Human Rights
E.G.L.R.	Estates Gazette Law Reports
E.H.R.R.	European Human Rights Reports
E.R.	Exchequer Reports
E.R.	English Reports
E.T.S.	European Treaty Series
E.U.	European Union
E.W.H.C.	England and Wales High Court
E.W.C.A.	England and Wales Court of Appeal
Ex.D.	Exchequer Division
Ed.	Edition
F.C.T.	Federal Capital Territory
F.S.C.	Federal Supreme Court
F.W.L.R.	Federation Weekly Law Reports
Gev. LJ	Georgia Law Journal
Har. L. Rev.	Harvard Law Review
H.L.C.	House of Lords Cases
H.L.	House of Lords
H.M.	Her Majesty
H.R.A.	Human Rights Act
Ir. Eq. Rep.	Irish Equity Reports

J.C.A.	Justice of the Court of Appeal
J.S.C.	Justice of the Supreme Court
K.B.	King's Bench
LTD.	Limited
L & T	Law of Landlord and Tenant
LASPO Act	Legal Aid Sentencing and Punishment of Offenders Act
L.D.	Legislative Division
L.F.N.	Laws of the Federation of Nigeria
L.J.	Law Justice of Appeal
L.L.R.	High Court of Lagos Law Reports (Nigeria)
L.P.A.	Law of Property Act
L.Q.R.	Law Quarterly Review
L.R.	Law Reports
L.R.A.	Land Registration Act
L.R.L.	Land Instrument Registration Law of Lagos State
L.R.P.G.	Land Registry Practice Guide
L.T.	Law Times Reports
L.U.A.	Land Use Act
M & W	Meeson & Welshy's Reports
Mi.L.R.	Miami University Law Review
M.P.	Member of Parliament
Nig.	Nigeria

Nw. U. L.R.	New York University Law Review
N.L.J.	Nigerian Law Journal
N.L.R.	Nigerian Law Reports
N.M.L.R.	Nigerian Monthly Law Review
N.N.L.R.	Northern Nigeria Law Review
N.S.C.C.	Nigerian Supreme Court Cases
N.S.W.	New South Wales
N.W.L.R.	Nigerian Weekly Law Reports
OAU	Organization of African Unity
Para.	Paragraph
Pt.	Part
P & CR	Planning (Property) and Compensation Reports
P.C.	Judicial Committee of the Privy Council
Ph.D	Doctor of Philosophy
Q.B.	Queen's Bench
Q.U.T.	Queensland University of Technology
R.T.A.	Registration of Titles Act
S.C.	Supreme Court
S.R.	State Reports
Taunt.	Taunto's Reports
T.B.E.	Tropical Built Environment Journal
U.B.H.L.	University of Botswana Law Journal
U.N.T.S.	United Nations Treaty Series

U.K.	United Kingdom
U.K.H.L.	United Kingdom House of Lords
U.K.S.C.	United Kingdom Supreme Court
Vol.	Volume
V.S.C.	Victoria Supreme Court
W.A.C.A.	West Africa Court of Appeal
Wash C.A.	Washington's Court of Appeal
W.L.R.	Weekly Law Reports
W.R.	Weekly Reports

CHAPTER 1
GENERAL INTRODUCTION

1.0 A Digest of the Book

This book engages a study of the English doctrine of adverse possession in relation to land[1] as applied by the Nigerian courts, against the backdrop of different legal frameworks, the peculiarities of existing local circumstances and the plural land tenure system, subject to the Land Use Act. The thrust of the book is basically and particularly doctrinal and meant to ascertain the relevance and effectiveness of the doctrine within the context of Nigerian law.

Although Nigeria statutorily received the English law comprising of the common law,[2] equity and English statutes of general application[3] consequent upon almost a century of British rule,[4] the imperial law was made subject to local circumstances, and local statutes for the time being

---

[1] Adverse possession in relation to chattels is beyond the scope of this book.

[2] The English common law is that part of the law of England that was formulated, developed and administered by the old common law courts of King's (or Queen's) Bench, Court of Common Pleas and Court of Exchequer.

[3] These were statutes in force in England on the 1st of January 1900 applicable to any civil or criminal court and to all classes or all members of any particular class of people. However, in the old Western Region of Nigeria now Ogun, Oyo, Osun, Ondo, Ekiti, Edo and Delta States of Nigeria, the enactment of the Laws of England (Application) Law Cap 60 Laws of Western Nigeria 1959 limiting applicable English statutes of general application to those incorporated as within the legislative competence of the Region and prohibiting further enforcement of all "Imperial Acts hitherto in force within the Region." (s.4 of the Law). See generally, JO Asein *Introduction to Nigerian Legal System* 2nd ed. 2005 Ababa Press Ltd, Lagos-Nigeria, 101-113.

[4] The British colonial rule in Nigeria took effect from the signing of the Treaty of Cession in 1861 by King Dosumu of Lagos up until 1960 when Nigeria became an independent country. For the Reception statutes, see the Law (Miscellaneous Provisions) Act Cap 89 Laws of Nigeria 1958, s.45; The Interpretation Act Cap 132 Laws of the Federation of Nigeria, 2004, s.32; and the High Court Laws of the various States in Nigeria.

in force.[5] It follows therefore that the application of the English common law and by implication, the English land tenure system, the doctrines of equity, and statutes of general application including the English statutes of limitations that were in force in England on January 1 1900 were made applicable in Nigeria.[6]

However, there were indigenous laws and institutions[7] including the indigenous land tenure systems[8] already in place before the advent of colonial rule, and consequently operating parallel to the English system of land tenure. This interaction between the English and the Nigerian land tenure systems and the enactment of the Land Use Act in Nigeria in 1978 (an Act meant to harmonise them), form the *corpus juris* of what is known today as the Nigerian land law.

1.1 What is Adverse Possession?

'Adverse possession' is defined as:

> ...the process by which a person can acquire title to someone else's land by continuously possessing it [with the requisite intention and without the consent of the owner] for a set limitation period, in circumstances where the owner either has, or is deemed to have the right to recover the land.[9]

---

[5] Law (Miscellaneous Provisions) Act (n 4), s.45(2); The Interpretation Act (n.4), s.32(2).

[6] ibid (n.5), s.45(1), and s.32(1) respectively.

[7] The High Court Laws of the various States within the Federation of Nigeria contain provisions on the application of customary law in Nigeria. See e.g. the High Court Law of Lagos State Cap H3 2003, s.26; and section 28 of the High Court Law applicable in the Northern states of Nigeria.

[8] *AmoduTijani v Secretary Southern Nigeria* (1921) AC 399.

[9] S Jourdan and O Radley-Gardner, *Adverse Possession,* 2nd ed. Bloomsbury Professional Limited 2011, West Sussex, England – U.K. at 3.

In *Adedeji v. Oloso,*[10] the Supreme Court of Nigeria describes adverse possession as one which derogates from and is inconsistent with the ownership title of a person who claims to be the true owner of the land. Failure of the owner to take legal steps to recover the land within the period set by the statute of limitations extinguishes his title in favour of the adverse possessor in the case of unregistered title, and in the case of registered title, entitles the adverse possessor to be registered as the new registered proprietor in place of the previous registered proprietor.[11] The set limitation period and the circumstances under which adverse possession may arise vary as between jurisdictions.[12]

Whilst a squatter in occupation of abandoned land may qualify as an adverse possessor in circumstances cognizable at common law,[13] adverse possession may also arise in other cases.[14] Many cases of adverse possession take place by way of encroachment upon neighboring land either intentionally or inadvertently.[15] It may arise from situations in which a formal relationship earlier existed between parties at common

[10] (2007) 5 NWLR (Pt 1026) 133.

[11] ibid at 4.

[12] For a detailed comparative study in this regard, see the *Report of the British Institute of International and Comparative Law for Her Majesty's Court Service,* September 2016, available online at https://www.biicl.org/files/2350_advposs_sept_ftnsv3.pdf. Accessed on October 3, 2019.

[13] See *Ellis v. Lamberth LBC* (1999) 32 HLR 596; *JA Pye (Oxford) Ltd v. Graham* [2003] 1 AC 419; *Bello Salami & Anor v. Adetoro Lawal* (2008) 6-7 SC (Pt II) 242.

[14] It is said that: "The typology of adverse possession is richly varied and it is likely that consciously wrongful seizure of land nowadays constitutes its least common form. Adverse possession rules are rather more frequently invoked to resolve ownership disputes which originate either in relatively innocent circumstances of entry under colour of title or in defective conveyancing practice…The areas of land involved in contemporary claims of long possession are rarely large tracts of uncharted wilderness": K Gray & SF Gray, *Elements of Land Law* 5th ed. (2009) OUP 1165, 9.1.13.

[15] *Bridges v. Mees* (1957) Ch 457; *Prudential Assurance Co. Ltd v. Waterloo Real Estate Inc.* [1999] 2 EGLR. 85.

law but not anymore, such as where a former contractual tenant,[16] licensee[17] or mortgagee[18] holds land adversely to the interest of the landlord, licensor or mortgagor respectively. Also a purchaser of land who enters into possession under an incomplete contract of sale or at a time that the transfer of title by the vendor is incomplete may end up being an adverse possessor throughout the limitation period and may be entitled to claim a transfer of title to him.[19] In all these situations, possession must fulfill all the conditions laid down at common law,[20] and must have been enjoyed by the adverse possessor continuously for a sufficient period of time prescribed by the statute of limitation.

In many common law jurisdictions including Nigeria, one of the potent ways of acquiring or proving title is through acts of possession with *animus possidendi* (that is, the intention to possess) over a long period of time.[21] This not only forms the basis of action by the 'real' owner against squatters and trespassers in particular, but has been recognised in law generally as justification for the claim in adverse possession by such squatters and trespassers, and as a defence in an action for declaration of title by the 'real' owner under a system of unregistered conveyancing.[22]

---

[16] A typical example is a tenant at sufferance at common law where time begins to run from the commencement of the tenancy. "This is because a tenancy at sufferance is really not a tenancy at all, but is adverse possession": C Harpum et. al, *The Law of Real Property* 8th ed., Sweet and Maxwell (2012) 1474 , 35-032. For a discourse on whether this position applies to a statutory tenant in Nigeria, see Chapter 5 *infra.*

[17] A licensee whose license is revoked by the licensor becomes a trespasser at common law and time ipso facto runs in his favour. For a discourse on whether this position applies in Nigeria where such erstwhile licensee may qualify as a statutory tenant in Nigeria, see Chapter 5 *infra.*

[18] *Young v. Clarey* [1948] Ch. 191.

[19] *Belotti v. Bickhardt* 127 NE 239at 243-244 (1920); *Kohua Pty Ltd v. Tai Ping trading Pty Ltd* (1985) 3 BPR 9705 at 9707.

[20] See Chapter 5 *infra.*

[21] See *Pye (Oxford) Ltd &Ors v Graham &Anor*[2002] UKHL 30 at 41, 43, 70 76; *Buraimoh v Bamgbose*(1989) 3 NWLR (Pt 109) 352 at 355.

[22] *Oyebamiji v Lawanson* (2008) 15 NWLR (Pt 1109) 122, *Duzu v Yunusa* (2010) 10 NWLR (Pt 1201) 80

Sequel to putting in place a system of title registration in some of the common law jurisdictions,[23] it may be necessary for the adverse possessor to register his or her title thereby defeating the interest of the pre-existing registered owner.

The claim of the adverse possessor at common law has been bolstered up by the statutes of limitation put in place in different jurisdictions stipulating the period within which the 'real' owner is expected to bring an action in court against the adverse possessor for declaration of title, or have his or her title extinguished in favour of the adverse possessor after the time prescribed by law. Thus, a valid adverse possession claim under Anglo-Nigerian law is dependent on meeting the legal requirements for adverse possession at common law coupled with the lapse of time under the relevant limitation statute.

1.2 Nature of Anglo-Nigerian Law of Adverse Possession

The Anglo-Nigerian law of adverse possession is a product of a divergent system of land tenure applicable in England and Nigeria.[24] Whilst the English land law and relevant statutes[25] apply in England and Wales in a uniform manner within a monolithic legal system, Nigerian land tenure system is an amalgam of both the English and the indigenous systems of land tenure operating side by side within a plural legal system, but

---

[23] See for example, the Land Registration Act, 2002 applicable in England and Wales, and the Land Registration Law of Lagos State Nigeria, 2015.

[24] While both jurisdictions are known to have the common law tradition which recognises the rule of adverse possession, Nigeria, unlike England and Wales, operates a plural legal system consisting of customary law and Islamic law in addition to the English common law, while the Nigerian Land Use Act enacted in 1978, harmonises these systems and streamlines landholding in accordance with its provisions.

[25] Such statutes include the Limitation Act, 1980; and the Land Registration Act Cap 9 2002

subject to the Nigerian Land Use Act,[26] which is the principal legislation regulating title to land.

Thus, while the English common law doctrine of adverse possession is applicable in both the English and Welsh jurisdiction as well as in the Nigerian jurisdictions, the indigenous land tenure systems in Nigeria and the Land Use Act are systems unknown to England and Wales. The essence of this book therefore, is to demonstrate the application of the doctrine of adverse possession under diverse considerations as dictated by the peculiar circumstances of the different land tenure systems, and to show that whilst the doctrine may generally be of universal application in both the common law and civil law jurisdictions,[27] its application as a means of acquiring title to land varies.[28]

While England and Wales have a uniform legislation on limitation of actions and land registration (both having a bearing on application of the doctrine of adverse possession), in Nigeria, the content of the legislation on land registration vary as to whether registration pertains to land instrument or land title – a difference unknown to English law. Consequently, while the law on limitation of actions is generally the same across the component states within the Nigerian federation, registration law varies as between Lagos State and the Federal Capital Territory on the one hand, and the other states of the federation on the other hand.[29]

---

[26] Cap L5 Laws of the Federation of Nigeria, 2010.

[27] See the *Report of the British Institute,* supra (n 12).

[28] For example, apart from the fact that the period after which the 'real' owner may no longer bring an action to repossess his land varies across jurisdictions, the effect of proof of good faith or lack of it on the part of the adverse possessor may determine the Limitation period. Also, the question whether the land is registered or not may determine the application or otherwise of the rule of adverse possession: See the *Report of the British Institute,* supra (n 12).

[29] While Lagos State and the FCT have a Law on title registration, other states have the Land Instrument Registration Laws in place.

1.3 Scope of the Book

This book engages the question whether the Nigerian land tenure system can accommodate the application of the doctrine of adverse possession as known to England and Wales, in view of the Land Use Act and other municipal laws in place. It examines the efficiency or otherwise of the Land Registration Law of Lagos State of Nigeria 2015 which, unlike the Land Registration Act (LRA) 2002 applicable in England and Wales, allows the adverse possessor to register legal title without giving the owner the opportunity to object.

Whilst a combination of the common law and the Limitation Laws applicable in England and Nigeria appears to automatically extinguish the title of the owner in favour of the adverse possessor after 12 years of adverse possession in the case of the individual and 20 years in the case of the State, section 48 of the Nigerian Land Use Act makes the doctrine of adverse possession applicable in Nigeria subject to the provisions of the Act. Under the Land Use Act, no title is acquired except by grant - actual or deemed; or by way of formal alienation with the consent of the Governor or the Local Government. Any other form of acquisition of title is subject to the provisions of the Act. Under this dispensation, it is necessary to examine the efficacy of the doctrine in Nigeria.

This book discusses the historical credentials of the doctrine of adverse possession at common law as a fall out of the English doctrine of *seisin*,[30] the applicability of the doctrine under Nigerian customary and Islamic law of land tenure and the legitimacy or otherwise of the retention of the doctrine under the Nigerian land tenure system following the advent of the Nigerian Land Use Act.[31] The book also examines the effect of adverse possession under the land registration regime in England and Nigeria.[32]

---

[30] 'Seisin' refers to the measure of interest in land under English law.

[31] Land Use Act 1978 Cap L5 Laws of the Federation of Nigeria, 2010.

[32] The land registration regime in Nigeria consists of the Land Instruments Registration Law applicable in the federating states except in Lagos state where

The question whether the doctrine is subject to human rights challenge under Nigerian law is engaged against the backdrop of the extant legal and Constitutional regimes, and in light of applicable international instruments. The thorny issue of criminalisation of peaceful entry and peaceable possession in Nigeria is examined with emphasis on specific Laws passed by the legislature in Nigeria.[33]

In undertaking a discourse of the Anglo-Nigerian doctrine of adverse possession, this book covers the following questions:

1. Whether the application of the doctrine of adverse possession under a unified system of land tenure applicable in England and Wales the same in content and effect under the Nigerian plural system of land tenure harmonised by the Land Use Act?
2. With the advent of the Nigerian Land Use Act, has there been a radical departure from the English model of adverse possession as a mode of acquiring title to land in Nigeria?
3. Whether the land registration regime under the Anglo-Nigerian law has rendered the doctrine of adverse possession impotent in content and effect?
4. Whether the doctrine of adverse possession is challenged under the Anglo-Nigerian law by both the local and international legal regimes on the sanctity of right to property and the entrenched right to compensation upon violation?
5. Whether the criminalisation of peaceful entry and peaceable possession by an adverse possessor under the Anglo-Nigerian law has defeated the efficacy of adverse possession as a mode of acquisition of title to land?

---

the Lands Registration Law applies, and in the Federal Capital Territory where the Registration of Titles Act applies.

[33] See for example, ss. 81, 82 of the Criminal Code Act Cap C42 Laws of the Federation of Nigeria 2004; s.279(2) of the Criminal Law of Lagos state 2011 and Lagos State Property Protection Law, 2016.

In engaging these questions, this book explores the principles of common law, customary and Islamic law relating to adverse possession; pieces of legislation applicable in relation to the content and application of the doctrine of adverse possession under English and Nigerian law, the Limitation Laws, and the Land Registration Laws. Also discussed are the human rights provisions in the European Convention on Human Rights domesticated as the Human Rights Act applicable in England and Wales, the Constitution of the Federal Republic of Nigeria 1999 and the provisions of the African Charter on Human and Peoples' Rights domesticated as such in Nigeria, as well as case law generally emanating from within and outside Nigeria.

From the perspective of a comparative study of the doctrine of adverse possession in England and Wales, and in Nigeria, the work deduced various evolutionary changes in the functionality and efficacy of the rule of adverse possession as a mode of acquisition and enjoyment of land titles within social contexts.

However, while the main thrust of this book is strictly doctrinal and comparative, it incorporates a discussion of the wider developments in the allied areas of squatting, eviction, homelessness and state responsibility in the human rights domain. The essence is to further appreciate the application of the doctrine of adverse possession within social contexts and against the backdrop of the human rights provisions in the constitutions of some jurisdictions such as South Africa, and Brazil.

In attempting a comparative study of the application of the doctrine of adverse possession under English and Nigerian law, this work identifies with and adopts the most recent methodology on comparative studies. Tourkochoriti, in her essay on Law and Methodology[34] identifies three main approaches in this regard, pointing out that 'the methods that

---

[34] I. Toukochoriti, 'Comparative Rights Jurisprudence: An Essay on Methodologies.' Special Issue-Comparative Law LaM November 2017, DOI: 10.5553/REM/.000030. Although the article dealt specifically with comparative rights jurisprudence, it is a useful guide on methodologies on comparative study generally.

can be helpful to a comparative legal research depend on the research question and the goal of the researcher.'[35] According to her, there is first the interdisciplinary approach which focuses on the socio-political context of discourse, enabling the researcher to understand the social basis for differences;[36] second, there is the normative enterprise approach in which the 'legal similarities or differences under comparison would provide inspiration for theoretical arguments for and against a solution in one area or another;'[37] and third, an amalgam of the two approaches earlier mentioned. In the case of the third approach, the aim could be to challenge 'the socio-political frame that led to the emergence of legal rules,'[38] where injustice or other iniquities could result from the application of the rules in concrete cases; it could be aimed at reaching 'a reflective equilibrium 'between the *is* and the *ought* – a back and forth movement from the formation and operation of the rules in their context to a normative principle as to how they should be operating and the other way round.'[39]

The foregoing approaches amount to the jurisprudential rule of law either as a product of social factors (the first approach); or as an instrument of social dynamics the second approach); or as an amalgam of the two. This work adopts the third approach in which the essence of law in the social context could explain the peculiarities in the application of the doctrine of adverse possession, and in determining its efficacy as a mode of acquisition of title under English and Nigerian law. Consequently, whilst for example, the peculiar socio-political dynamics of each jurisdiction under study could explain the social underpinnings of the application of the doctrine of adverse possession in those jurisdictions, the way in which the extant laws tend to harmonise its operation in light of land rights and other legal considerations, provides a stimulus for a case study in applied legal philosophy in re-conceptualising the operation

[35] ibid.

[36] ibid.

[37] ibid.

[38] ibid.

[39] íbid.

of the doctrine of adverse possession towards law reform. Thus this book analyses the content and application of the rule of adverse possession in England and Nigeria and assesses how the relevant concepts of land use, control and management impact on the application of the doctrine.

1.4 Summary of Chapters

Apart from this chapter which is a general overview, Chapter 2 discusses the historical evolution of the doctrine from remote antiquity through its development at common law. It examines its nexus with the limitation statutes at different times, its content and scope, and its application to registered and unregistered land. An x-ray of the development of limitations statutes and impact on the operation of the doctrine are critical in appreciating the nature, scope and limitations of the doctrine.

Chapter 3 discusses the theoretical foundation for the work by taking a general overview of the traditional theories of the doctrine of adverse possession as a mode of acquisition of title to real property, and also as indicators of justification for sustainability of the doctrine. A critical evaluation of the theories reveals not only the pitfalls in them but also, and in particular, the gaps in them in relation to relativity and relevance of the doctrine under different legal backgrounds necessitating an engagement with such modern theories such as the *relativity theory,* the *grant theory,* the *'vulnerability theory'*, the *'indefeasibility theory,'* and the *'incompatibility theory'*. These modern theories lay a foundation for the discourse in this book.

Chapter 4 focuses on the rationale behind the application of the doctrine. Many of the arguments for and against the relevance of its application in modern times revolve around a consideration of the rationale behind the doctrine and have been explored by the courts in its application. The rationale underlying the application of the doctrine has guided the courts in England and Nigeria in resolving cases bordering on alleged violation of human rights and in defending the application of the doctrine despite the act of the State in criminalizing entry into residential premises.

Chapter 5 deals with the doctrinal analysis of adverse possession under the Anglo-Nigerian law. The chapter deals robustly with the dichotomy between adverse possession and allied concepts in property law; the elements of adverse possession; specific cases of application of the doctrine; the effect of time running and circumstances under which time would not run.

Chapter 6 discusses the application of the doctrine under the Nigerian plural land tenure system harmonized by the Land Use Act. It examines the applicability of the doctrine under the customary and Islamic law of land tenure and its compatibility with the provisions of the Land Use Act 1978 – the principal legislation harmonizing the land tenure systems in Nigeria. Its impact on the dual systems of land registration applicable in Nigeria, and its effect on the system of unregistered land are engaged.

Chapter 7 deals with the application of the doctrine of adverse possession under the Land Registration regime. It examines the English Land Registration Act 2002, the land registration regime in Nigeria and the limitations in its application where no distinction is discernible between the application of the doctrine under both registered and unregistered land.

Chapter 8 examines the question whether the application of the doctrine is subject to human rights challenge. The position in England as encapsulated in the *Pye* Case, the rationale for the decision of the Grand Chamber in that case, and the effect of the European Court of Human Rights in *Pye* are discussed. From the Nigerian perspective, the relevant provisions of the Nigerian Constitution, the African Charter on Human and Peoples' Rights, and the effect of these instruments on the application of the doctrine are analysed and discussed.

Chapter 9 deals with squatter's right against eviction, the position of English law from the trespass paradigm to Human Rights paradigm; informal settlements in Nigeria and the role of the courts. The lessons from the Republic of South Africa and Brazil are also explored.

Chapter 10 deals with criminalization of illegal occupation of land and adverse possession. From the standpoint of the English position, the provision of section 144 of the Legal Aid Sentencing and Punishment of Offenders Act, and the regime of adverse possession as interpreted by the English Court of Appeal in *Best v. Chief Registrar and Secretary of State for Justice* are discussed. The Chapter delves into the background to the Nigerian position on the criminalization of illegal occupation, and the effects of the criminal law jurisprudence in that jurisdiction on the regime of adverse possession.

Chapter 11 juxtaposes the application of the doctrine of adverse possession under English and Nigerian law. It commences with a comparative analysis of the different land ownership structures existing in both jurisdictions and the dichotomy in the land rights that may be acquired in these jurisdictions, which underpins the variation in the applicability of the doctrine. The Chapter engages a comparative analysis of the effect of the peculiar local circumstances on ground in the jurisdictions under study, and impact of the diversity of the land tenure systems on the doctrine of adverse possession. It addresses the application of the doctrine under different registration systems; and the question whether the doctrine is susceptible to human rights challenge from a comparative perspective. It also compares the criminalization policies in the different jurisdictions, in determining the effect on the application of the doctrine. From a comparative perspective, the responses or otherwise of the two jurisdictions to the constitutional and human rights developments regarding forceful evictions, and the state responsibility towards the homeless, are discussed. In engaging the comparative study, issues are classified and dealt with, each with a summary at the end.

Chapter 12 explores the future of the doctrine in England and Nigeria. It focuses on the trend in many common law jurisdictions in view of certain legal parameters trailing the effective application of the doctrine. The possibility or otherwise of continued survival of the doctrine in the face of effective equitable remedies and in-built mechanisms for tackling issue of stale claims are discussed.

It also outlines various recommendations for reforms and draws conclusions from the discourse in earlier Chapters accordingly. Recommendations proffered ranges from a general re-think of the doctrine of adverse possession and its application under diverse legal systems and peculiar social circumstances prevailing at any time, to an appraisal of major determinants for its just application. Suggestions are also made against the backdrop of the constitutional and human rights development in some jurisdictions.

A pioneering work on a comparative study of the application of the doctrine of adverse possession under English and Nigerian law, the book demonstrates the limitations facing the application of the doctrine as a result of the variations in social circumstances, the diversity in the legal and institutional frameworks between the English and Nigerian jurisdictions, and the differences in state policies formulated against the backdrop of peculiar challenges facing acquisition of title to land by adverse possession. This book identifies the pitfalls in the application of the doctrine in diverse circumstances and makes recommendations as appropriate.

On the whole, the work provides a veritable window for subsequent researchers in this area of study to appreciate the fact that whilst the doctrine may be universally recognized in the common law and civil law jurisdictions, the historical and social antecedents of their land tenure systems and the peculiarities of the state land policies may streamline the application of the doctrine.

CHAPTER 2
HISTORICAL BACKGROUND

2.1 Origin in Remote Antiquity

The origin of adverse possession could be traced to remote antiquity. As far back as 2000 BC, King Hammurabi of Babylon, Mesopotamia laid out one of the first set of laws.[1] Law 30 of the code provides:

> "If a chieftain or a man leaves his house, garden and field…and someone else takes possession of his house, garden, or field and uses it for three years: if the first owner returns and claims this house, garden, and field, it shall not be given to him, but he who has taken possession of it and used it shall continue to use it."[2]

This coincides with the historic view that "land was not seen to be of intrinsic value," but valuable only when put into productive use.[3] Thus, while the social policy underlying many legal systems is generally the protection of the rights of the citizenry including their property rights while penalising violators of those rights, the doctrine of adverse possession postulates that a land owner who failed to put his land to productive use[4] is considered a "legal wrongdoer."[5] It is said that a neglected or abandoned land may become a nuisance and a financial

---

[1] Out of the 282 rules, three focus on adverse possession: See J. Hiatt and J. Hladik, "Adverse to Change: A modern look at adverse possession." Center for Rural Affairs, 2019 at 2. Available at https//www.cfra.org/sites/www.cfra/files/publications. Accessed on 5/10/19.

[2] "Code of Hammurabi: Translated by L.W. King," Yale Law School. Lilian Goldman Law Library, The Avalon Project, 2008, Avalon.law.yale.edu/ancient/hamframe.asp. Accessed 5/10/19.

[3] J. Hiatt and J. Hladik, supra (n 1).

[4] Productive use could mean passive or active use. It is said that "fallowed fields and static wetlands are just as much considered a productive use as planted fields." See J. Hiatt and J. Hladik, supra (n 1).

[5] ibid.

burden for owners and the State, while lowering the value of neighboring land owners.[6]

The two exceptions to the doctrine of adverse possession provided by the Hammurabi's Code namely: its non-applicability in the case of a soldier-landowner "captured or killed during a battle, or in the case of a landowner's juvenile son,"[7] afforded underlying justification for the neglect or abandonment of land by the land owner. These, among other reasons, may constitute the defence of disability or lack of capacity in a claim of adverse possession in modern times.

2.2 The Concept of Possession

In the old Roman law under which the common law concept of property drew its major components, possession was taken to be nine-tenths of the law, and a person having possession of land had greater claim to it than the paper title holder who was not in possession.[8] This Roman law concept formed the basis of the doctrine of adverse possession in many common law and civil law jurisdictions.[9]

---

[6] ibid.

[7] ibid, at 2.

[8] It is said that the "[a]ncient Romans believed the land itself had a spirit that had to be nurtured and cared for by the person using the land. This gave the person who possessed the land greater claim to it than the person who merely held paper title to the land…" See J. Hiatt and J. Hladik, supra (n 1).

[9] The rule applies generally in all common law jurisdictions. Thus, apart from the United Kingdom, Nigeria and other common law jurisdictions such as Australia, New Zealand and the United States, it applies to civil law jurisdictions. Prominent amongst the civil law jurisdictions are France (Art 2229C Civ); Spain (Art 41 of the Spanish Civil Code); the Netherlands (Art 3.99(1), 3.105(1)); Sweden (Cap 16 Real Property Code); Hungary (s. 121(1)) Civil Code Act IV 1959); Poland (Art 172-176 Polish Civil Code); Germany (Para 900 BG-B German Civil Code): See the Report of the British Institute of International and Comparative Law for Her Majesty's Court Service, September 2006 on 'Adverse Possession' accessed online at http:www.biicl.org/files/2350_advposs_sep_ftnsv3.pdf on 10/10/2019.

Historically, "[t]he common law tradition in England went through a substantial transformation from a system that promoted heredity and limited access to land to a systemthat emphasised protection of individual property rights and free alienation."[10] In those feudal times, land was essentially the pivot of the society and "the monarchy in England maintained property rights through primogeniture[11], ultimogeniture[12] and other hereditary system that kept land from being freely alienated."[13]However, with the development of the middle class in the 14th Century, an economy based upon wages as opposed to rendering services led to the emergence of individual property rights in real property.[14]

The nearest equivalent of the Roman legal concept of possession known to the English land tenure was *seisin* which was the landholder's interest in a freehold estate.[15]*Seisin* in the old English law was an estate in land amounting to possession of land by one who owns it for at least a period of his life, and having the right to possession of it as against all others.[16] It was supplemented by the writ of "novel *disseisin*" which was an action in which "the plaintiff alleged a recent, novel *disseisin* by the

---

[10] B. Gardiner, Squatters' "Rights and Adverse Possession." [1997] IND. International and Comparative Law Review, vol. 8:1 at 125.

[11] The 'right of primogeniture' is the ' superior or exclusive right possessed by the eldest son, and particularly, his right to succeed to the estate of his ancestor, in right of his seniority by birth, to the exclusion of younger sons: See Black's Law Dictionary 6th ed. at 1191

[12] Compared with 'primogeniture,' últimogeniture' is a principle of inheritance in which the right of successionbelongs to the youngest child: See Oxford Dictionary of English, 3rd ed. 2010 (online).

[13] ibid.

[14] J.Dukeminier & J. Krier, Property 112 (1981) cited in B. Gardiner supra n.11 at 126.

[15] H. Hausmaninger, R. Gamauf, *A case book on Roman Property Law.* Oxford University Press, USA 2012, 1.

[16] M. Rayned, *Adverse Possession of Land.* Encyclopaedia Britannica, last updated February 2020, accessed on 3/03/2020.

person now seised of the land in dispute."[17] It does not matter that the action was brought by a person who acquired *seisin* wrongfully.[18]The known remedy for loss of possession at the time was to "oust the *disseisor* by force...[and] if one did not do so promptly, one lost the right ."[19]

2.3 Possession and the Statutes of Limitations

The limitation period for real actions at the time depended on the judges' discretion and subsequently on Acts of Parliament with fixed dates being chosen "before which allegations of the *seisin* of an ancestor might not be made."[20] The Statute of Westminster of 1275 limited claims of *seisin* starting after 1189, and effectively established an 86-year statute of limitations on adverse possession claims. However, "the establishment of this fixed date for *seisin* greatly disadvantaged those who were trying to establish adverse possession claims since it became more difficult to establish clear claims as the years passed."[21] This State policy changed with the passing of the Limitations Act of 1623 which fixed the period of limitation for 20 years.

The modern English land law has since de-emphasised *seisin* as root of title to land and freehold estates could then be transferred by deed and registration. But whilst proof of unregistered title in English law would often take the form of production of deeds or other instruments of title showing transfer of title to land from one person to another beyond the period of limitation and showing in practical terms that it is secure against adverse claims, "they do not prove that the transferor was in possession or entitled to possession."[22] English courts have held that in proof of title to land, mere production of document of title without proof

---

[17] S. Jourdan, O. Radley-Gadner, *Adverse Possession* 2nd ed, Bloomsbury Professional Limited, UK 2011, 19 para 2-01.

[18] ibid.

[19] Thompson on Real Property para. 87(David A. Thomas ed. 1994) cited by B. Gardiner, supra, n.11.

[20] Jourdan and Radley-Gadner, supra(n.17) at 19 para 2-02.

[21] B. Gardiner, supra n.10 at 126-127.

[22] Jourdan and Radley-Gardner, supra, (n 17) at 61 para 4-07.

of possession is to no avail; the party adducing the documentary evidence as proof of title must support it by proof of possession.[23]

The early statutes of limitation in England[24] recognised the tenacity of possessory rights and protected it by barring the right of action in court for recovery of possession by the holder of a superior title after a period of time prescribed by statute, while keeping his title intact. Thus, prior to the Real Property Limitation Act 1833, an entry on land by whatever means (short of an action in court) by a superior title holder after the limitation period was possible, since "the older statutes barred only the remedy and not the right."[25] The right of the superior title holder ('the paper owner') caught by the limitation statute was not extinguished.

2.3.1 The Limitation Act 1632

The enactment of the Limitations Act of 1632 set the limitation period for the action of ejectment for 20 years. The expiration of the limitation period barred an action to recover the land as opposed to extinction of the true owner's title; in other words, there was no divesting of estate, only the remedy was barred.[26] Although the Act laid down what appeared to be a single limitation period for rights of entry and ejectment, the courts developed a rule that before time would run under the statute, there had to be adverse possession.[27] However, the question whether possession was adverse or not was dependent on circumstances of the possession. For example, case law decided that "possession by a person with the

[23] Summing up the position of the English courts in *Lord St Leonards v. Ashburner* (1870) 21 LT , 595 at 596 Bramwell B said: "Title deeds come to little without evidence of actual enjoyment, for otherwise anyone might pretend to give away the lands of anybody else. Parchment, of itself, comes to little; the real question is as to actual enjoyment." See also *Malcolmson v. O'Dea* (1863) 10 HLC 593 at 614; *Bristow v. Cormican* (1878) 3 App Cas 641 at 668; *Johnston v. O'Neill* (1911) AC 552.

[24] See e.g. the Statute of Westminster 1275; Limitation Act 1623.

[25] *per* Griffith J. in *Bellew v. Bellew* [1983] ILRM 128.

[26] Jourdan and Radley-Gardner, supra (n 17) at 23 para 2-13.

[27] ibid, at 24 para 2-15.

consent of the true owner was treated as being under a tenancy at will, and was not adverse;[28] that "where the possession was at first lawful, it did not become unlawful by his continuance in possession after the period when he was in possession by right;"[29] and that where there were co-owners on property, the exclusive possession by one of them was treated as exclusive possession by all."[30]

The Limitation Act 1632 "reflected an early desire in England to prevent the waste of land resources,"[31] by encouraging landowners to put their land to productive use. It provided a warning signal for landowners to monitor their land and keep squatters in check. Also, "by avoiding legal actions and quieting title, it provided a framework for decreasing the often high transaction costs associated with land disputes, and allowed for greater economic development based on the new certainty of title."[32]

2.3.2 The Real Property Limitation Act 1833

The Real Property Limitations Act, 1833 ('the 1833 Act') laid the foundation for modern law of limitations in England.[33] It was enacted sequel to the First Report of the Commissioners on the Law of Real Property in 1829 which contained significant suggestions regarding limitation of actions for the recovery of real property.

---

[28] *Doe d Thompson v. Clark* (1828) 8 B & C 717; *Do ed Milburn v. Edgar* (1836) 2 Bing NC 498.

[29] *Roe d Pelatt v. Ferrars* (1801) 2 Bos & P542; *Doe d Souter v. Hull* (1822) 2 Dow & Ry KB 38.

[30] *Reading v. Royston* (1703) 91 ER 3687.

[31] B. Gardiner, supra (n 10) at 127.

[32] ibid.

[33] This Act was enacted following the First Report of the Commissioners on the Law of Real Property in 1829. Describing the state of the law on limitation of actions as "very unsystematic and very defective, the Commissioners made a number of recommendations culminating in the Real Property Limitation Act 1833.

The 1833 Act provided in section 2 that "no person shall make an entry or...bring an action to recover any land or rent but within twenty years next after the time at which to make such entry...or to bring such action shall have first accrued."[34]The time at which to make an entry or bring an action shall first accrue as provided for in section 3 of the Act which provided inter alia, that:

> "when the person claiming such land or rent, or some person through whom he claims, shall, in respect of the estate or interest claimed, have been in possession...or in receipt of such rent, and shall while entitled thereto have been dispossessed, or have discontinued such possession or receipt, then such right shall be deemed to have first accrued at the time of such dispossession or discontinuance of possession, or at the last time at which any such...rent ...was received."

There are other deeming provisions concerning the determination of the date of accrual of rights to make an entry or to bring an action to recover land in four other cases[35]

[34] This period was reduced to 12 years by The Real Property Limitation Act 1874 which shortened the limitation period(s.1) and was retained by the Limitation Act 1939 (s.4(3)) and subsequently by the extant Limitations Act, 1980 (s.15(1)).

[35] These other cases are: (i) In the case of successor in title of a deceased person who was before death entitled to an estate or interest in land or rent in respect thereto, the right is deemed to have accrued to such successor in title at the time of death of the title holder; (ii) In the case of a person entitled under an instrument (safe a will), to an estate or interest in land or rent in respect of same, the time was deemed to have first accrued at the time the person or the person through whom he claims is entitled to such possession or receipt by virtue of such instrument; (iii) In the case of an estate or interest in reversion or remainder or other future estate or interest, and no person had obtained possession of the land or receipt of profits or rent in respect thereto, such right was deemed to have accrued when such estate or interest became an estate or interest in possession; (iv) Where the person claiming land or rent or a person through whom he claimed became entitled by virtue of any forfeiture or breach of condition, such right was deemed to have accrued when such forfeiture was incurred or such condition was broken: These

A remarkable feature of the 1833 Act was its departure from the old construction of adverse possession "in the sense of requiring something more than a right for the true owner to recover possession from the squatter."[36] Interpreting the provisions of sections 2 and 3 of the Act, Lord Denman LJ in *Napean v. Doe d Night*[37] held that the two sections "have done away with the doctrine of non-adverse possession and…the question is whether twenty years have elapsed since the right accrued whatever be the nature of the possession." This was followed by a long line of judicial authorities.[38]

The consequences following from the expiration of the limitation period recommended by the Commissioners on the Law of Real Property in 1829 went the whole hog: it was recommended that "wherever by the provisions aforesaid all remedy is barred, the right shall be considered as extinguished to the party out of possession, and absolutely vested in the party in possession." But this recommendation was not fully implemented by the Act for, whilst the Act extinguished the right or title of the person against whom time had run upon the expiration of the

---

deeming provisions were retained by the Real Property Limitation Act 1874; retained in a modified form in the 1939 Act, ss. 5, 6.and 8 and retained in the 1980 Act as modified. Also, the Act provided that the right of a person holding an estate or interest in reversion to make an entry was due to accrue when the estate or interest fell into possession, even if the person had previously been in possession (s.5). The right to make an entry by the landlord in the case of a tenant at will was deemed to accrue from the determination of the tenancy, or if earlier, from one year after the commencement of the tenancy (s.7) As regards oral periodic tenants, it provided that the right to make an entry was deemed to accrue at the end of the first period or at the last time when rent was received, if later (s.8).

[36] Jourdan and Radley-Gadner, supra (n 17) at 33 para.

[37] 2 M&W 895; Barn & Adolph, 86.

[38] See *Smith v. Lloyd* (1854) 9 Exch 562; *Governors of Magdalen Hospital v. Knotts* (1878) 8 ChD 709; *Re Jolly*[1900] 2 Ch 616; *Paradise Beach and Transportation Co. Ltd v. Price-Robinson* [1968] AC 1072; *JA Pye (Oxford) Ltd v. Graham* [2003] 1 AC 419, paras 33-35, to mention a few.

period of limitation,[39] it did not vest such right or title in the party in possession.

Some of the common law rules which prevented possession from being adverse under the Limitation Act 1623 were reversed. For example, mere entry was not to be deemed possession,[40] and no continual claim on or near the land would preserve a right of entry.[41] There are also other important provisions regarding extension of the limitation period in cases of disability[42] or concealed fraud.[43]

2.3.3 The Real Property Limitation Act 1874

The Real Property Limitation Act 1874 which came into force in 1879 preserved the earlier legislation of 1833 with certain modifications.[44] Amongst other provisions, it reduced the limitation period from 20 years to 12 years for any action, entry or distress brought or made after its commencement;[45] it altered the rule regarding persons under disability by shortening the extension allowed from ten to six years with maximum extension allowed from 40 to 30 years; and it took out persons beyond the seas from the category of persons under disability.[46]

2.3.4 Adverse Possession and Registered Land

In the case of registered land, section 21 of the Land Transfer Act protected a registered proprietor from adverse possession by a squatter.

---

[39] Real Property Limitation Act 1833, s. 34. This was an important change from the previous law under which only the remedy and not the right to possession was barred by the expiry of the limitation period.

[40] ibid, s.10.

[41] ibid, s.11.

[42] ibid, ss. 16-19.

[43] ibid, s. 26

[44] Real Property Limitation Act 1874, s.9

[45] ibid, s.1.

[46] ibid, ss.3-5.

However, if at the date of registration of land with a possessory title time was already running against the applicant for registration under the Real Property Limitation Act of 1833 or 1874, it would continue to run against him after registration, and a title adverse to the registered title could be acquired.[47] To perfect the title of the adverse possessor, section 12 of the Land Transfer Act 1897 made provision for rectification of the register to accommodate a squatter who acquired title by possession to registered land; but the squatter's title would be defeated where there was a disposition of the land for valuable consideration before he was registered.[48]

Section 173 of the Law of Property Act 1922 which became substituted for the provision of section 12 of the Land Transfer Act 1897 contained provisions adopted by the Land Registration Act (LRA) 1925.[49] Section 75 (1) of the LRA 1925 provided that "the Limitation Acts shall apply to registered land in the same manner and to the same extent as those Acts apply to land not registered." However, where the estate of the registered proprietor would have been extinguished if it were not registered, "such estate shall not be extinguished but shall be deemed to be held by the proprietor for the time being in trust for the person who, by virtue of the said Acts, has acquired title against any proprietor, but without prejudice to the estates and interests of any other person interested in the land whose estate or interest is not extinguished by those Acts."[50] It is also provided that any person who claims to have acquired title under the Limitation Acts to a registered estate in land may apply to be registered as proprietor thereof and, if the Registrar is satisfied that the person is so entitled, register him with absolute, leasehold, qualified or possessory title as the case may be, but without prejudice to any estate or interest protected by any entry on the register which may not have been

---

[47] S. Jourdan, O. Radley-Gadner, supra (n 17).

[48] See the Land Transfer Act 1875, s.18 as amended by the Land Transfer Act 1897, Sch.1.

[49] See s.75 of the Act. The whole Act was subsequently repealed by the Land Registration Act 2002.

[50] ibid.

extinguished under the Limitation Acts.[51] Such registration shall have the same effect as the registration of a first proprietor and the applicant or any other person interested may apply to the court for the determination of any question thereby arising.[52]

2.3.5 The Limitation Act 1939

Following the publication of the Fifth Interim Report of the Law Revision Committee on Limitation of Actions in 1936, the recommendations of the Committee were substantially implemented by the Limitation act 1939. Although the Act re-enacted the provisions of earlier statutes to a large extent, it made a number of significant amendments.[53]

Significantly, the 1939 Act re-introduced the expression 'adverse possession' though not with the same meaning it had before 1833. Adverse possession was defined to mean "possession of some persons in whose favour the period of limitation can run."[54] This definition was retained by paragraph 8(1) Schedule 1 to the Limitation Act 1980.[55]

---

[51] LRA 1925, s. 75(2).

[52] ibid.

[53] Limitation Act 1939, 33b(b).Such amendments included introduction of new rules for limitation against the Crown; a 30 year period for "all actions to recover possession other than those relating to the foreshore, where the previous 60 year period was retained, and gold and silver mines, where no limitation period applied:" Limitation Act 1939, ss 4, 30. It also introduced new rules for the extension of the limitation period in case of disability, acknowledgement, part payment and fraudulent concealment: Limitation Act 1939, ss22-26; while new rules were introduced dealing with claims between beneficiaries and trustees: Limitations Act 1939, s.19.

[54] See s.10(1) thereof.

[55] Lord Brown-Wilkinson in *Pye (Oxford) Ltd v. Graham* (2003) AC 419 at 36 referred to the re-introduction of the expression 'Adverse Possession' as unfortunate for, it creates the impression that "in order for a squatter to gain title by lapse of time, he has to act adversely to the paper title owner... he has to "oust" the true owner in order to dispossess him; that he has to intend to exclude the whole world including the true owner; that the squatter's use of the land has to be inconsistent

2.3.6 The 21st Report of the Law Reform Committee

Following the publication of the 21st Report of the Law Reform Committee in 1977,[56] Parliament enacted first, the Limitation Amendment Act 1980 which amended the Limitation Act 1939, and subsequently, the Limitation Act 1980 which consolidated the existing Limitation statutes.

As part of the recommendations of the Committee relevant to adverse possession, the Committee recommended that there should be no change to the various limitation periods relating to actions for recovery of land;[57] that the law should be amended to ensure that no licence to possess the land is implied unless the evidence warrants it;[58] that in the case of tenancy at will, a gratuitous licence or a periodic oral tenancy, time shall not begin to run in favour of the occupier until the tenancy or licence has been determined;[59] that there should be no change in the law relating to the running of time against persons entitled to future interests in land;[60] that there should be no limitation period for rectification of the land register;[61] that a claim for indemnity in cases of erroneous registration of title should not be defeated by a defence of limitation except where, had the land not been registered, the claim to the right itself would have been lost by lapse of time;[62] and that a trustee who was also a beneficiary who acted prudently and honestly in distributing trust property should be able to rely on a defence of limitation except in respect of the share which he

---

with any present or future use by the true owner...[M]uch confusion and complication would be avoided if reference to adverse possession were to be avoidedso far as possible and effect given to the clear words of the Acts. The question is simply whether the defendant squatter has dispossessed the paper owner by going into ordinary possession of the land for the requisite period without the consent of the owner."

[56] Cmnd 6923 (1977).

[57] ibid, paras 3.38-3.42.

[58] ibid, para 3.52.

[59] ibid, paras 3.55, 3.56.

[60] ibid, para 3.65.

[61] ibid, para 3.72.

[62] ibid, paras 3.77-3.79.

would have had to pay to the late-comer had all the beneficiaries (including himself) been sued in time.[63]

2.3.7 The Limitation Amendment Act 1980

This Act which came into force consequent upon the various recommendations of the Law Reform Committee contained in the 21st Report on the limitation of actions applied in all causes of action accruing, and things taking place before and after the commencement of the Act.[64]It provided that no action may be brought which was barred by the Limitation Act1939 before its commencement, nor affected any action or arbitration commenced before its commencement, nor the title to any property which was the subject of any such action or arbitration.[65] It abolished the rule that time ran against a landlord under a tenancy at will from the anniversary of the grant of the tenancy.[66]A new provision of the Limitation Act1939 was introduced in its section 10(4) which provided that "there was to be no implication of law that a squatter's occupation was by permission of the person entitled to the land merely by virtue of the fact that the squatter's occupation was not inconsistent with the person entitled to the land's present or future enjoyment of the land."[67]

2.3.8 The Limitation Act 1980

The extant Limitation Act 1980 consolidated the pre-existing limitation statutes and repealed the Limitation Act 1939 and the Limitation Amendment Act 1980.[68]In addition, it contains transitional provisions so far as it relates to adverse possession cases. In particular, it provides that

[63] ibid, paras 3.84.
[64] The Limitation Amendment Act 1980, s.12(2).
[65] ibid, s.12(1).
[66] ibid, s.3(1).
[67] ibid, s.4. The provision is incorporated in the extant Limitation Act 1980 in Schedule 1, para 8(4).
[68] Limitation Act 1980, s. 40(3) and Sch 4.

nothing in the extant law shall enable any action barred by the previous statutes to be brought premised on the provisions of the extant law.[69]

The relevant provisions of the Limitation Act 1980[70] ('the Act') which applies in the case of unregistered title generally are sections 15(1), 17, Schedule I paragraphs 1-8.

Section 15(1) of the Act provides:

> "No action shall be brought by any person to recover any land after the expiration of twelve years from the date on which the right of action accrued to him or, if it first accrued to some person through whom he claims, to that person."

The right of action is said to accrue in case of present interests on land, on the date when a person entitled to possession or a person claiming through him is dispossessed or discontinued his possession.[71] In the case of a deceased person who was, on the date of his death, in possession of the land being the last person entitled to the land in possession, the right of action is deemed to accrue on the date of his death.[72]

Section 17 of the Act provides:

> "Subject to-
>
> (a) section 18 of this Act, [...]

---

[69] ibid, Sch 2, para 9(1).

[70] The Limitation Act 1980, c58.

[71] Schedule 1 paragraph 1.

[72] Schedule 1 paragraph 2. In the case of an estate or interest insured otherwise than by will to him, or to some person through whom he claims and the person making the assurance was on the date when the assurance took effect was in possession of the land charged and no person has been in possession of the land by virtue of the assurance, the right of action is deemed to accrue on the date when the assurance took effect: See Schedule 1 paragraph 3. For accrual of right of action in case of future interests, see Schedule 1 paragraphs 4-6.

> at the expiration of the period prescribed by this Act for any person to bring an action to recover land (including a redemption action) the title of that person to the land shall be extinguished."

As for accrual of right of action to recover land, Schedule 1(1) of the Act provides:

> "Where the person bringing an action to recover land, or some person through whom he claims, has been in possession of the land, and has while entitled to the land been dispossessed or discontinued his possession, the right of action shall be treated as having accrued on the date of the dispossession or discontinuance."

The expression, "Adverse possession" is contained in the provisions of Schedule 1

paragraph 8(1) and (2) which provide:

> "(1) No right of action to recover land shall be treated as accruing unless the land is in the possession of some person in whose favour the period of limitation can run (referred to below in this paragraph as 'adverse possession'); and where under the preceding provisions of this Schedule any such right of action is treated as accruing on a certain date and no person is in adverse possession on that date, the right of action shall not be treated as accruing unless and until adverse possession is taken of the land
>
> (2) Where a right of action to recover land has accrued and after its accrual, before the right is barred, the land ceases to be in adverse possession, the right of action shall no longer be treated as having accrued and no fresh right of action shall be treated as accruing unless and until the land is again taken into adverse possession

The foregoing provisions are clear and unambiguous: First, an action for recovery of land is barred after 12 years of accrual of the cause of action to recover the land. The right of action accrues in this case when the land is in the possession of a person in whose favour the period of limitation can run (i.e. adverse possession), provided that the right of action shall not accrue unless there is a person in adverse possession of the land both at the time the right of action accrued and before the right of action is barred. Secondly, after the period of limitation, the title of the person outside possession is extinguished.[73]

2.4 Nature and Source of Title of the Adverse Possessor

While the requirement of adverse possession is germane in determining the running of time under the Limitation Act 1980, there is still a thorny issue to be dealt with as a result of the patent lacunae in the Act. The argument goes that it is not sufficient that the title of the paper owner is extinguished after the limitation period, the nature of the interest acquired by the adverse possessor is germane. While it is trite from statutory provisions earlier discussed that the person in whose favour time has run has title to the land, there have been disagreements over the nature and source of that title. This is particularly important since the Limitation Act 1980 does not specifically vest any form of title in the adverse possessor at the end of the limitation period and upon the extinguishment of the owner's title.

One view based on the *parliamentary conveyance theory* is that upon the expiration of the limitation period, the estate of the owner is statutorily conveyed to the adverse possessor. This is a legal fiction meant to ensure efficacy of the provisions of the law, and it was the view taken by the Real Property Commissioners in their first report on Limitation of action in respect of real property,[74] culminating in the Real Property Limitation Act 1833. The Commissioners had recommended that "wherever by the provisions aforesaid all remedy is barred, the right shall be considered as extinguished to the party out of possession, and absolutely vested in the party in possession."[75] This recommendation was

[73] ibid, s.17.

[74] First Report of the Commissioners on the Law of Real Property, 1829.

[75] ibid, at 81.

not implemented by Parliament in enacting the Real Property Limitation Act 1833 or subsequent limitation statutes including the Limitation Act 1980. Although favoured by some old English cases,[76] the parliamentary conveyance theory was rejected unanimously by the Court of Appeal in *Tichborne v. Weir,*[77]*Fairweather v. St. Marleybone*[78] and *Buckinghamshire County Council v. Moran.*[79] Indeed, the provision of section 17 of the Limitation Act[80] 1980 contradicts this theory. It also appears illogical to conceive of a transfer of title which has been extinguished by statute, for 'extinguishment imports annihilation'; while 'transfer imports continued existence'[81]

Some logic was found in the *commensurate estate theory* by Darby and Bosanquet who held the view that the "rights...remaining un-extinguished [after the limitation period] is clearly commensurate with the interest which the rightful owners have lost by the operation of statute...and must therefore,...have the same legal character..."[82] Apart from the fact that section 17 of the Limitations Act 1980 runs contrary to this theory, the theory has generated criticism by legal commentators both in form and content,[83] and has been rejected by the House of Lords in *Fairweather v. St Marleybone* where Lord Ratcliffe said:

---

[76] See *Doe d Jukes v. Sumner* (1845) 153 ER 380, 381; *Cp Incorporated Society v. Richards* (1841) 1 Dru & War 258, 289; *Scott v. Nixon* (1843) 6 Ir Eq Rep 8, 17; *Dawkins v. Lord Penrhyn* (1877) 6 Ch D 318(CA) 323.

[77] (1892) 67 LT 735

[78] [1963] AC 510 (HL) 535(Lord Radcliff) 544 (Lord Denning) 553 (Lord Morris)

[79] [1990] Ch 623, 644 (Nourse LJ).

[80] The provision of this section provides that, upon the expiration of the limitation period, 'the title...to the land' of the person against whom time has run 'shall be extinguished.'

[81] See Cp. AC Meredith, 'A paradox of Sugden's' (1918) 34 LQR 253, 255.

[82] JGN Darby and FA Bosanquet, *A Practical Treatise on the Statute of Limitations in England and Ireland* (W Maxwell & Son 1867) 390.

[83] See for example, W Hayes, *An introduction to Conveyancing* (5th edn, Sweet 1840) vol 1, 269-270; N Curwen, 'The Squatter's Interest at Common Law' [2000] Conv 528, 532-33.

> [a squatter] has not the title or estate of the owner or owners whom he has dispossessed nor has he in any relevant sense an estate 'commensurate with' the estate of the dispossessed. All that this misleading phase can mean is that, since his possession only defeats the rights of those to whom it has been adverse, there may be rights not prescribed against...which are no less enforceable against him in respect of the land than they would have been against the owners he has dispossessed.[84]

While the theory may sit well with the position of an adverse possessor of registered land under the Land Registration Act 2002 where the law entitles the adverse possessor to be entered into the register as against the registered proprietor who is disqualified where he qualifies to be so registered,[85] it does not explain the situation with unregistered land on which he acquires no estate commensurate to that of the person against whom time has run.

It would appear that the modern view on the source of the squatter's title lies in *presumption of possession as legal evidence of ownership*. This presumptive status of possession may be traced to the words of Cozen-Hardy MR in the case of *Re Atkinson and Horsell's Contract*[86] that:

> "whenever you find a person in possession of property that possession is prima facie evidence of ownership in fee, and that prima facie evidence becomes absolute when once you have extinguished the right of every other person to challenge it..."

This view was adopted by Fletcher Moulton LJ that:

> "Possession is prima facie evidence of right, and that evidence becomes conclusive when the rights of all other people are extinguished. That is the effect of the [statute of limitation]."

[84] supra, (n 67) at 536.

[85] Land Registration Act 2002, Sch 6; Sch 6 para 9(1).

[86] [1912] 2 Ch 1 (CA) 9.

This presumption is not irrebuttable, as there may be superior title to which the possessory title may be subject and which may defeat it. This point was made clear by Holroyd Pearce LJ in *Marylebone Property Co. v. Fairweather*[87] when he said:

> "In such circumstances, the squatter obtains a pragmatic or defeasible fee simple. If the title which the squatter has destroyed is the true immediate fee simple, then he has in practice acquired the best available title and he will prevail against all. If, however, the title that he has destroyed is not the true immediate fee simple, but some lesser title, he is still vulnerable, for he can be ejected when he is subsequently challenged by a stronger immediate title. While that stronger title is only a title in reversion, he is safe, but when the reversion comes into possession, the reversioner's right to eject him arises."

The logical implication of the exercise of a possessory title therefore is that it gives rise to a possessory right which is alienable[88] and not possession-dependent;[89] a right to non-interference;[90] and a power to convey it inter vivos, or to devise the interest by will.[91] But the interest of the adverse possessor remains defeasible and vulnerable if the title destroyed is not an immediate fee simple absolute in possession but a form of lesser title with a reversioner holding a fee simple absolute with the right to enter into possession and defeat the interest of the adverse possessor. This is actualised in modern time by bringing an action of ejectment against the adverse possessor. There lies the frailty of the doctrine of adverse possession under English law, which frailty affects its efficacy as a mode of acquisition of title to land.

---

[87] [1962] 1 QB 498 (CA) at 513.

[88] *Asher v. Whitlock* (1865) LR 1QB 1; *Perry v. Clissod, Ex parte Winder* (1877) 6 Ch D 696.

[89] *Ezekiel v. Fraser*[2002] EWHC 2066 .

[90] This is a basic attribute of exclusive possession.

[91] *Asher v. Whitlock* (supra) n. 59; *Wheeler v. Baldwin* (1934) 52 C.L.R 609 (High Court of Australia); *Allen v. Roughley* (1955) 94 C.L.R 98 (High Court of Australia).

2.5 The Land Registration Act 2002

The advent of the Land Registration Act in 2002 streamlined the application of the doctrine of adverse possession by giving the registered proprietor of registered land the opportunity of discovering the presence of a squatter on his land. Where the registered proprietor failed to take steps to eject the squatter within a certain period stipulated by law, the adverse possessor may be put on the register as the new registered owner and the register rectified without compensating the former proprietor. The effect of the Act on the doctrine of adverse possession is examined fully in a subsequent chapter.[92]

2.6 Application of English Law in Nigeria, Adverse Possession and the Statute of Limitations

Before the advent of British rule in the various territories later known as Nigeria, the customary and Islamic land tenure systems were in operation predominantly in the South, and the North respectively.[93] These land tenure systems had parallel rules regulating their application in those territories.[94]

The doctrine of adverse possession did not apply under the Customary land tenure system and adverse claim to possession of communal or family land for any length of time was not recognised. Although Islamic law recognised acquisition of title by long possession known as *hauzi*, this was subject to onerous conditions and not subject to the same common law conditions for establishing adverse possession under English law.

With the advent of British rule, English law became applicable in Nigeria either by way of its direct extension through the English

---

[92] See Chapter 7*infra*.

[93] See I.O.Smith, *Practical Approach to Law of Real Property in Nigeria*. 1983 Ecowatch Publications Nig Ltd, Lagos-Nigeria, 5-6.

[94] ibid.

legislation upon British rule in 1862,[95] or by way of its reception through the Nigerian local legislation after independence.[96] The former consists of the common law of England, the doctrines of equity, English statutes and subsidiary legislation, made on or before October 1 1960, but not yet repealed by the appropriate authority in Nigeria. Such Laws apply subject to local circumstances, legislation and jurisdiction, and continue to apply in Nigeria by its own force until repealed, notwithstanding its repeal in England at any time. The latter as a source of Nigerian law consists of the common law of England, the doctrines of equity, and statutes of general application applicable in England on January 1, 1900, received into Nigerian law by local legislation.

Going by the foregoing narrative, the doctrine of adverse possession was introduced into the Nigerian law as part of the English common law, while the Limitations statutes in force in England from 1874 through to 1939 were made directly applicable to Nigeria. However, local legislation passed after independence repealed and replaced the English statute of limitation, and by 1966, the first local statute of Limitation – the Limitation Decree (now Act), was passed as a federal legislation in Nigeria. Subsequently, the federating states enacted Limitation Laws, while the Limitation Act 1966 applies to the Federal Capital Territory.

On 29th March 1978, the Land Use Act came into force. The Act vests radical title to land within the territory of each state in the governor of the state. Individual unlimited right in land in the form of fee simple was converted to right of occupancy granted or deemed granted by the Governor or the local government. Section 48 of the Act preserves the pre-existing land tenure systems, subject to its provisions.

Consequently, it preserves the customary and Islamic land tenure systems including the principles pertaining to stale claims, the English common law including the doctrine of adverse possession, and local statutes including the statutes of limitation in force, but subject to the provisions

[95] This was consequent upon the Treaty of Cession 1861 between Her Royal Majesty, the Queen of England and King Dosumu of Lagos

[96] See e.g. the Law (Miscellaneous Provisions) Act, Cap 89 Laws of Nigeria, 1958.

of the Act. This development has far reaching implications for the relevance and application of the doctrine of adverse possession in Nigeria.

CHAPTER 3
THEORETICAL FRAMEWORK

3.1 Introduction

Understanding the theoretical foundation of the doctrine of adverse possession is a clue to appreciating its content and application from remote antiquity to the present time. It explains the justification or otherwise for the application of the doctrine under the English and Nigerian law, and provides the foundation for inquiry into its efficacy from a comparative perspective. It also demonstrates how existing theories influence judicial law-making process in England and Nigeria.

3.2 The Two Segments of Theoretical Foundation

The theoretical foundation has two segments. First, there are the traditional theories[1] well known as the bedrock of the doctrine and as the basis of arguments sustaining its rationale and application. These traditional theories are alluded to in the existing literature on the subject, and form the basis of parliamentary reactions and government policies on the application of the doctrine. Some of these traditional theories informed the reasoning underlying judicial pronouncements in both jurisdictions as rationale for their tenacious application by municipal and international courts.

Second, there are certain theories developed from the peculiar circumstances of a land tenure system such as the non-applicability of the doctrine under the Nigerian customary and Islamic land tenure systems (the 'relativity theory'); or from the peculiar nature of landholding introduced by the regime of the Nigerian Land Use Act and the emergence of the compulsory state grant (the 'grant theory') exhibiting peculiar characteristics unknown to English law; or resulting from the emergence of the regime of title registration in both jurisdictions and

---

[1] The traditional theories are the occupation theory; the labour theory; the utilitarian theory; the personhood theory, the economic theory and the social function of property theory discussed in this chapter: See subheads 3.4.1, 3.4.2, 3.4.3, 3.4.4, 3.4.5, 3.4.6 respectively.

consequently, the emergence of the 'indefeasibility theory' sometimes alluded to as a factor rendering the doctrine irrelevant in modern times. Also inclusive in this category are the 'sanctity of property right theory'- a product of the local and international legal regimes applicable in both jurisdictions; and the 'incompatibility theory' resulting from the criminalization of certain forms of trespass which ordinarily is a civil wrong.

The distinction between these two categories of theories is one with a difference. While the first category of theories (the traditional theories) relate to the rationale behind the recognition of the doctrine of adverse possession as a universal concept, the second category directly focuses on the operation of the doctrine and determines its efficacy or otherwise in each jurisdiction under study. A study of one without the other would amount to an exercise in futility for, although a probe into the efficacy of the doctrine must essentially proceed from the question whether there are justifications for it at all; but that may not explain whether it is efficacious or not. The efficacy of the doctrine can only be determined through a study of its application and functionality given certain circumstances and peculiarities.

3.3 Theories of Adverse Possession and Private Property

The justificatory theories of the doctrine of adverse possession are intertwined with the theories of private property in modern property law. Getzler[2] categorised the theories of property law into two in his writing as follows:

[2] J. Getzler, "Theories of Property and Economic Development." Journal of Interdisciplinary History, XXVI: 4 (1996). See also J. Waldron, *The right to Private Property* (Oxford, Clarendon Press, 1988); S. Munzer, *A Theory of Property* (Cambridge University Press, 1990; M.J. Radin, *Reinterpreting Property* (University of Chicago Press, 1993).

> There is a notion of property as pre-social, a natural right expressing the rights of persons which are prior to the state and law, this being the view of Hugo Grotius, Samuel von Pufendorf, John Locke, Immanuel Kant, and George W.F. Hegel; and there is a notion of property as social, a positive right created instrumentally by community, state, or law to secure other goals-the theory of Thomas Hobbes, David Hume, Adam Smith, Jeremy Bentham, Emile Durkenheim and Max Weber.

This classification depicts the divide between the natural law theorists and the positivists.

The natural law theorists on the one hand postulate that "the earth's resources were given to mankind in common."[3] In the words of Blackstone:

> The earth…and all things therein are the general property of mankind, exclusive of other beings, from the immediate gift of the creator…all was in common among them, and that everyone took from the public stock to his own use such things as his immediate necessities required.[4]

This was derived from the general notion of property as a natural right existing prior to the state and law and to which positive law is susceptible. This natural law theory underlines the justification for the 'occupation theory' and lays the foundation for the 'labour theory' and the 'personhood theory' of adverse possession discussed below, and it is said to be the basis for the legal maxim that "possession is nine-tenth of ownership" often alluded to as the bedrock of adverse possession under the Anglo-Nigerian law of adverse possession.

---

[3] See H. Grotius, *On the Law of War and Peace,* Book 2 Ch.2, 1, 4-5 (Kesley translation, Oxford Clarendon Press, 1925); S. Pufendorf, *Of the Law of Nature and Nations,* J. Churchill et.al. (ed) (1703).

[4] *Blackstone's Commentaries on the Laws of England.* Available online at http//Avalon.law.yale.edu>blackstone_bk2ch1. Accessed on 4/10/2019.

On the other hand, the positivists regard property as a positive right (as opposed to a natural right) created by the instrumentality of the law. In the words of Bentham,[5] "law and private property are born together and die together". "Without laws" he says, "there is no private property." He argues that all laws flow from the state and deprecates the idea of natural rights as "...rhetorical nonsense - nonsense upon stilts."[6] This forms the basis for the 'utilitarian theory' or 'economic theory' sometimes alluded to as justification for the doctrine of adverse possession. These theories are also discussed below.

The traditional theories often canvassed in favour of adverse possession include the *occupation theory*; the *labour theory*; the *utilitarian theory*; the *personhood theory*; the *economic theory;* and the *social function of property theory.*Each of these theories provides the supposed rationale for the pervasiveness of the doctrine as a means of acquiring title to real property in modern times.

However, apart from the various shortcomings identified with these theories in this chapter, it is observed that the theories presuppose the existence of unregistered titles in land where possession is the hallmark of title and adverse possession is seen as the clue to title to land at any given time. The regime of title registration applicable in the various common law jurisdictions including England, Wales and Nigeria has allegedly set limitations to the perspectives of the role of adverse possession as a potent instrument of construction of title based on possession,[7] while it is argued that the peculiarities of the legal and constitutional frameworks in Nigeria have eroded the efficacy of the doctrine and necessitated an appraisal of some other theories with adverse consequences.[8]

---

[5] J. Bentham, "Anarchical Fallacies" Nonsense *upon stilts:* Bentham, Burke, and Max on the rights of Man, J. Waldron ed., (London, Methuen, 1987) 53.

[6] ibid.

[7] See Chapter 7 *infra.*

[8] ibid.

3.4 The Traditional Theories

3.4.1 The Occupation Theory

The occupation theory of private property suggests as a rule that "objects become the private property of individuals when such individuals have taken occupation of them."[9] Occupation is actualised when there has been an unambiguous act of appropriation which has been communicated to the whole world.[10] It is said that "pursuits and acts which fall short of such an unequivocal act of appropriation, are insufficient because of the problem of assigning possession when there are two or more overlapping efforts to take occupation."[11]

Panesar explains that the "essence behind the occupation theory is that, given that all material resources are given to mankind in common, such material resources become the private property of individuals through the consent of, or agreement with the rest of mankind."[12] He posits that the division of such property is by reference to either an express agreement that the property would be distributed on a mutual understanding, or under an implied agreement to be found on the basis of first occupation, giving rise to private property which amounts, in the words of the common law, to the maxim that "possession is the root of title."[13]

This theory justifies the fulcrum of the doctrine of adverse possession which is the act of possession coupled with *animus possidendi*. It is different from the labour theory[14] because the prospective occupier or squatter is not required to exert labour in any form to be in possession; it suffices like an adverse possessor, that he has appropriated the property

---

[9] S. Panesar, (2000) "Theories of Private Property," Denning Law Journal, vol. 15, 113 at 118.

[10] ibid.

[11] ibid.

[12] ibid, at 116.

[13] ibid.

[14] See sub-head 3.4.2 next.

and communicated the same to the whole world by evincing the intention to possess in any form adverse to the interest of the true owner.

In the law and policy relating to adverse possession of land like the occupation theory, "rule of notice and communication sufficient to give occupation"[15] is a key requirement, "and the principle of adverse possession recognises that long and uncontested possession of land by a trespasser confers upon such a person an effective title to the land."[16]

It has been queried whether the occupation theory has any significance in contemporary property law. Lowie[17] criticises the theory as "a mere description of the origin of property, without any significant relevance to property law concept."[18] It is said that the theory "is based on facts which are both historical and primitive,"[19]adding that the situation prevalent during the time of Grotius and Pufendorf (the natural law theorists) when resources were commonly held, do not apply to a complex system of resources in contemporary societies where resources are parceled into private property. The greatest challenge of the theory "relates to the actual point at which and the amount of labour needed to take first possession", especially when there are overlapping efforts to take possession.[20]

However, despite the claim that the theory belongs to the realm of facts "which are both historical and primitive."[21] Panesar recognises its importance to "present day property law"[22] for various reasons: Apart from explaining how the chain of ownership began, he says the principles enunciated by the theory are relied upon by the courts in resolving "modern day property law disputes", and particularly in adverse

---

[15] Panesar, n.9 at 120.

[16] ibid.

[17] R. Lowie, "Incorporeal Property in Primitive society" 37 Yale Law Journal at 551 (1928).

[18] ibid.

[19] ibid, at 118

[20] Panesar, supra (n 9) at 116-117.

[21] ibid.

[22] ibid.

possession cases where the courts find the rule of notice and communication useful in resolving adverse possession disputes.[23] He reckons that the occupation theory facilitates trade and functioning of an effective market, adding that "such clear titles facilitate trade by introducing certainty in the marketplace."[24]

3.4.2 The Labour Theory

Locke, in his *Second Treatise on government,*[25] finds justification for the rule of adverse possession in the old labour theory. He argues that the interest of a squatter who has improved the property through concerted labour has overriding interest in it over an owner who has abandoned it. The *raison d'etre* of this theory is that since labour belongs to the person performing it, exerting it in developing or cultivating the land brings the land out of the commons and makes it a subject matter of acquisition by the labourer to the exclusion of all claims by other persons.[26]

Locke however qualifies his theory by stating that it would only become a valid method for acquiring property "at least where there is enough left in common for others"[27] suggesting that the labour theory suffices as long as there remains enough un-owned things in the commons for others to appropriate.[28] He states that no person is free to appropriate from the commons than he is able to enjoy otherwise, the person appropriating is taking to be 'spoiling' the remainder which will

---

[23] ibid, at 119-120.

[24] ibid, at 122.

[25] J. Locke, "Two Treatises of Government (1690, Laslet P ed. 1963) Oxford Blackwall (1966) para 25.

[26] ibid at paras 26-28.

[27] ibid at paras 27, 33.

[28] ibid.

revert to the commons from where other persons are able to appropriate them.[29]

The theory suggests that land being a finite resource is best when being used, and has limited value when neglected or abandoned.[30] Consequently, neglected or abandoned land may "become a financial burden for owners, state and local governments, and neighboring property owners."[31] A piece or parcel of land not maintained becomes a nuisance and diminishes the value of surrounding properties resulting in infringement of the rights of others by the absentee owner.[32]

This theory however presupposes land that was not originally the subject matter of ownership or possession ('the commons'), which is not the situation in adverse possession cases. Adverse possession deals with the extinguishment of the existing right of the owner of land who has either abandoned it or who has been dispossessed of it by an adverse possessor, which makes any improvement on it illegitimate and wrongful. Also, it is said that "without a prior theory of ownership, it is not self-evident that one owns even the labour that is mixed with something else."[33]

The Lockean labour theory does not determine how much labour need be expended before the labourer becomes entitled to the property in cases where other people have equally exerted labour on the property, and left unanswered the question as to whether labour has to reflect the value added to the resource in question.[34] However, the labour theory justifies the recognition of the possessory rights of the squatter who has

---

[29] Ibid, at paras 31-32. See also K. Green, "Citizens and Squatters: Under the surfaces of land law" in S. Bright & J.K Dewar (eds) *Land Law: Themes and Perspectives* (1998) 229 at 243.

[30] J. Hiatt and J. Hladik, *Adverse to change: A modern look at Adverse Possession.* Centre for Rural Affairs, 2019 at 1, accessed online at www.cfra.org on 25/09/2019.

[31] ibid.

[32] ibid.

[33] C.M Rose, "Possession as origin of property." 52 Univ. Chicago L. Review 73 (1985)

[34] ibid, 73-74.

developed or put the acquired land to use, and not allowing it to lie fallow.

3.4.3 The Personhood Theory

This theory which may justify adverse possession of both private and public property[35] recognises that a squatter in possession of land after a certain time, forms a personal attachment to it than the actual owner "who has presumably become detached from the land."[36] In the words of Oliver Wendell Holmes: "A thing which you have enjoyed and used as your own for a long time whether property or an opinion, takes root in your being and cannot be torn away without your resenting the act and trying to defend yourself, however you came by it."[37]

Describing the essence of the theory, Radin says the strength of a person's relationship with an object is measured by taking into account the kind of pain that would be suffered should the object be lost in some way: an object is closely bound up with the custodian's personhood if its loss causes pain that cannot be relieved by replacing that object with its monetary value.[38] Radin refers to two different types of property relationship namely, 'personal property' involving property to which individuals are attached; and 'fungible property' to which the individuals are not. The first kind of relationship, according to her, gives rise to a stronger moral claim than the other, and in the case of adverse possession, it could be argued that the personal relationship existing between the

---

[35] See generally, A. Klass, "Response Essay: The Personhood Rationale and its Impact on the Durability of Private Claims to Public Property." 103 GEO L.J 41 (2014) available at http://scholarship.law.umn.edu/faculty_articles/53.

[36] A. Klass, supra (n 35) at 45.

[37] O.W.Holmes, "The Path of the Law," 10 Harvard Law Review 457, 477 (1897). As Holmes succinctly put it: "[t]he true explanation of title by prescription seems to me to be that man, like a tree in the cleft of a rock, gradually shapes its roots to his surroundings, and when the roots have grown to a certain size, can't be displaced without cutting at his life." See Holmes, supra at 476-477.

[38] M.J. Radin, "Property and Personhood" (1982) 34 Stanford Law Review 957 at 959.

squatter and the land, is more worthy of protection than the absentee owner's fungible relationship with his property.

Finding justification for the doctrine of adverse possession in this theory, Singer states that:

> ...the adverse possessor comes to expect and may have come to rely on the fact that the owner will not interfere with the possessor's use of the property. If the adverse possessor were to be ousted from the property, she would experience a loss. The adverse possessor's interests grow stronger over time as she develops legitimate expectations that the true owner will continue to allow her to control the property.[39]

This is true especially in situations where the adverse possessor values the property more than the true owner by using and cultivating it if it is "constitutive to such squatter's personhood."[40]

In the context of homeless persons, Rosendorf[41] posits that "property theories [such as this] provide a means to argue for recognition of limited property interests in abandoned or government owned buildings based on both economic utility and a squatter's personal identification with the property." Squatting by the homeless, according to him, has proven to be an effective tool for the homeless, not only in the direct manner of producing low-income housing, but also as "a means of mobilising public opinion."[42]

However, the theory is not foolproof. First, it undermines the interest of the true owner and of society generally in preserving the

---

[39] J.W. Singer, "The reliance interest in property," 40 Stanford Law Review 611 at 666-667 (1988). Also, M.J. Radin, "Time, Possession and Alienation," 64 WASH U L.Q 739, 739-74.

[40] ibid.

[41] D.L. Rosendorf, "Homelessness and the Uses of Theory: An Analysis of Economic and Personality Theories of Property in the Context of Voting Rights and Squatting Rights. 45 U. Miami L. Rev. 701, 722 (1990-1991) .

[42] ibid, at 724.

integrity of the set of entitlements grounded in law.[43] Following Bentham,[44] there is a presumption that property rights are creatures of law as opposed to unilateral expectations outside the law.[45] It is said that "a policy of transferring entitlements to individuals in order to protect extra-legal expectations would inevitably undermine the general security of property rights."[46]

The theory makes an assumption that the true owner out of possession no longer believes in his ownership;[47] an assumption which may turn out to be rebuttable in circumstances where the land is left fallow for the purpose of recuperation of the soil or pending when a development loan is released by a lender. Sometimes, the true owner still values his ownership but is unaware of the fact of adverse possession of his property.[48]

It has also been argued[49] that "squatters are not a homogenous group" for, whilst some have a genuine need of the property, some may have political objectives, some may prefer the "lifestyle of squatting and its cheapness,"[50] and others may be "a disaffected group or individuals who welcome the freedom and anonymity of squatting"[51] among other reasons.

---

[43] T.W Merrill, "Property Rules, Liability Rules, and Adverse Possession," 79 Nw. U.L.Rev. 1122 at 1132 (1985).

[44] See J. Bentham, Theory of Legislation 111-13 (1914).

[45] T.W. Merritt, supra note 19.

[46] ibid.

[47] See J. E. Stake, "The Uneasy Case for Adverse Possession" (2001) 89 Georgetown Law Journal 2419, 2474

[48] See *J.A Pye (Oxford) Ltd and Another v. Graham and Another* [2000] Ch. 676.

[49] Department of Environment, Consultation paper on squatting (London, HMSO 1975).

[50] ibid.

[51] ibid.

3.4.4 The Utilitarian Theory

Utilitarianism is generally known in legal theory as promoting "the greatest happiness of the greatest number," regarding this as "the measure of right and wrong."[52] J.S Mill in his *Principles of Political Economy*[53]says that: "in the case of land, "no exclusive right should be permitted in any individual which cannot be shown to be productive of positive good." "When land is not intended to be cultivated," he says, "no good reason can in general be given for its being private property."[54] He states that possession ought to be recognised as ownership if it has not been challenged within a moderate number of years, pointing out that "revival of a claim which had long been dormant, would generally be a greater injustice, and almost always [cause] a greater private and public mischief, than leaving the original wrong without atonement."[55] This reasoning has its root in rule-utilitarianism[56] which states that utility is maximized in a legal system by having a rule, namely, the acquisition of property through adverse possession, thereby resolving conflicting claims and promoting legal certainty.

However, apart from the fact that 'use of land' or 'productive use' is not a legal requirement for a valid adverse possession, the basic consequence of adverse possession both at common law and under the Statute of Limitations goes beyond mere recognition of use of land by the adverse possessor, but fundamentally and automatically extinguishes the

---

[52] J.A. Bentham, "Fragment of Government and an Introduction to the principles of Morals and Legislation" (1776, Harrison W ed 1948) 3 para 2.

[53] J.S. Mill ,*Principles of Political Economy* (1902), University of Chicago Press 1993 at 35.

[54] J.S. Mill (n 17).

[55] ibid.

[56] Knowles distinguishes between two types of utilitarianism namely: 'act-utilitarianism' which takes the consequences of an act into account to determine whether that act maximize utility; and 'rule utilitarianism' which takes the view that utility is maximized in a legal system by having a rule which resolves conflicting claims and promotes legal certainty, regardless of consequences. See D. Knowles, *Political Philosophy* (2001) 25.

owner's title in favour of the adverse possessor who may go ahead to register his 'statutory title.' The fact that the 'paper owner' of the land had no knowledge of squatter's presence on the land is of no moment and the use of the land by the adverse possessor may be detrimental to the overall interests of the adjacent land or the general public.

Also, there is no empirical evidence to show that adverse possession of land would have a positive impact on the socio-economic expectations of society. For example, it is said that the interpretation of "productive use" in contemporary times could mean passive as well as active use;[57] "fallowed fields and static wetlands are just as much considered a productive use as planted fields."[58] This view is corroborated by Clarke[59] who does not see "productive use" of property as a potent rationale behind adverse possession. Citing the position of the U.S Supreme Court on the point in *Lessee of Ewing v. Burnet*,[60] he argues that "activities of the adverse possessor mimicking the legal role of a true owner, such as ejecting trespassers and paying taxes, established adverse possession."[61]

---

[57] J. Hiatt and J. Hladik, *Adverse to change: A modern look at Adverse possession.* Centre for Rural Affairs, www.cfra.org 1.

[58] ibid.

[59] J.A Clarke, "Adverse Possession of Identity: Radical Theory, Conventional Practice." Oregon Law Review vol. 84 (2005) 563 at 566-567.

[60] 36 U.S. 41, 49 (1837). In that case, Ewing claimed a sand and gravel lot adjacent to his property relying on evidence of tax payments on the lot, exclusive right of digging and removing sand and gravel, and brought an action of trespass against others who attempted to remove sand and gravel without his permission. Accepting these acts as evidence of adverse possession, the Supreme Court held that "[n]either actual occupation, cultivation nor residence, are necessary to constitute actual possession, when the property is so situated as not to admit of any permanent useful improvement, and the continued claim of the party has been evidenced by public acts of ownership, such as he would exercise over property which he claimed in his own right, and would not exercise over property which he did not claim."

[61] Clarke, supra (n 59) at 567.

While generally, contemporary utilitarian scholars justify possession of squatters in adverse possession on the ground that it promotes "investment, commercialisation, civic diversity and political decentralization,"[62] modern society "now routinely enforces and, one presumes, places social utility in conservation and preservation restrictions"[63] and sometimes, "less productive uses may be best for society."[64]

3.4.5 The Economic Theory

The economic theory provides a rationale for adverse possession from the perspective of economic efficiency. Providing a structure for assessing such efficiency, Calabresi and Melamed argue that legal rules should allocate entitlements efficiently in order to reduce societal costs or costs to third parties.[65]

The theory is predicated on "the assumption that production and use are socially preferable to stagnation and disuse"[66] with positive effect on valuation of property. In allocating entitlements, it is said that "society should assess the end-result of distributional goals sought to be achieved"[67] adding that "[t]here are also preferences which are linked to

---

[62] E.R Claeyes, Locke Unlocked: Productive Use in Trespass, Adverse Possession, and Labour Theory. George Mason University Law and Economics Research Paper Series February 21 2012 at 61.

[63] ibid.

[64] J.E Stake, "The Uneasy Case for Adverse Possession" 89 Geo L.J 2419 at 2435 (2001).

[65] G. Calabresi and A.D Melamed, "Property Rules, Liability Rules, and Inalienability: One view of the Cathedral," 85 Harv. L. Rev. 1089, 1093-94 (1972).

[66] M. R Baron, "Weeks v. Krysa: Cultivating the Garden of Adverse Possession" 62 Me. L. Rev. 289 (2010). Available at: http://digitalcommons.mainelaw.maine.edu/mlr/vol62/iss1/10 .Accessed on 27 September 2019, citing G. Calabresi and A.D Melamed, supra (n 30) above.

[67] ibid, at 297.

dynamic efficiency concepts" such as "producers ought to be rewarded since they will cause everyone to be better off in the end."[68]

Apart from adding productivity to the social network, Posner[69] points out that adverse possession has the advantage of shifting a property right from the passive title owner who attaches no significant economic value to the property, to another who has shown a higher valuation through use. Also, Demsetz is of the view that "the general welfare will be better served if material resources are owned and controlled by private individuals."[70]

The economic approach to adverse possession has found rationale in minimising transaction costs where a party to a potential transaction is absent, holds out or fails to accurately assess the market value of the property. In such cases, property owners should be subject to potential adverse possession, encouraging them to make themselves known thereby reducing transaction costs for any potential buyer.[71]

3.4.6 The Social Function of Property Theory

One of the theories advanced as justification for the doctrine of adverse possession in contemporary time is the social function of property. The social function of property theory deprecates the idea of property as a subjective and nearly absolute right to property.[72] It opposes the idea of the classical liberal conception of property that property is an independent positive exercise of bundle of rights to private property such

---

[68] Calabresi and Melamed, supra (n 65) at 1098.

[69] R.A. Posner, "Savigny Holmes, and the Law and Economics of Possession"86 VA.L.Rev. 535, 559-60 (2000).

[70] H. Demsetz, "Towards a Theory of Property Rights." American Economic Review: Proceedings and Papers, 57 at 348 (1967).

[71] T.W. Merrill, "Property Rules, Liability Rules, and Adverse Possession," 79 NW. U. L. Rev. 1122, 1130-31 (1985).

[72] See generally SR Foster & D Bonilla, 'The Social Function of Property: A comparative Law Perspective.' Fordham Law Review [2011] vol. 80 101.

as the right to use, reap the benefits of and dispose of assets"limited only by the legal order and the common good."[73]

Duguit,[74] a proponent of this theory, argues that "property is not a right but rather a social function."[75] The idea is, creating an obligation on the part of the owner of property to put it at the service of the community which is tantamount to putting it into production- an obligation which the state superintend by intervention when there is a breach.[76] The rationale for this theory lies in interdependence between people as the central element of social reality.

Duguit criticises the individualism of the liberal right to property on three main grounds: First, he argues that a foundation resting on the presumption of the existence of an isolated individual "does not correspond with an accurate description of reality;" individuals are interconnected beings that need each other to meet their physical and spiritual needs.[77] Secondly, he says there is inconsistency between the idea of an isolated individual exercising the right of property and the negative duties on third parties, since third party obligation would not be necessary where property rights are enjoyed by isolated individuals. Thirdly, that it is puzzling that "classical liberal property exists only to serve individual interests."[78] This obscures the greater function of property which is to serve the larger interests of the community and tantamount to putting it into production. It is said that "the wealth concentrated in property cannot remain unproductive" and may lead to

---

[73] L Lomansky, *Persons, Rights, and the Moral Community* 111-51 (1987) cited in Foster and Bonilla, supra (n 72).

[74] L Duguit, *Las Transformaciones Del Derecho Publico Y Privado* (Editorial Heliasta 1975).

[75] Duguit, supra (n 74) at 236. According to him, the idea of property right dates back to the Declaration of the Rights of Man of 1789 (Art 2) and the Napoleonic Code (Art 544 and 545). See Foster & Banilla, supra (n 72) at 104.

[76] The intervention may be by way of taxation and expropriation. See Foster & Bonilla, supra (n 72).

[77] Duguit, supra (n 74) at 181 cited in Foster and Bonilla, supra (n 72) 104-105.

[78] ibid 237.

negative social circumstances thereby putting social cohesion in jeopardy.[79]

This theory underscores the extinction of title over unproductive land at the end of the limitation period in many jurisdictions[80] and informs constitutional provisions safeguarding public interest in the occupation and use of abandoned land.[81] Many international instruments[82] on the protection of right to private and family life, the state obligation in making provision for adequate and affordable housing available for the homeless are all reminiscent of the social function of property.

3.5 Limitations to the Traditional Theories and the Emergence of New Theories

Apart from the general critique against the traditional theories of adverse possession earlier discussed, it would appear that there are limitations to the perspectives of the role of adverse possession in modern property law, necessitating an appraisal of other theories affecting the efficacy of the doctrine from a broader perspective.

The application of the concept of property in modern times is not constant but dynamic depending, inter-alia, on the existing legal and

[79] Foster & Bonilla, supra (n 72) at 105.

[80] See for example, the Limitation Act 1980 applicable in England and Wales discussed in chapter 5 *infra* and the Limitation Act 1966 applicable in Nigeria and discussed in chapter 6 *infra*.

[81] See for example, s. 44(2)(i) of the Constitution of the Federal Republic of Nigeria 1999 as amended which excludes acquisition of land by the operation of the statute of limitation from the ambit of provision for compensation. See also s. 26 of the Constitution of the Republic of South Africa, 1996 in balancing competing interests and, in particular sub section (3) on protection of squatters' rights.

[82]See for example, International Covenant on Civil and Political Rights (ICCPR), Art. 6 with a corresponding provision on Right to adequate standard of living including Housing as contained in the International Covenant on Social, Cultural and Economic Rights (ICSCER), Art. 11.

institutional frameworks in operation within the jurisdiction(s) in view at the relevant time. It is also said that "the traditional rationales fall short," as "some rest on shaky or on outdated normative foundations [while] others do not fit the doctrinal contours."[83] It is said, the fact that the doctrine of adverse possession applies in varying circumstances has been responsible for the difficulty in finding a rationale for it.[84] Whilst the doctrine may be associated with title disputes generally, it may be contextual in the sense that it may not relate substantially to the question of ownership over the entire land, but may be narrowed down to the extent of ownership in boundary dispute matters, necessitating justification under different rationales.[85]

The perceived universality of the doctrine of adverse possession is subject to local circumstances thereby subjecting it to the '**relativity theory**' and making it inapplicable. This is the case under the Nigerian legal system where the legislature has expressly made the Statute of Limitation inapplicable under customary law,[86] thereby obviating the application of the doctrine of adverse possession.[87] In England[88], and to some extent Nigeria,[89] the regime of title registration would propel the '**indefeasibility of title theory**' or the '**security of title theory**' operating on the doctrine of adverse possession and tweaking its application and *ipso facto*, the basis for it.[90] Also, the regime of the Land Use Act in Nigeria has paved way for the **grant theory of title** resulting in adverse consequences for the efficacy of the doctrine. The human rights regime in

---

[83] J.E Starke, supra (n 64) at 2421.

[84] ibid.

[85] ibid.

[86] Limitation Act 1966, s.1(2).

[87] The Act provides that time runs in favour of an adverse possessor only.

[88] See the Land Registration Act 2002.

[89] See e,g, the Lagos State Land Registration Law No.1, 2015.

[90] In the England and Wales for example, an adverse possessor intending to protect his acquired title is expected to register it, while the application for such registration is brought to the notice of the actual owner, thereby giving him the opportunity to oppose such registration and to eject the adverse possessor.

both jurisdictions have been affected by local[91] and international[92] instruments on the sanctity of land rights resulting in the evolvement of the **sanctity of property rights theory**. Also, the criminalisation policy affecting adverse possession in both jurisdictions has brought about a controversial regime of **incompatibility** between a property law right premised on civil law, and the act of adverse possession tagged 'criminal trespass' and penalised with terms of imprisonment. These developments as this literature demonstrates, have given another dimension to the effectiveness of adverse possession as a mode of acquiring title in both jurisdictions under discourse.

As could be seen from the ensuing discussion, these modern theories are fall-outs from decades of judicial pronouncements, various reception statutes overtime, constitutional provisions, specific pieces of local legislation and international human rights instruments.

3.5.1 The Relativity Theory

One of the legacies of colonialism in many parts of the world and particularly in Africa, is the reception of foreign law by the colonised.[93] In

[91] The Human Rights Act, United Kingdom, 1998 applicable in England and Wales; Constitution of the Federal Republic of Nigeria, 1999, as amended, s. 43.

[92] Protocol 1 of the European Charter on Human Rights applicable in the United Kingdom; African Charter on Human and Peoples' Rights domesticated and passed as an Act of the National Assembly in Nigeria: See Cap A9 Laws of the Federation of Nigeria, 2010.

[93] This is known as legal transplant. This could come in different shapes and sizes. It could be major or minor; voluntary or imposed. It is voluntary where a country never experienced the domineering might of colonialism but propelled by the drive to attain radical transformation, embarked on the process of legal transplantation. This drive made countries such as Turkey, Ethiopia and Thailand to mention a few, to borrow alien systems to their advantage. Legal transplant is imposed consequent upon conquests and/or colonisation. This was the situation in the 19th Century Europe with the dissemination of the Napoleonic Code following conquests by Napoleon Bonaparte resulting in countries such as Spain, Portugal, Austria and the Germanic States to mention a few, adopting the Code. Also,

Nigeria where English law was received through an Act of Parliament,[94] the legal transplant took place subject to local laws and local circumstances.[95] The relevant clauses to that effect make the application of English law in Nigeria subject to local Laws and local circumstances, and the application of the doctrine of adverse possession is not an exception.

One characteristic feature of legal systems affected by a process of legal transplant[96] is the existence of indigenous laws and institutions albeit in rudimentary form prior to the advent of colonialism. This has generated socio-cultural conflicts and the need to adapt the foreign laws to suit same.[97] In Nigeria for example, this has resulted in the enactment of reception statutes stipulating conditions for the application of the English common law and statutes[98] But as discussed later,[99] there is a conundrum of uncertainties in applying the English land tenure concepts to local systems of landholding, particularly with the advent of the Land Use Act 1978.

---

many countries in Africa such as Nigeria, Ghana, Sierra Leone and other commonwealth countries which experienced colonisation at one time or the other, had no option but to adopt the laws of their colonial masters. See generally, W. Allan, *Legal Transplants,* 1974 Edinburg Scottish Academic Press Ltd, 21; JH Beckstrom, 'Reception of Law in Ethiopia', American Journal of Comparative Law, vol 21, 557; AN Allot, New *Essays in African Law,* Butterworth at 10; AN Allot, *The Future of African Law,* Butterworth at 220; IO Smith, 'Legal Transplant in a Developing Society: A critical Appraisal of the Reception of English Law in Nigeria.' Lagos State University (1987) Faculty of Law Seminar Series, vol. 1 at 1; IM Valderrama, 'Legal Transplants and Comparative Law.' Available online at: https//researchgate.net/publication/256014383_Legal_Transplants_and_Comparative_Law (December 2004); JO Ogbonnaya, H Chioma, 'Jurisprudential Issues Arising from Legal Transplant: An Appraisal.' Journal of Law, Policy and Globalisation vol 50 (2016).

[94] See the Law (Miscellaneous Provisions) Act Cap 89 Laws of Nigeria 1964.

[95] ibid, s.45 (2) and (3).

[96] See n. 93 above.

[97] See literature cited in n.93 above.

[98] See n.93 above.

[99] See chapters 6, 8 and 10*infra.*

The relativity theory played out in the comment of Lord Denning in *Nyali v. Attorney General*[100]wheninterpreting the clause: 'subject to such qualifications as local circumstances may render necessary, as contained in the East Africa Protectorate Order in Council 1900 as follows:

> ...the common law cannot be applied in a foreign land without considerable qualification. Just as with the English oak, so with the English common law. You cannot transfer it to the African continent and expect it to retain the tough character, which it has in England. It will flourish indeed but it needs careful tending. So, with the English common law. It has many principles of manifest justice and good sense which can be applied with advantage to peoples of every race and colour all over the world, but it has also many refinements, subtleties and technicalities which are not suited to other folks. These offshoots must be cut away. In these far off lands, the people must have a law which they understand and which they will respect. The common law cannot fulfil this role except with considerable qualifications.

The relativity theory has been put to use by the legislature in Nigeria where the doctrine of adverse possession is made inapplicable under customary law by legislative fiat,[101] and it does not apply post Land Use Act 1978[102], although Nigerian courts are often not at home with this reality.[103] A study of the traditional theories on adverse possession offers no explanation for this diversity.

---

[100] [1955] 1 All ER 646 at 652-653.

[101] For a detailed analysis on this, see Chapter 6 *infra*.

[102] Cap L5 Laws of the Federation of Nigeria, 2010. This is so because section 48 of the Act which preserves pre-existing land tenure systems makes them subject to the provisions of the Act; provisions which have rendered the doctrine of adverse possession impotent. For a detailed analysis, see Chapter 6 *infra*.

[103] In fairness to Nigerian judges, running through decided cases, that point has never been canvassed by counsel before them. For a critique of these decades of decisions post 1978 when the Land Use Act was enacted, see Chapter 6 *infra*.

3.5.2 The Indefeasibility Theory

The theory of indefeasibility of title proposes that once a person is registered as a proprietor of a certain estate or interest in land, such title cannot be vitiated except as prescribed by the registration of title law itself.[104] It is said that the regime of registered title not only protect the title of the registered proprietor from unregistered interests, but also obviates the need to go "behind the register in order to investigate the validity of title or possible rival claims to the land."[105]

As discussed later in Chapter 10, the English Land Registration Act 2002, and to some extent, the Lagos State Registration Law 2015 in Nigeria provide for a system of title registration which serves as 'mirror' of title, and sometimes prompting the real owner to act timeously to protect his or her title to land. The UK Land Registration Act 2002 applicable in England and Wales provides an alert for the paper owner to challenge the occupation of the adverse possessor, makes the basis of title primarily the fact of registration as opposed to possession, and makes it generally difficult for the adverse possessor to be registered as a proprietor.[106] To the extent that the indefeasibility theory makes the register as opposed to possession the relevant fact in the acquisition of title to land, it runs contrary to the traditional theories of adverse possession.

---

[104] See *Custodian of Expropriated Property & Anor v. Tedep&Ors*[1964] 113 CLR, 331-332; and the Nigerian case of *Majekodunmi v. Abina* (2002) 1 SC 92.

[105] See S.L Martin, "Adverse Possession: Practical Realities and an Unjust Enrichment Standard." Frank G. Zarb School of Business, 2008. Available online at alsb.roudtablelive.org/Resources/Documents/NP%202008%20Martin.pdf.
Accessed on 10/10/2019; Griggs, "Possession, indefeasibility and Human Rights."(2008) 8(2) QUT Law JJ. 286; *Gibbs v. Messer* [1891] AC 248 at 204.

[106] For the flip side of the indefeasibility theory applicable in title registration, see M. Pawlowski and J. Brown, "Adverse Possession and the Transmissibility of Possessory rights–The dark side of Land Registration." [2017] (2) Conv. 116-131. Also available online at www.https://research.aston.ac.uk

3.5.3 The Grant Theory

The regime of the Land Use Act[107] in Nigeria has brought radical changes to the ownership structure in Nigeria[108] resulting in a new concept of 'right of occupancy' which confers no absolute right of ownership,[109] and with radical title vested absolutely in the chief executive of the state,[110] who has the sole prerogative to make a grant of statutory right of occupancy.[111] From the Land Use Act arises the **'grant theory'** impacting on the natural effect of adverse possession known to common law which recognises absolute but relative title; a title which simply passes to an adjudged adverse possessor without much ado.[112]

In a situation such as the regime of the Nigerian Land Use Act where radical title is vested in the Governor of the State (or in the Minister on behalf of the President with regard to the Federal land) who makes a grant, actual or deemed[113] to a holder of a right of occupancy having only

---

[107] Land Use Act, Cap L5 Laws of the Federation of Nigeria, 2010.

[108] Absolute ownership became streamlined and reduced to a right of occupancy which is, for all intent and purposes, a lease: See *Majiyagbe v. AG Northern Nigeria* (1957) NNLR 158, a case decided under the old Land Tenure Law of the old Northern Region with similar provisions to those of the Land Use Act 1978; *Savannah Bank (Nig) Ltd v. Ajilo*(1989) 1 NWLR (Pt. 97) 305 at 328. For a contrary argument as to whether a right of occupancy is a lease, see Chapter 6 *infra.*

[109] As to whether the Land Use Act gives a term of years, See Chapter 6 *infra.*

[110] ibid, s.1.

[111] ibid, s. 5(1). The Local Governments in the state may also register a person as a holder of a customary right of occupancy. Title holders existing before the advent of the Land Use Act continue to hold the land as deemed grantees of right of occupancy: See the Land Use Act, supra (n 107), ss. 34 and 36.

[112] Whereas adverse possession in its pristine state generally presupposes the existence of the real owner and the adverse possessor, the position under the Land Use Act involves three parties namely, holder of a right of occupancy, the claimant of adverse possession (if recognised by law) and the State represented by the Governor, or the Minister, or the Local government.

[113] Actual grant is made directly to a citizen of Nigeria by the Governor under section 5(1) of the Act whether the land is situate in urban or non-urban area, whilst all holders of unlimited interest in land such as the fee simple estate or

a right to occupy and use land, and, in some cases, for a definite term, the effect of the 'statutory conveyance' of title after the extinction of the paper owner's title cannot be the same. This is complicated by the prohibition of false claims to land and the provisions of sanctions for breach.[114] This argument is canvassed robustly in Chapter 7.

3.5.4 Sanctity of Property Right Theory

In England, the Human Rights Act 1998[115] which domesticated the European Convention on Human Rights[116] on the one hand, and in Nigeria, both the Constitution of the Federal Republic of Nigeria 1999 as amended, and the African Charter on Human and Peoples' Rights as domesticated by an Act of the National Assembly[117] on the other hand, have the right to property enshrined in them. These instruments have made it generally wrongful or unlawful to deprive a person of his or her right of property except in some limited justifiable circumstances,[118] and created international obligations on the part of both jurisdictions to uphold the sanctity of property rights. However, while the fore-mentioned legal instruments are literally clear in their intent, judicial

---

customary right before the advent of the Land Use Act in 1978 had their titles streamlined and converted to rights of occupancy by the Act under sections 34 and 36 of the Act respectively. In the same vein, the President of the Federal Republic of Nigeria through the Minister of the Federal Capital Territory can make an actual grant with regard to Federal lands in the State or lands within the Federal Capital Territory: See s. 47 of the Act.

[114] Land Use Act supra, n.107, ss. 37, 43.

[115] Human Rights Act Cap 42, 1998. Information on this is online at https//www.Legislation.gov.uk.

[116] See in particular, Protocol 1 Art. 1 of the Protocol to the Convention for the Protection of Human Rights and Fundamental Freedoms. Paris, 20.III.1952.

[117] Cap A10 Law of the Federation of Nigeria, 2004.

[118] See e.g. proviso to Art. 1, Protocol 1 of the European Convention for the Protection of Human Rights and Fundamental Freedoms; s.44(1) of the Constitution of the Federal Republic of Nigeria 1999 as amended; and Art. 14 of the African Charter on Human and Peoples' Rights. See Chapter 8 *infra*for a full discussion on this.

interpretation of their provisions may constitute a barrier to the realisation of the social objective. This discourse is taken further in Chapters 8.

3.5.5 The Incompatibility Theory

In both England and Nigeria, there are laws criminalising fraudulent claims of title through illegitimate and wrongful possession amounting to "land theft,"[119] making the trespasser or squatter liable to prosecution despite his legitimate claim and 'smart' reliance on the limitations statute to bolster up a claim in adverse possession. The effect of this is the incongruity of different civil and criminal law intendments, and a 'comedy' of confusion in the administration of justice in both jurisdictions under study. While the ensuing conundrum of uncertainty in this regard awaits the court's intervention in Nigeria, the English Court of Appeal held in *Best v. Chief Land Registrar and the Secretary of State for Justice*[120]that the adverse possessor's application for registration should be allowed by the Registrar on the ground that Parliament did not intend that adverse possession "be prevented because it was based on criminal trespass."[121] From this incongruous model of the civil and criminal dispensation arises the '**incompatibility theory**' behind the legal maxim, '*ex turpi causa non oritur actio*' with far reaching consequences. This argument is taken further in Chapter 10.

The foregoing developments tend to affect the efficacy of the rule of adverse possession in both jurisdictions with far reaching consequences.[122]

---

[119] See the Criminal Law of Lagos State 2011(Nigeria); and the Legal Aid, Sentencing and Punishment of Offenders .Act 2012 (United Kingdom) for provisions on criminal trespass.

[120] *R (on the application of Best) v. The Chief Land Registrar and the Secretary of State for Justice* [2015] EWCA Civ 17.

[121] ibid, para 34.

[122] For a practical implications of these developments, see chapters 6, 10 and 11 *infra*.

3.6 Conclusion

This Chapter has demonstrated that whilst the traditional theories underline the rationale behind the doctrine of adverse possession as discussed later in Chapter 4, the contemporary theories which dictate the contextual application of the doctrine underline its efficacy as discussed in Chapters 6, 7, 8, 9, 10 and 11.

CHAPTER 4
RATIONALE UNDERLYING THE DOCTRINE OF ADVERSE POSSESSION

4.1 Introduction

Many jurisdictions[1] allow a squatter who has been in uninterrupted but adverse possession of another's land over a period of time to lay claim to it, while the original owner has his/her title extinguished without payment of compensation by the squatter.[2] Proponents and adversaries of the doctrine of adverse possession rely on certain rationale to either welcome or condemn the doctrine of adverse possession which has made this possible, while some often cite certain objectives of the rule as justification for its application.

This chapter identifies and discusses the various rationale underlying the application of the doctrine and engages its main objectives with a view to assessing the application of the doctrine in England and Nigeria. This Chapter critically assesses the efficacy of the doctrine in these jurisdictions against the backdrop of the rationale and objectives of the rule.

---

[1] These jurisdictions include all common law jurisdictions including the United Kingdom, the United States of America and Nigeria; and the civil law jurisdictions such as France, Spain, The Netherlands, Sweden, Hungary, Poland and Germany. See the Report of the British Institute of International and Comparative Law for Her Majesty's Court Service, September 2006 on 'Adverse Possession.' Available online at http:www.biicl.org/files/2350_advposs_sep_ftnsv3.pdf. Accessed on 10/10/2019.

[2] Apart from the various common law jurisdictions (See e.g. UK Limitation Act 1980, Nigeria Limitation Act 1966), prominent amongst the civil law jurisdictions with Limitation Laws are France (Art 2229 of the French Civil Code); Spain (Art 41 of the Spanish Civil Code); the Netherlands (Art 3.99(1), 3.105(1) of the Netherlands Civil Code); Sweden (Cap 16 Real Property Code); Hungary (s. 121(1) Civil Code Act IV 1959); Poland (Art 172-176 Polish Civil Code); Germany (Para 900 BG-B German Civil Code): See the Report of the British Institute of International and Comparative Law for Her Majesty's Court Service, September 2006, supra note 1 above.

The rationale behind the rule of adverse possession may vary depending on whether the subject matter of dispute relates to title to land, or the extent to which ownership claim extends as in the case of boundary disputes.[3] It may also depend on whether the claimant is an individual or the state;[4] or on the type of property-whether it is meant as a place of abode (e.g. a home) or meant for investment or intended so,[5] or, whether

---

[3] In the words of Stake, ''[O]ne of the difficulties in finding a rationale for this doctrine is that it applies in widely varying situations…the issue can always be boiled down to whether a given person owns a given piece of land. But the context of the disputes varies in ways that could be important. In title disputes, the basic issue is whether some person owns anything at all. In boundary disputes, the issue is not who owns land, but how far geographically that ownership extends.'' 'See J.E Stake, ''The Uneasy Case for Adverse Possession.'' Articles by Maurer Faculty. Paper 221. Available online at http//www.repository.law.indiana.edu/facpub/221 2419 at 2421. Accessed on 25/10/2019.

[4] Marra draws a distinction between justification for individual and government adverse possession. In the first place, he says that the assumption that "the record owner has property rule interest in her property and an ejectment right against the trespasser'' does not apply when government is the adverse possessor as the owner's property right of ejectment does not apply to government as the latter has the power of eminent domain which entitles it to take the land subject to payment of compensation. Second, the assumption that "society has a robust interest, above all else, in quiet marketable titles" does not apply when government is the adverse possessor, apart from "ensuring that the state does not abuse its power or…trespass on land rather than exercise its eminent domain power." Third, the idea that a trespasser develops "robust reliance interest over time," does not apply where the adverse possessor is the state for, not only is government not psychologically attached to land unlike an individual, the unlikelihood of ejectment carries less risk of loss of investment on its part. See W.C Marra, "Adverse Possession, Takings and the State." University of Detroit Mercy Law Review (2011) vol. 89 No.1, 1 at 2, 3.

[5] This factor operated on the minds of the Justices of the Grand Chamber of the European Court of Human Rights in *J.A Pye (Oxford) Ltd v. UK* (2006) 43 EHRR 45, provoking public protests and negative media commentary, following the Colorado court's judgment in *McLean and Stevens v. DK Trust and Kirlin*, (2007)

indeed, the adverse possessor exhibited good or bad faith in exercising adverse possession among others.[6] These and other underlying factors are examined in more detail in this Chapter.

4.2 Suggested Rationale

A number of rationale have been suggested by writers[7] for the application of the rule of adverse possession namely: discouraging owner's tardiness; quieting titles; facilitating market transfers; protecting investments in aid of development; reducing boundary uncertainties; protecting rights of those with a compelling fairness claim to ownership; and protecting third party rights.

4.2.1 Discouraging Owner's Tardiness

The law applicable in the common law jurisdictions including England and Nigeria cherishes vigilance on the part of the landowner and abhors indolence, tardiness or slow response to encroachment on land.[8] In the same vein, the civil process of ventilating rights or claims in court places time limitation on bringing action in court when the cause of action arises. The reason for this stance of the law is to discourage stale claims and ensure an end to litigation. Consequently, the Statute of Limitation prescribes the time within which actions including action for declaration of title to land and claim for possession of land shall be taken. This has a

---

Boulder District Court Case No. 06 CV 982. Both decisions are discussed in Chapter 6*infra*.

[6] While this consideration may be relevant in title disputes generally, it may be of no moment in land boundary disputes. See generally, E. Cooke, *The New Law of Land Registration* (Hart Publishing 2003) 134; R.H Helmholz, "Adverse Possession and Subjective Intention" (1983) 61 Washington University Law Quarterly 331, 332.

[7] See generally, Stake, supra (n 3); H. Conway and J. Stannard (2013) NILQ 64(1) 75 at 76,77; W.C Marra, supra, (n 4) at 14-22.

[8] The court of equity frowns against delays or indolence, which underlines the maxim: "Equity aids the vigilant and not the indolent."

number of consequences on the conduct of the owner of land in a claim of adverse possession by a squatter.

One of those consequences is to impose penalty on a landowner who slept on his/her right. Such land owner is often referred to as a 'wrongdoer' who ought to be penalised by losing the right of possession on the land.[9] It is said that this "balances the scales of justice."[10] It is also said that "[t]he doctrine prods lazy owners into putting their land into production."[11]

However, these two justifications have been faulted by writers. It is argued that the "assumption of our economic and legal system is that we protect rights in land…with what…have famously been named property rules that require someone who wants to obtain a thing to buy it from the owner."[12] In the words of Stake,[13] "…the person who leaves unattended or refrains from suing someone is not culpable; he has not behaved reprehensibly and does not deserve to lose his right."

On "putting the land into productive use" as justification for the rule of adverse possession, societal needs in modern times may support preservation of land for the purpose of recuperation of the soil, or for conservation in order to protect natural habitat or endangered species, and these are often the subject of legislative interference.[14] The courts have also recognised conservation easement in the form of servitudes for 'nature conservancy.'[15] Non-productive use of land by the owner may be justified if future use would generate proportionately less positive externalities than current use in which case, "the owner's self-interested decision will also serve society's interest."[16] The fact that the owner may avoid loss of title by constant monitoring of the land shows that the

[9] W.B. Stoebuck and D.A Whitman, The Law of Property, 853, 860 (3rd ed. 2000).

[10] J.E Stake, supra (n 3) at 2435.

[11] ibid.

[12] ibid, at 2421.

[13] ibid, at 2435.

[14] ibid.

[15] ibid.

[16] ibid, at 2436.

statute of limitation may be "a poor stick" for actualising the policy of putting the land into productive use.[17]

Another notable consequence of the statute of limitation and the rule of adverse possession abhorring owner's tardiness is to ensure that the owner monitors his/her land to discover any squatter thereon. This gives the owner the opportunity of early discovery and an opportunity of bringing action to recover possession timeously.[18] The advantages of suing the squatter without delay lie in minimizing costs and avoiding evidence getting stale, "less trust worthy or more ambiguous."[19] It could also afford buyers the opportunity to communicate their offers to purchase.

However, while the statute of limitation and the rule of adverse possession may be advantageous to parties and the courts in that it may obviate the time and trouble of going into history of the title in dispute, there remains the arduous task of proving actions and intent of the adverse possessor over a long period of time. On the part of the owner, there is the need to determine whether the owner has ä cause of action to regain possession and when that cause of action arose.[20]

4.2.2 Quieting Title

A popular rationale often advanced for the statute of limitation is that it quiets title, making it more settled and certain.[21] It is claimed that the rule of adverse possession provides a quicker and cheaper method of ascertaining title and ensures security of tenure.[22] Since security and

---

[17] ibid.

[18] In the words of Merrill, "[a] rule requiring prompt resolution of claims is...efficient in that it helps to minimise the costs of litigation and trial." See T.W Merrill, "Property Rules, Liability Rules, and Adverse Possession." 79 Nw. U. L. Rev. 112, 117 (1984).

[19] J.E Stake, supra (n 3) at 2438.

[20] ibid, at 2439.

[21] ibid, at 2441.

[22] J.E Stake, supra (n 3) at 2442.

certainty of title are the hallmark of valid transfers and furnishes the prospect and opportunity required to access credit, adverse possession appears to be a safety valve.

However, the proliferation of title insurance in the modern day transactions involving land titles, and the regime of title registration in some jurisdictions appear to provide better ways of quieting titles and raise the question whether adverse possession is still of potent utility. In both England and Nigeria, title insurance is a remarkable safety valve in transactions involving title to land, while the regime of title registration, as will be discussed,[23] would make title indefeasible and more reliable.

4.2.3 Facilitating Market Transfers

It is claimed that adverse possession facilitates market transfers and makes transactions involving land reliable and secure.[24]Empirical support is found for this rationale by Netter, Hersch, and Manson[25] in a recent study on title registration, assuming that "certainty can be added by giving additional weight to the record." Their position"assume that shortening a statute of limitations increases a prospective purchaser's certainty," suggesting that "shorter statutes were adopted where land was more valuable."[26]

Apart from tightening lose ends of title for a prospective purchaser relying on the owner's record when indeed, there is an adverse possessor on the land, adverse possession fills the missing gap where the owner is missing with no assurance that he/she would show up and reclaim the land.[27] Merrill also argues that in the absence of adverse possession, there would be more defects in title resulting in higher

---

[23] See Chapter 7 *infra.*

[24] See J.M Netter et.al., "An Economic Analysis of Adverse Possession Statutes." 6 Int'l Rev. L. & Econ 217, 220 (1986).

[25] ibid.

[26] ibid.

[27] J.E. Stake, supra (n 3) at 2442, 2443.

insurance premium and consequently, in a downturn in the market for land transactions.[28]

But while assisting prospective purchaser in getting a reliable title from the owner, it is said that "the existence of the doctrine of adverse possession makes it more costly for owners to prove their ownership to judges, and therefore, to potential buyers."[29] Prospective purchasers cannot afford the time to be lost, and the owner, the expense to be incurred on litigation.

4.2.4 Protecting Investments in Aid of Development

It is claimed that "[a]dverse possession...promotes development by clearing up errors in the records and increasing certainty of ownership."[30] Where title is uncertain, the possibility of underinvestment is high with adverse consequences on economic development. Security of title is a factor estate investors cannot compromise, making it imperative to have in place a clear record of title. Adverse possession is therefore a potent way of assuring the investor of security of tile.

However, a number of pitfalls are known to overrun the said justification for the rule of adverse possession as a protector of investment. In the first place, the existence of the record owner does not obviate the presence of an adverse possessor unknown to the investor, and the realisation of this overriding interest in future may throw up a conundrum of uncertainties resulting in loss of valuable improvements on land by the investor. It is said therefore that "[t]oday, adverse possession is one of the primary reasons why the record is not accurate."[31]

---

[28] T.W Merrill, supra (n 18) at 1129.

[29] J.E Stake, supra (n 3) at 2442, 2443.

[30] ibid, at 2444.

[31] ibid.

Also, the presumption of good title in respect of ownership dating back to a certain period prescribed by law[32] may furnish a better and more reliable protection than adverse possession.[33] In the case of jurisdictions with improver statutes, "the record owner pays the possessor the market value of improvements made in good faith;" a provision assuring the developer that "a good part of his investment will be returned to him if the land turns out to belong to someone else."[34] The improver statute, when applied along with title insurance and marketable title acts, provides a panacea for insecurity of title and undermines "that proffered justification for the doctrine of adverse possession."[35] Consequently, the view is held that while "a rationale focusing on incentives for investment in land improvements has some appeal,...[it] ultimately cannot justify the scope of the traditional doctrine today."[36]

4.2.5 Reducing Boundary Uncertainties

Reducing uncertainty about boundaries is seen as the major benefit of adverse possession considering the regularity of minor incursions into the land of another, and the inadvertent conduct associated with such encroachment. In disputes resulting from adverse possession, boundary

---

[32] Under a system of unregistered conveyancing in both England and Nigeria ownership traceable to forty years before the transfer is evidence of good title.

[33] Certain advantages have been identified by Starke as accruing to this marketable title acts which make them superior to adverse possession. In his words: "...marketable acts are superior to adverse possession in three ways. First, they terminate old claims even more effectively. Second, marketable title acts do not shift attention from the record to unrecorded and unrecordable evidence, but rather restrict attention to the newer instruments in the record, making disputes cheaper to resolve. Third, marketable title acts do not generate as much useless monitoring by record title holders. A possible fourth benefit is that marketable title acts do not deprive true owners of their property as often as does adverse possession." See J.E Starke, supra (n 3) at 2444.

[34] ibid, at 2445.

[35] ibid.

[36] ibid, at 2446.

disputes appear to be in the majority,[37] often arising from comparably smaller project of construction such as erection of fences in which case, reliance is placed on the use of survey rather than reliance on adverse possession, at low costs.

However, disputes involving major and expensive improvements encroaching on neighbour's land may necessitate reliance on the rule of adverse possession, "reducing the likelihood that the improvement will have to be removed..."[38] In any case, it is argued that the continued relevance of survey especially in this age of technology when the use of the GPRS is in vogue at lower costs, makes reliance on adverse possession in boundary disputes increasingly insignificant.[39]

4.2.6 Protecting rights Having Compelling Fairness Claim to Ownership

There is usually an individualist assumption that under the statute of limitation and *a fortiori* under the rule of adverse possession, there is a clean separation of the owner whose interest is extinguished at the end of the statutory period and the squatter who becomes an adverse possessor whose interest the statute protects.[40] This may not always be the situation in all cases for, the protection afforded by the statute of limitation may vary depending on circumstances. From the perspective of state policy for example, Ballantine opines that:[41]

> "The state has not for its object to reward the diligent trespasser for his wrong nor yet to penalise the negligent and dormant owner for sleeping on his rights; the great purpose is automatically to quiet all

[37] Netter, et al., supra (n 24) at 219.
[38] J.E Starke, supra (n 3) at 2447.
[39] ibid.
[40] See for example, the views of D. Ames, Lectures, Legal History, 197; A. Teisen III Am. Bar Assoc Journal, 127 (April 1917).
[41] H.W Ballantine, "Title by Adverse Possession." 32 Harv. L. Rev. 135, 135 (1918).

titles which are openly and consistently asserted, to provide proof of meritorious titles, and correct errors in conveyancing."

Thus, apart from quieting titles, other major objectives of adverse possession are: "to provide proof of meritorious titles, and correct errors in conveyancing." The circumstances under which these may happen vary. For example, a record owner with a defective or void title but who has been in adverse possession of land purportedly conveyed has not lost everything. In a situation such as this, "possession is better evidence of true or just ownership than the evidence from recorded documents," and same is protected by law.

The validity of such adverse possession is hinged on the relation-back theory which relates title by adverse possession back to the first day of adverse possession thereby making the adverse possessor non-liable for "trespasses occurring before the statute of limitation has run."[42] This illustration demonstrates that adverse possession offers protection mainly to rights having compelling fairness claim to ownership.

This rationale of 'protecting the true owners' by adverse possession is not free from lapses. It is said that the perception "of what is just are based in part on the legal system" so that "[i]f our title system were based wholly on the record, we might see little justice in claims based on facts outside the record."[43] Again, to the extent that a bad faith adverse possessor may gain title by adverse possession, "the law would seem quite unfair."[44] Furthermore, it is said that "true owners do not always get a chance to prove that their cause is just"[45] and "once the adverse possessor proves the elements, the doctrine makes evidence from the record and any other evidence on the record owner's behalf irrelevant."[46] It is also said that "[as] the record increases in reliability, the

---

[42] J.E Stake, supra (n 3) at 2452.

[43] ibid, at 2454.

[44] ibid.

[45] ibid, at 2455.

[46] ibid.

ratio of injustice to justice resulting from adverse possession also increases."[47]

4.2.7 Protection of Third Party Rights

Various third party rights may exist consequent upon possession by an adverse possessor which may be protected consequent upon protection of adverse possession by the statute of limitation. Amongst these rights are the right of easement or restrictive covenant and the right of creditors. In all these cases lies another rationale of the rule of adverse possession. The presumption that the person exercising peaceful, open but adverse possession on land is the owner of that land is in tandem with the notion of property right in law.

Prominent amongst the third party rights is the right of creditors to recover from the debtor, the cost of credit facility advanced to the debtor in the event of default. For example, access to credit by purchaser of goods and services may be given by the vendor based on the knowledge that the purchaser has lived on land for a substantial number of years. It is argued that "[b]y increasing the chances that the purchaser actually owns the land the vendor assumes he owns, the law increases the chances that the vendor will be able to collect on the debt"[48] based on the requisite guarantee of adverse possession.

However, the possibility of relying on possession of real property as a guarantee of ownership is fast becoming increasingly rare in modern times, and the likelihood is to "rely on the records of land ownership in extending credit instead of merely relying on the knowledge of the borrower's possession of land."[49] Consequently, it is argued that elimination of adverse possession would encourage vendors to "turn to

---

[47] ibid.

[48] ibid, at 2441.

[49] ibid.

the records" rather than the exhibited possession of the debtor in determining the latter's creditworthiness.[50]

4.3 Variation in Apportioning Rationales

The rationale underlining adverse possession may vary depending on a number of factors as earlier indicated. These factors have been responsible for the positive or negative public opinion influencing appropriate law making responses and judicial attitude over the years.

4.3.1 Title to Land or Boundary Disputes

Many of the rationale applicable in cases of disputes over wholesale parcels of land may not apply in cases of boundary disputes. In the first place, the area of encroachment may be relatively small or inconsequential to the general interests of parties to deserve the kind of attention and emotional outbursts compared with what is generated or experienced in cases of disputes over wholesale land title disputes.[51] Second, while possession over encroachment may be manifest in both cases of land titles and boundary disputes, the intent and motive differ as between the two for, while adverse possession in boundary cases is often found to be exercised in good faith (e.g. in the belief by the adverse possessor that the land belongs to him), courts are usually saddled with circumstances warranting a determination whether an adverse possessor of parcels of land acted in good or bad faith.[52] Third, it is most likely that an adverse possessor of the strip of land the subject of encroachment may be ready and willing to settle with the record owner by paying the price of the land rather than resort to litigation, since it may not be cost effective to do so considering the high costs of litigation, outcome of which may

[50] ibid.

[51] See generally, H. Conway and J. Stannard(n 7) at 81.

[52] See generally, Fennell, "Efficient Trespass: The case for bad faith Adverse Possession." 100 Northwestern University Law Review 1037 (2006).

not be too certain.[53] In addition, recourse to survey or making use of modern technology to resolve boundary disputes add up to make the rule of adverse possession of less importance in those cases.

4.3.2 Who the Adverse Possessor is

The adverse possessor may be an individual or government with different rationales or justifications for adverse possession, based on varying assumptions.[54] In the case of the individual squatter, there is a disincentive to trespass as a result of the property rule interest in the property of the owner entitling the latter to eject the trespasser.[55] However, this is not the case where government is the adverse possessor in which case, the record owner has only a "liability rule entitlement against the state" for compensation.[56]

While the assumption of adverse possession law "that society has a robust interest" above everyone else "in quiet marketable titles" may apply in the case of the individual adverse possessor, it does not apply as a rationale when government is the adverse possessor; the main objective of the law in the latter case is ensuring that "the state does not abuse its power or face a perverse incentive to trespass on land rather than exercise its power of eminent domain."[57]

Furthermore, while "adverse possession law assumes that the individual trespasser develops robust reliance interests over time," making it unjust for the record owner to eject him and appropriate his investment, such assumption does not apply in the case of government in adverse possession for, "government cannot be ejected from land, and there is less likelihood that it will lose its investment."[58] Also, the notion that "the more time the trespasser spends on the land, the more

---

[53] ibid.

[54] See generally, W.C Marra, supra (n 4).

[55] ibid, at 13.

[56] ibid.

[57] ibid, at 14.

[58] ibid.

psychologically attached to land he becomes" does not apply as rationale in the same way to government.[59]

4.3.3 Type of Property

In determining what rationale to ascribe to what category of adverse possession, it may be necessary to know what type of property is involved. For example, while adverse possession may be justifiable in the case of large expanse of land meant for investment purposes on the ground that the law would have to balance the interest of the lazy and unproductive record owner against the economic interest and development of the society at large,[60] it may generate negative emotions and may be condemned in totality in the case of property meant as a home.[61]

4.3.4 Motive of the Adverse Possessor

It is said that "cases do clearly show that the trespassers who knows he is trespassing stands lower in the eyes of the law…than the trespasser who acts in honest belief that he is simply occupying what is his already."[62] While it may be justifiable to turn a 'blind eye' on minor encroachments

---

[59] ibid.

[60] What weighed more in the minds of the House of Lords and both Chambers of the European Court of Human Rights in the English case of *J.A Pye (Oxford) Ltd v. Graham* (2003) 1 AC 419 (HL) (2006) 43 EHRR 3 and (2008) 46 EHRR 45, was the fact that the adverse possessor was an individual who was cultivating the large expanse of land in the public interest as opposed to a corporate record owner who was not putting the property to use.

[61] In the Colorado case of *McLean and Stevens v. DK Trust and Kirlin,* Booulder District Court Case No. 06 CV 982 (filed 4 October 2006), a non-consideration of this factor by the court in reaching its decision generated unprecedented public reactions leading to "sweeping amendments to the law of adverse possession in the state of Colorado making it virtually impossible for a similar claim to succeed in the future": See H. Conway and J. Stannard supra (n 7) at 81, 83.

[62] R.H Helmholz, supra (n 6).

and boundary disputes and "to tolerate the innocent, good faith squatter" who mistakenly encroached on the land of another, "the same cannot be said of the opportunistic 'bad faith' squatter who deliberately sets out to acquire land by adverse possession."[63]Judges sometimes tend to bend backwards and realising the manifest injustice to be done by contemptuous infringement of property right of the record owner, often "raise the legal threshold...by making it more evidentially difficult for such 'unconscionable' squatter to meet the two vital requirements of adverse possession namely, the 'intention to possess' or 'factual control of the land.'[64] Cooke notes a recurring attitude of English judges in adverse possession cases which tilts towards striving "to make things difficult for the squatter by setting the requirements...rather higher than they need be."[65] Thus, the current trend in judicial intervention regarding the motive of the adverse possessor tweaks the traditional rationale behind adverse possessor in favour of justice and fairness.

4.4 Assessment of Suggested Rationale and Arguments Against Adverse Possession.

There are arguments against the application of adverse possession from the foregoing appraisal of the suggested rationale. It is said that the rule has either become anachronistic and fast becoming irrelevant in the dynamic contemporary societies,[66] or has failed the notion of justice and fairness in the allocation of land rights.[67]

Efforts by law to sustain the rule often comes at certain costs which cannot be glossed over. Stake[68] identifies such costs among others,

---

[63] H. Conway and J. Stannard, supra (n 7) at 81.

[64] ibid at 85.

[65] E. Cooke, *The New Law of Land Registration* supra (n 6). See also Helmholz, supra (n 6) 339-34, for the same trend being noted by the courts in the United States.

[66] In the words of Stake, "...regardless of how well they served in the past, none of the justifications...will be entirely satisfactoryin the future, as the same benefit can now be achieved in less costly ways." See J.E Stake, supra (n 3) at 2455.

[67] ibid, at 2434.

[68] ibid, at 2432-2434.

as "the diminishing utility by discouraging owners from letting others use their land"[69] thereby preventing optimal use of land; "the cost of monitoring" in the search of possessors by the record owner, amounting to waste of resources;[70] cost of improvements made by squatter with a view to acquiring adverse possession, amounting not only to waste of resources, but also creating "an opportunity to steal land;"[71] and the cost imposed on the judicial system.[72] All these diminishes the utility of adverse possession and prods writers,[73] and the courts[74] for a re-think.

It is said that the legitimate aim if at all, of adverse possession "are irrelevant when it comes to the emotional reactions engendered" by it.[75] The emotional reaction of anger and disgust ventilated against the squatter and the regime of adverse possession is not without justification. In the words of Conway and Stannard:[76]

> "Ownership of property, and land in particular, is inextricably linked with certain social and cultural values. Land is much more than a precious natural resource which is vital for the sustenance of mankind; it is a potent and socially recognised symbol of material wealth, identity, social standing and financial security for the owner. The old mantra that 'an English man's home is his castle conjures up important notions of dominion and control, with ownership conveying a sense of 'economic power, individual self-meaning and personal self worth.' Adverse possession represents a direct attack, on these basic constructs and the feelings of happiness, well-being and personal satisfaction associated with ownership."

---

[69] ibid, at 2432.

[70] ibid, at 2433.

[71] ibid. The view that adverse possession is land theft has been deprecated as misconceived: See for example, L.A Fennell, supra (n 52).

[72] ibid, at 2434.

[73] See e.g Stake, supra (n 3), 2419; H. Conway and J. Stannard, supra (n 7), 75.

[74] See Chapter 12 (n 47)–(n 55) infra.

[75] H. Conway and J. Stannard, supra (n 7) at 77.

[76] ibid.

The English society thus attaches individual connection with land as a result of deep sense of emotional attachment, and "because every piece of land is unique and potentially irreplaceable." In the same vein, the Nigerian society recognises a strong emotional attachment to land reminiscent of the African tradition and cultural values. Under the traditional land tenure system, land is said to belong to the living, the dead and to generations yet unborn, and must therefore be preserved.[77] It is said to be an evidence of social status and cultural cohesion; encroachment by strangers is frowned upon, while transfer to them is required to be only with the consent of the community or family.[78]

The reception of English system of land tenure which resulted in individual ownership and commercialisation of land[79] and the advent of the Land Use Act[80]which streamlines the land tenure system in Nigeria have not altered the traditional believes or doused emotions associated with land ownership.[81]

Argument has also been canvassed that the notion of property right connotes reciprocal respect for ownership and that respect for ownership plays "an important part in how we relate to others, and how we 'imagine' ourselves as part of a broader collective community and a civilized nation."[82] Consequently, "interference with these rights by the

[77] West African Lands Commission, 183, para 1048.

[78] See *Adejumo v. Ayantegbe* (1989)3 NWLR (Pt 110) 417 at 444 para H & 448 para B;*Alao v. Ajani* (1989)4 NWLR (Pt 113) 1; *Ojoh v. Kamalu* (2005) 18 NWLR (Pt 958) 523.

[79] See e.g. *Oshodi v. Balogun* (1936) 2 All ER 1632.

[80] Cap L5 Laws of the Federation of Nigeria 2004.

[81] In the words of the Supreme Court of Nigeria in *Ogunola v. Eiyekole* (1990) 4 NWLR (Pt 146) 632 at 653: "Land is still held under [customary] law even though dominion is in the Governor. The most pervasive effect of the Land Use Act is the diminution of the plenitude of the powers of the holders of land. The character in which they hold remain substantially the same."

[82] H. Conway and J Stannard, supra (n 7) at 78.

squatter is regarded as an immoral act" by both the original owner and the whole community.[83]

While it is expected that the state would protect private property rights through law, the passing of statute of limitation by the state and allowing a squatter to successfully encroach or take over the control of the record owner's land, compromised the position of the state by ultimately "failing in its duty to protect its citizens against what is perceived to be an unlawful appropriation by others."[84] It is observed that while the criminal law and the law of tort would generally punish "only those who have performed affirmative act or failed to act to avoid creating an unreasonable risk of harm," adverse possession penalises the inactivity of landowners which poses no threat of harm to others.[85]

[83] ibid, at 79.
[84] ibid.
[85] ibid.

CHAPTER 5
DOCTRINAL ANALYSIS

5.1 Introduction

The position of the law both in England and Nigeria is that, for the statute of limitations to extinguish the title of the record owner of land, there must have been an adverse possessor who has met the requirements of the law.[1] In other words, for an adverse possessor to take advantage of the statute of limitations, it must be established that his possession "was actual, hostile, open and notorious, exclusive, and continuous for the period of the statute of limitations."[2] An occasional squatter or trespasser without a claim of right cannot take advantage of the statute of limitations, and shall instead be liable in the tort of trespass to land.[3]

This chapter examines the nature, content, scope and limitations of the rule of adverse possession as a mode of acquisition of title to land in England and Nigeria. The essence is first, to identify the core of the rule of adverse possession and remove the penumbra of uncertainties created by other rights having the colour of adverse possession in appearance but exhibiting certain characteristics different from it. Secondly, it is to engage the legal requirements of adverse possession and the effect of its application. Thirdly, it is to explore the parameters of the rule and factors that may lead to its extinction. In undertaking the doctrinal analysis, the relevant common law principles shall be engaged through judicial decisions in England and Nigeria.

---

[1] *Ogunko v. Shelle*(2004) 6 NWLR (Pt. 868) 17 at 43-44, para. F-A.

[2] J.E Stake, "The Uneasy Case for Adverse Possession." (2001) Articles by Maurer Faculty, Paper 221, 2419 at 2423 citing Stoebuck& Whitman, *The Law of Property*, 853, 860 (3rd ed. 2000); Richard Helmholz, "Adverse Possession and Subjective Intent, 61 Wash. U. L. Q 331, 334 (1983). The possession must be 'hostile' only to the extent that the squatter's presence is 'hostile to the title of the owner' See *Beever v. Spaceline Engineering Property Ltd* (1993) 6 BPR 13270 at 13283 per Bryson J.

[3] It is said that there ought to be a manifestation of an intention to possess to show that the squatter was not merely a persistent trespasser: See *Powell v. McFarlene*(1977) 38 P. & C.R 452 at 480.

5.2 Adverse Possession and Other Land Rights

Certain land rights exist in different forms resulting in varying legal consequences. Some of these rights may exhibit certain characteristics of adverse possession and may be confused with it except certain distinctions are drawn. At least four of such rights may be identified such as the right of prescription; laches and acquiescence; occupational right; and derivative title.

While there are clear cut distinctions between adverse possession and those other land rights mentioned under English law, Nigerian case law has not demonstrated a clear-cut understanding of the concepts as shown in the analysis that follows.

5.2.1 Right of Prescription

Prescription has been defined as "primarily a common law doctrine[4] by which certain incorporeal rights (such as easements and profits) can be acquired over the land of others."[5] It is usually a presumption of grant by the owner of land "and therefore, of a title derived through him."[6] The essence of the right of prescription "is that the law should attribute a lawful origin to a use of land which has continued openly for a long time, without the use of force, and not pursuant to any express permission given by the owner."[7] In prescription, the long exercise of a right is an evidence that the right has a lawful origin which is why the law requires that the right of prescription in incorporeal hereditaments such as easements and profits lie in grant, and not in the possession of land, unlike adverse possession.

---

[4] This common law doctrine has been extended by statute: See e.g the English Prescription Act of 1832 applicable in Nigeria as a Statute of general application pursuant to the Law (Miscellaneous Provisions) Act 1964.

[5] C. Harpum, S. Bridge, M. Dixon, *The Law of Real Property* 8th ed. Sweet and Maxwell (2012) 1457, para 35-002.

[6] ibid.

[7] S. Jordan O. Radley-Gardner, *Adverse Possession,* 2nd ed. Bloomsbury Professional Ltd (2011) 7 para. 1-13.

Adverse possession based on the statute of limitations "is the antithesis of prescription and rests on wrongful possession rather than any presumption of right."[8] Unlike prescription, adverse possession is statutory, and is concerned with the title to the land itself rather than an incorporeal hereditament. Also, unlike prescription which operates positively like a conveyance, adverse possession operates negatively "by eliminating the claim of a person having a superior title, without any 'parliamentary conveyance'[9] or transfer from that person."[10] By extinguishing the right of the owner to recover the land, "the squatter's possession becomes impregnable giving him a title superior to all others."[11]

It is significant to note that prescription is a mode of acquiring title to an incorporeal hereditament (such as easements and profits a *prendre),* by immemorial or long continued enjoyment;[12] it is not a mode of acquiring title to land. Being a common law concept, it forms part of Nigerian law and may be applied by the Nigerian courts as such.

Unfortunately, courts in Nigeria apply the concept interchangeably with adverse possession[13] and sometimes coin a

---

[8] C. Harpum, S. Bridge, M. Dixon, supra (n 5) at 157-1458 para. 35-002, relying on the court's decision in *Buckinghamshire County Council v. Moran* [1990] Ch 623 at 644.

[9] The notion of 'Parliamentary Conveyance' is applicable in the case of a registered land where a registered adverse possessor is substituted as a new registered proprietor in place of the previous one in which case, there is 'Parliamentary Conveyance.'

[10] ibid, 1458.

[11] *Buckinghamshire County Council v. Moran* supra (n 8) at 644B.

[12] Black's Law Dictionary, 4th ed. 1345.

[13] For example, in *Mora v. Nwalusi* (1962) 1 All NLR 681 at 684, the court per Lord Evershed remarked in relation to customary land tenure system in Nigeria, that: "There is in Nigeria no law corresponding to the English rule of prescription for conferring title to land..." By this statement, the law lord actually meant, in relation to title to land under customary law, the doctrine of *adverse possession* as opposed to *prescription.*

nomenclature such as "adverse possession by prescription;"[14] which is not only a contradiction in terms, but unknown to the received English law applicable in Nigeria. In particular, under Islamic law, 'Hauzi' is interpreted to mean prescription or long possession entitling a party who had been dealing with the land in all manners as to show that he is the absolute owner for a minimum period of ten years, to the ownership of it.[15] 'Hauzi' is not tantamount to adverse possession as the right does not arise under the statute of limitations in Nigeria. It is not tantamount to prescription at common law or under the Prescription Act of 1832 in relation to an incorporeal hereditament; it is rather a right based on long possession of land under Islamic law. It is therefore a case of laches and acquiescence on the part of the true owner for a period of ten years or more as prescribed by Islamic law.

5.2.2 Laches and Acquiescence

Laches and acquiescence are equitable defences against an action in court brought by a party who by his tardiness, indolence, or lack of due diligence has put another party in a situation such that it would be inequitable or unconscionable to sustain such action by insisting on the same right of action afterwards.

Although they are similar equitable defences against stale and or unconscionable claims, laches and acquiescence are not the same.[16]

---

[14] This nomenclature was wrongly used by the Nigerian Court of Appeal in *Tsome v. Peverega* (2001) 2 NWLR (Pt. 698} 556 at 574 para. H, 575 paras D-E.

[15] *Abubakar & Anor v. Bashir* (2017) LPELR 43272 (CA)

[16] In the old English case of *Lindsay Petroleum Co. v. Hurd* (1874) L.R.S.P.C. 221, the doctrine of laches is said to apply where it would be "unjust to give a remedy, either because the claimant has, by his conduct, done that which might fairly be regarded as equivalent to a waiver of it, or where by his conduct and neglect he has...put the defendant in a situation in which it would not be reasonable to place him if the remedy were afterwards to be asserted, [and] in either of these cases, lapse of time and delay are most essential." Thus, laches is not about delay alone; some other factors such as conduct equivalent to a waiver, and knowledge on the part of the claimant of all the facts giving him a cause of action must exist. This

Whereas acquiescence means "conduct from which it can be inferred that a person has agreed to a certain state of affairs affecting his legal rights,"[17] laches means "culpable delay by a party when he takes no steps to enforce his rights."[18] In the words of Tobi JCA (as he then was) in the Nigerian case of *Ezekwesili v. Onwuagbu*[19]:

> "Laches and acquiescence are neither synonymous nor equivalent expressions. They are rather cognate terms. While laches implies the neglect on the part of the plaintiff to do what he should or ought to do to protect his rights on or over property, acquiescence implies that the plaintiff either submits to or shows a character of silent appearance of consent or nonchalance in respect of the adverse conduct of the defendant on or over the land."

Being cognate terms however, laches and acquiescence do overlap. It has been said that "[a]cquiescence primarily means conduct from which it can be inferred that a party has waived his rights" and that "[i]ndeed, lapse of

---

was adopted by the Supreme Court of Nigeria (per Iguh JSC) in *Kayode v. Odutola* (2001) 11 NWLR (Pt 725) 659 at 683. Acquiescence is a term used where a party whose right is being infringed upon by another stood by in such a manner as really to induce that other party committing the infringement to believe that he assents to it. In the words of Lord Cranworth in the English case of *Ramsden v. Dyson* (1866) LR 1 HL 129: "If a stranger begins to build on my land supposing it to be his own and I perceiving his mistake, abstain from setting him right and leave him to persevere in his error, a court of equity will not allow me afterwards to assert my title to the land on which he had expended money on the supposition that the land was his own. It considers that when I saw the mistake into which he had fallen , it was my duty to be active and to state my adverse title; and that it would be dishonest to me to remain wilfully passive on such an occasion, in order afterwards to profit by the mistake which I might have prevented..." This dictum was adopted and applied by the Nigerian courts in *Akpan Awo v. CookeyGam*(1913) 2 NLR 100 at 101; *Angbazo v.Sule* (1996) 7 NWLR (Pt 461) 479 at 493 paras D-H.

[17] *Nsiegbe v. Mgbemena* (1996) 1 NWLR (Pt 426 607 at 622-623 paras H-A.

[18] ibid.

[19] (1998) 3 NWLR (Pt 541) 217 at 241 paras G-H.

time is an important element in considering whether there has been acquiescence."

The equitable doctrines of laches and acquiescence apply generally in Nigeria as part of the received English law. It has been applied under customary law,[20] while Islamic law has adopted it with modifications.[21]

While it is the case that both the statute of limitations and the doctrines of laches and acquiescence are "designed to promote justice by preventing surprises through the revival of claims that have been allowed to slumber,"[22] the two spring from different sources, they are available under different considerations and face varying consequences. The doctrines of laches and acquiescence are rooted in equity which does not stipulate lapse of specific period for a claim to fail, whereas the statute of limitations specifically prescribes the limitation period after which an action is not only barred, but in the case of title to land, such title becomes consequently extinguished. Also, under a system of title registration such as the English Land Registration Act[23] or the Land Registration Law of Lagos State in Nigeria,[24] an adverse possessor may apply to register his adverse title, whereas the doctrines of laches and acquiescence mainly

---

[20] See *Akpan Awo v. Cookey Gam* supra (n 16).

[21] Under that rule of Islamic law, where a person has been in undisturbed possession of land for a period of ten years or more while the true owner stood by and watched, and did nothing to claim back his property, and the parties are not related by blood or marriage, the person in possession acquires title: See *Yaro Ningi v. Dan Katsina*(1991) 3 NWLR (Pt 177) 76. However, while the Islamic rule is somehow similar to the English doctrines of laches and acquiescence, there are striking differences between their application under the two legal systems. First, whereas, laches and acquiescence under English law do not depend on enjoyment of rights within a *specific* time frame and each case depends on its own peculiar circumstances, Islamic law stipulates a time frame required for a right of prescription to accrue. Secondly, the requirement of non-relationship by blood or marriage under Islamic law does not apply under English law.

[22] *Sulgrave Holdings Inc v. FGN* (2012) 7 NWLR (Pt. 1329) 309 at 343, paras. E-F.

[23] Land Registration Act 2002.

[24] Registration of Titles Law 2015 applicable in Lagos State-Nigeria.

offer a defence which may be raised against a holder of title in respect of the reliefs sought.

The requirement of laches and acquiescence that, "the person expending money suppose himself to be building on his own land," is not a *mandatory* legal requirement of adverse possession. Although this requirement is usually met in cases of mistaken encroachment or encroachment in 'good faith' by an adverse possessor,[25] adverse possession is no less so at common law because the adverse possessor exercised his right in 'bad faith,' that is, conscious of the fact that the land does not belong to him.

While the real owner's knowledge of encroachment is a requirement for application of the doctrines of laches and acquiescence, it is not a requirement for adverse possession.[26] The requirement that the defendant must have altered his position to his detriment in the case of laches and acquiescence, is not applicable in adverse possession cases. The statute of limitations prescribes a fixed period required for the right of the title holder to be extinguished in the case of adverse possession, a defence of laches and acquiescence may be exercised after a relatively longer or shorter time than the period prescribed by the statute of limitations and is determined based on the circumstances of each case.

5.2.3 Occupational Right

Occupation of land may be lawful such as a license,[27] or unlawful, such as where the occupant enters the land without the permission of the title

[25] This is often the case in land boundary disputes.

[26] There is a plethora of cases that knowledge of the title holder of adverse possession is immaterial to the claim of the adverse possessor. See *Ajibona v. Kolawole* (1996) 10 NWLR (Pt. 476) 22; *Akibu v. Azeez*(2003) 5 NWLR (Pt. 814) 643; *Elabanjo v. Dawodu*(2006) 15 NWLR (Pt. 1001) 76; *Mulima v. Usman* (2014) 16 NWLR (Pt 1432) 160 at 202 paras. D-F.

[27] A license is a personal privilege in the form of authority or permission granted a person by another to enter and use premises or perform some acts therein which

holder such as a squatter or a trespasser. Whereas a licensee cannot be exercising a right adverse to that of the title holder as his interest is created by the latter,[28] a squatter or trespasser may exercise a right inconsistent with the right of the owner provided such right is exercised *nec vi, nec clam, nec precario.*[29]

5.2.4 Derivative Title

Title may be original or derivative. While the title holder or 'owner' is said to hold an original title, other lesser rights deriving there from such as leasehold interests are derivative titles inferior to the original title and therefore, cannot be adverse to it.[30] However, a tenant at sufferance who holds over after the expiration or determination of his lease or tenancy and against the will of the landlord-title holder, is an adverse possessor. Being an adverse possessor, time runs in his favour and upon the expiration of the period prescribed by the statute of limitations within which the title holder shall bring an action to eject him, he shall be vested with the title over the record owner's property.

5.3 Legal Requirements

At common law applicable in England and Nigeria, a squatter or other persons[31] relying on adverse possession to claim title under the statute of

---

would otherwise be wrongful or amount to trespass: See *Mobil Oil Ltd v. Johnson* (1961) 1 All NLR 93.

[28] *Powell v. McFarlane* (1977) 38 P & CR 452 at 469

[29] Meaning, without violence, without secrecy and without permission.

[30] *Hayward v. Chaloner* [1968] 1 QB 107, at 122; *Adedeji v. Oloso* (2007) 5 NWLR (Pt. 1026) 133 at 173 paras. E-G.

[31] While the appellation 'squatter' is used in decided cases to describe a person in adverse possession, the word may be inappropriate to describe other persons in adverse possession such as "a mortgagee or mortgagor in possession, a tenant under an oral periodic tenancy after the end of the first period where rent is not paid and a person without title who takes possession believing he is the true owner...": See S. Jourdan, Radley-Gardner, *Adverse Possession,* Second ed.

limitations is required by law to prove certain legal requirements to succeed. It is not enough that the claimant is able to show that he has been in possession of land for the requisite number of years under the statute of limitations;[32] he must go further to prove the following legal requirements[33] to the satisfaction of the court, namely that:

(i) The defendant has been in factual physical possession of land with the requisite intention to possess (*animus possidendi*);

(ii) The possession is adverse;

(iii) The defendant's stay has been continuous for the period of limitation set by the requisite statute of limitations;

(iv) Possession has been peaceful and uninterrupted; and

(v) Possession has been open and notorious.

5.3.1 The Act of Physical Possession Coupled with the Requisite Intention to Possess

This requirement of physical possession coupled with the requisite intention to possess has been adumbrated by the courts in England and Nigeria. In *Pye v. Graham,*[34] the House of Lords defined factual possession as "a sufficient degree of physical custody or control"[35] while an "intention to possess" is defined as "an intention to exercise such custody and control on one's own behalf and for one's own benefit."[36] In the same vein, the Supreme Court of Nigeria, in *Buraimoh v. Bamgbose,*[37]defines legal possession as "effective physical or manual control or occupation of

---

Bloomsbury Professional Ltd, West Sussex, UK (2011) at 3. See also the Nigerian case of *Davies v. Ajibona* (1994) 5 NWLR (Pt 343) 234.

[32] *Majekodunmi v. Abina* (2002) 3 NWLR (Pt. 755) 720 at 745 para E; 746 paras. B-C

[33] By way of a preliminary but vital consideration, the property must be in existence and must either be owned or be a registered land.

[34] [2003] 1 AC 419 HL.

[35] ibid, *per* Lord Browne-Wilkinson, at para 40.

[36] ibid.

[37] (1989) 3 NWLR (Pt 109) 352.

land...[coupled with] *animus possidendi* together with that amount of occupation or control of the land which is sufficient to exclude other persons from interfering..."[38]

5.3.1.1 Act of Physical Possession

The possession required is factual possession, signifying an appropriate degree of exclusive physical control.[39] What acts constitute a sufficient degree of exclusive control depends on the circumstances of each case particularly, "the nature of the land and the manner in which land of that nature is commonly used or enjoyed."[40] The most obvious of what constitutes exclusive physical control is the physical enclosure of the land,[41] physical presence or cultivation of land,[42] or the making of unexhausted improvements[43] thereon. However, it may not always be necessary for the defendant to take such active steps in relation to the land, for the type of conduct which indicates possession must vary with the type of land.[44] It is however important to show that the defendant had

[38] ibid, *per*Nnaemeka-Agu JSC at 355.

[39] *Powell v. McFarlane* (1977) 38 P & CR 452, per Slade J. at 470; *Pye (Oxford) Ltd v. Graham* [2003] 1 AC 419.

[40] ibid.

[41] *Ayinde v. Salawu*(1989) 3 NWLR (Pt. 109) 297 at 318;*Pye (Oxford) Ltd v. Graham,* supra (n 39).

[42] ibid..

[43] ibid.

[44] Per Lord Guest in the Privy Council case of *Wuta- Ofei v. Danquah* (1961) 3 All ER 596 at 600 cited with approval by the Supreme Court of Nigeria in *Ayinde v. Salawu* supra (n 41) at 317. It is said that "where land is suitable for very limited uses, it will be easier to demonstrate the required degree of physical control." Thus, in *Red House Farms (Thornton) Ltd v. Catchpole* [1977] 2 EGLR 125, a small island formed when a river changed course was found to be unsuitable for any agricultural purpose, in which case, a trespasser, who was regularly using it for hunting, was able to establish adverse possession.

an appropriate degree of physical control of the land "sufficient to exclude other persons from interfering."[45]

The test which has been adopted by the courts in recent years is whether the squatter "has been dealing with the land in question as an occupying owner might have been expected to deal with and that no one has done so."[46] However, the fact that the squatter might have done more will not be sufficient to defeat a claim for adverse possession,[47] nor is it required that the use made of the land is profitable in a commercial sense.[48]

In addition, the possession must be singular and not shared severally[49] by persons, for the law does not allow concurrent possession of land by adverse parties.[50] The possession must be exclusive in that, the possessor exercises act of possession to the exclusion of all other persons including the true owner.[51]

5.3.1.2 Intention to Possess (*Animus Possidendi*)

There must be the intention to possess the land (*animus possidendi*)[52]; but this does not imply an intention to own it.[53] It also involves the intention

---

[45] Per Nnaemeka-Agu JSC in *Buraimoh v. Bamgbose* (1989) 3 NWLR (Pt. 109) 352 at 355. Thus, in *Powell v. McFarlane* (1977) 38 P&CR 452 at 470, it was held that "grazing of cows coupled with making hay and limited repairs to fencing" were not sufficient; but "enclosing the land by erecting a new fence" as in *Buckinghamshire County Council v. Moran* [1989] 2 All ER 225 or "fitting new locks to doors" as was the case in *Lambeth LBC v. Blackburn* (2001) 82 P&CR 494, "are generally the types of action that will be required."

[46] *Powell v, McFarlane* supra (n 39) at 470-471.

[47] See *Purbrick v. London Bureau of Hackney* [2004] 1 P & CR 34 at paras 22-23.

[48] See *Roberts v. Swangrove* [2007] 2 P & CR 17 at para 39.

[49] *Onovo v. Mba*(2014) 14 NWLR (Pt. 1427) 391 at 439 paras. F-H. Possession by many squatters jointly however amounts to single possession.

[50]*Onovo v. Mba* supra (n 49).

[51] See *Pye (Oxford) Ltd v. Graham* supra (n 39).

[52] Rejecting Counsel's argument in *Pye (Oxford) Ltd v. Graham* supra (n 39) that there was no need to demonstrate an intention to possess in order to establish

to exclude others and to show that the squatter "was not merely a persistent trespasser but was seeking to dispossess the true owner."[54] In the words of Slade L.J in *Powell v. McFarlane,*[55]..."the animus possidendi involves the intention, in one's own name and on one's own behalf, to exclude the world at large, including the owner with the paper title if he be not himself the possessor, so far as is reasonably practicable and so far as the processes of the law will allow."[56]

This mental element of possession entails both the subjective intention to possess and some outward manifestation of such intention "which makes clear that intention to the world at large"[57] otherwise known as the objective intention. The court will normally infer the squatter's subjective intention from his conduct;[58] but in addition, there must be the manifested intention to exercise control over the land for the time being, excluding all others including the true owner from possession.[59] This is easily proven by the defendant showing that he made full use of the land as the owner of the land would have done; but where the conduct of the squatter is equivocal, it is expected that additional evidence be adduced to establish intention to possess.[60]

---

actual possession, the court, per Lord Browne-Wilkinson, held that "...there has always, both in Roman law and in common law, been a requirement to show an intention to possess in addition to objective acts of physical possession. Such intention may be, and frequently is, deduced from the physical acts themselves...So far as English law is concerned, intention as a separate element is obviously necessary."

[53] *Buckinghamshire County Council v. Moran* [1989) 2 All ER 225; *Topplan Estates Ltd v. Townley* [2005] 1 EGLR 89

[54] That was the situation in *Buckinghamshire County Council v. Moran,* supra (n 53) above.

[55] (1977) 38 P&CR 452 at 471-472.

[56] This dictum was approved by the House of Lords in *Pye (Oxford) Ltd v. Graham,* supra (n 39).

[57] *Smith v. Waterman* [2003] EWHC 1266 (Ch) at para 19.

[58] ibid.

[59] ibid.

[60] *Per* Lord *Hutton in Pye (Oxford) Ltd v. Graham,* supra (n 39).

Where the squatter enters into possession under a mistaken belief that he owns the land, the necessary intention is formed, and there is no requirement that the squatter intends to exercise exclusive physical possession over the land wrongfully.[61] In the same vein, a mistaken believe that a tenancy exists in favour of a squatter does not affect the requisite intention to possess the land by him.[62] However, there are conflicting decisions on the question whether a licensee, believing that his license may be terminated at any time has the intention to possess,[63] but it has been argued that "[t]here is no practical difference between the intention of a tenant holding under a tenancy which can be determined at any time by notice from the landlord and a licensee entitled to exclusive possession"[64] as "[b]oth intend to possess for the time being for their own benefit, and both know that they may be required to vacate at any time."[65]

Once there is a manifested intention to exercise control over the land by the squatter, it is of no moment that the true owner makes limited use of the land, although not in a way amounting to effective control of the land.[66] The intention required is not an indefinite one; it is one to possess the land in the meantime, that is, during the period of limitation. Thus, an intention to exercise control pending when the actual owner would need it, does not detract from the squatter's *animus possidendi*.[67]

Since proof of intention to possess requires a manifested intention to exercise exclusive control of the land, allowing access to the land by a third party (e.g. by handing over the keys to the main entrance to him)

[61] *Pye (Oxford) v. Graham* [2001] Ch 804.

[62] See *Tower Hamlets London Borough Council v. Barrett* [2006] P & CR 132 at para 42. Cited with approval in Pye's case.

[63] See e.g. *Adams v. Trustees of Micheal Batt Charitable Trust* (2001)82 P & CR 404; *Clowes Developments (UK) Ltd v. Walters* [2005] EWHC 669 (Ch) at paras 39-40 where the courts held that there was no intention to possess; and *Wretham v. Ross* [2005] EWHC 1259 (Ch) at para 41, *Alston & Sons Ltd v. BOCM Chemicals Ltd* [2009] 1 EGLR 93 at paras 86-105, where a contrary decision was reached.

[64] S. Jourdan and O. Radley-Gardner, *Adverse Possession,* (n 7) at 201 para 9-51.

[65] ibid.

[66] ibid, at 130 para 7-51.

[67] See *Buckinghamshire County Council v. Moran* (1990) Ch 623 at 643E.

without an unequivocal assertion that the squatter retains control over access to the land, would deny the squatter of intention to possess.

A squatter who offers to buy disputed land or pay rent for it does not cease to have *animus possidendi*. While such conduct may amount to an acknowledgement by the squatter of the true owner's title which would affect the running of the limitation period, it does not alter the squatter's intention to possess.[68]

5.3.2 Adverse Possession

For the period of limitation to run against the title holder under the statute of limitations, it must be proven by the defendant that his possession was adverse to the title of the real owner.[69] To make a possession adverse, there must be an entry under the colour of right claiming title inconsistent with that of the true owner, and against the whole world. In other words, the possession must be inconsistent with, and in denial of the true owner, and must be without legal title. In the words of Romer LJ:[70]

> "...if one looks to the position of the occupier and finds that his right to occupation is derived from the owner in the form of permission or agreement or grant, it is not adverse, but, if it is not so derived, it is adverse, even if the owner is, by legislation, prevented from bringing ejectment proceedings."

---

68 Per Lord *Browne Wilkinson in Pye (Oxford) Ltd v. Graham*[2003] 1 AC 419 at para 46.

69 It is said that time runs against the owner of land under the limitation statutes, "if the land is in continuous adverse possession for the limitation period." See Jourdan, Radley-Gardner, supra (n 7).

70 *Moses v. Lovegrove* (1952) 2 QB 533 at 539-540.

Thus, where possession is enjoyed pursuant to some agreement made with the title holder such as the existence of a lease or licence, it cannot be adverse.[71]

Proof of adversity of possession is crucial for three reasons:[72] In the first place, proof of adverse possession would show that the occupation was unauthorised by the title holder and that the occupation was hostile in the sense that it was meant to dispossess the owner. Secondly, the intention of the defendant to displace the title holder becomes manifest. Thirdly, the cause of action in trespass arose and the time would start running against the title holder under the statute of limitations from the moment adverse possession was being exercised. It is immaterial that the title holder had no knowledge of the presence of the adverse possessor[73] except the title holder is under some form of disability or the defendant is 'guilty' of fraudulent concealment,[74] nor is it of moment that he had a future use of the land in mind.[75]

Although possession by a squatter or a trespasser may generally qualify as an adverse possession, possession delivered by the title holder to another person may also turn out to be adverse in certain circumstances. For example, where a purchaser in possession of the land sold pays the purchase price without transfer made to him, his possession becomes adverse to that of the vendor who becomes a bare trustee for him, and consequently, the vendor's title would be extinguished after the limitation period.[76] In the same vein, a defendant with a defective document of title who remains in possession for the limitation period may plead adverse possession in defence if the plaintiff he dispossessed, or his

---

[71] *Buckinghamshire County Council v. Moran* supra (n 8) at 636, paras G-H; *Pye (Oxford) Ltd v. Graham* [2003] 1 AC 419 at para 37; *Adedeji v. Oloso*(2007) 5 NWLR (Pt. 1026) 133 at 173 paras. E-G.

[72] J.E Stake, "The Uneasy Case of Adverse Possession." supra (n 2) at 2426-2427.

[73] *Elabanjo v. Dawodu*(2006) 15 NWLR (Pt. 1001) 76. @142 paras. B-E.

[74] *Davies v. Ajibona* (1994) 5 NWLR (Pt. 343) 234.

[75] See *Pye v. Graham* supra (n 71).

[76] *Davies v. Ajibona*(1994) 5 NWLR (Pt. 343) 324.

successor- in- title, brings an action in court subsequently.[77] Also, a tenant at sufferance who initially entered into possession under an agreement with the landlord but who holds over against the will of the said landlord at the expiration of the lease or tenancy becomes an adverse possessor in favour of whom time runs, and may be entitled to title upon the extinction of the former landlord's title at the expiration of the limitation period.[78] The crucial question in all cases is whether the defendant, in whatever capacity, has been exercising a right inconsistent with the right of the title holder.

5.3.3 Continuous for the Period of Limitation set by the Requisite Statute of Limitations

Adverse possession must be continuous for the period set by the statute of limitations, for the title of the paper owner to be extinguished. It must run without a break in-between for that period, for anytime the squatter abandons his possession, the right of the title holder revives.[79]

Where there is a break in the adverse possession and a fresh intruder enters, there is a fresh dispossession; the period of limitation starts running afresh under the relevant statute of limitations, and a right of action accrues again to the title holder.[80]

The significance of the requirement of continuous possession is manifest in the case of successive squatters in adverse possession. Adverse possession of successive squatters may operate cumulatively to extinguish a pre-existing title only if the periods of adverse possession are strictly continuous. Thus, if A, a squatter who has occupied X's land for a continuous period of seven years out of twelve years limited by statute, transferred the land to D by conveyance, or by will, or on intestacy, X

---

[77] ibid.

[78] Harpum et. al., Megarry& Wade, *The Law of Real Property* 6th ed. Sweet & Maxwell (2012) para 17-107.

[79] *Roy v. Lagona*[2010] VSC 250 at para. 35; The English Limitation Act 1980 Sch 1 para 8(2).

[80] ibid.

would be barred after D has held the land continuously for another five years.[81]In the same vein, where a squatter X is dispossessed by another squatter Y, the latter may add X's period of occupation to his own as against the true owner.[82] Thus, time runs against the true owner from the time when adverse possession began, and so long as adverse possession is not broken.[83]

However, time of successive squatters cannot add up where a squatter abandons possession before the full period of limitation has run and some time passes before either someone else takes possession, or before he re-takes adverse possession of the land.[84] It follows therefore that during the gap between the two squatters, the owner has possession in law and there is no person he can sue. Consequently, the land ceases to be in adverse possession during that period, and when the second squatter comes in, a fresh cause of action accrues to the title holder.[85]

5.3.4 Peaceful and Uninterrupted Possession

It is imperative that the possession should be peaceful in the sense that entry must have been without violence; a forceful acquisition of possession is wrongful and cannot ripen into adverse possession.[86] Also, such peaceful possession must have continued uninterrupted by the true owner, or by a third party. Where the adverse possession is challenged from time to time so that it becomes intermittent and interrupted, it is not considered to be an adverse possession.[87] It follows therefore that each

---

[81] *Mount Carmel Investments Ltd v. Peter Thurlow Ltd*[1988] 1 WLR 1078.

[82] *Asher v. Whitlock* (1861) L.R 1 QB 1; *Willis v. Earl Howe* [1891] 2 Ch. 545.

[83] *Mount Carmel Investments Ltd v. Peter Thurlow* supra (n 78).

[84] *Roy v. Lagona*[2010] VSC 250 at para. 35; The English Limitation Act 1980. Sch 1 para 8(2). See also *Akibu v. Azeez* (2003) 5 NWLR (Pt. 814) 643 at 668;

[85] ibid.

[86] *Brown v. Perry* [1991]1 WLR 1297 at 1302A. It has been held, however, that aggressive defence of his boundaries reinforces his adverse possession claim rather than detract from it: See *Beever v. Spaceline Engineering Property Ltd* supra (n 2).

[87] *King (t/a Oakland Services UK) v. Job* [2002] EWCA Civ 181

time the adverse possessor relinquishes possession, the true owner is deemed to have resumed possession and the period of limitation stops counting, and would only start counting afresh upon encroachment by another adverse possessor[88]

Adverse possession need not be hostile[89] except in the sense of the squatter's presence being "hostile to the title of the true owner,"[90] since both the act of possession of the squatter and the title of the true owner are incompatible and irreconcilable. It follows therefore that adverse possession may occur "through ignorance or mistake" of the adverse possessor, or through lack of awareness of the true ownership of the property by the claimant.[91]

5.3.5 Open and Notorious Possession

It is said that "the sort of entry and exclusive possession that will ripen into title by adverse possession is the use of the property in the manner that an average true owner would use it under the circumstances."[92] The conduct of the possessor should be such that "marks the conduct of owners" in relation to "holding, managing and caring for property of like nature and condition";[93] the kind of conduct that would amount to holding out as the true owner of the property.[94] This may take the form of making unexhausted improvements on the land such as building, fencing or farming on the land, but it need not be; it is said that "[a]cting like a

---

[88] *Trustees, Executors and Agency Co. Ltd v. Short* (1883) 13 App. Cas. 793.

[89] *Pye (Oxford) Ltd v. Graham* [2002] 1 AC 347 per Lord Hope of Craighead at para 69.

[90] *Beever Spaceline Engineering Property Ltd* supra (n 2).

[91] K. Gray and S. F Gray, *Elements of Land law,* 5th ed. Oxford University Press (2009), 1183, citing *Pye (Oxford) Ltd v. Graham* [2001] Ch 804 per Mummery L.J at para 34(5).

[92] J. Dukeminier & J.E Krier, *Property*131 (4th ed. 1998).

[93] J.A.Clarke, Adverse Possession of Identity: Radical Theory, Conventional Practice, Oregon Law Review, vol.84 [2005] 563 at 566, relying on *Howard v. Kunto,* 477 P.2d 831, 861 (Wash C.A 1970).

[94] ibid.

landowner can mean mimicking the legal formalities of land ownership."[95] This can be actualised by public acts of ownership such as the adverse possessor would exercise if he was the true owner of the property.

However, it is not enough that the adverse possessor holds himself out as the owner; he must be seen and taken as such by the public at large.[96] It is therefore not so much of the subjective notion of the publicity or notoriety as perceived by the adverse possessor; but more of an objective perception of the publicity or notoriety by the public.

5.4 Adverse Possession and Specific Legal Relationships

Certain legal relationships may exist in relation to adverse possession the implication of which recognised legal principles regulate. Such legal relationships include that of adverse possessor, the landlord and his tenant; adverse possession by a trustee; and adverse possession by co-owners. These are dealt with next.

5.4.1 Adverse Possession Regarding Leaseholds

The law is that a tenant cannot acquire title against his landlord during the period of the lease because the possession of the tenant is not adverse to that of the landlord;[97] but the landlord's right to recover arrears of rent or an instalment of any rent due from the tenant is barred after six years from the payment default,[98] and the landlord's right of re-entry is barred if not exercised for a period of twelve years.[99] A squatter who is an adverse possessor against the interest of the leaseholder acquires the lease

[95] J.A Clarke, supra (n 93).
[96] J.A. Clarke, supra (n 93).
[97] *Hayward v. Chaloner* [1968] 1 QB 107, at 122.
[98] See the English Limitation Act 1980, s.19 Limitation Act Cap 522 Laws of the Federal Capital Territory, Nigeria, 2007, s.19
[99] ibid, s.15.

at the expiration of the limitation period,[100] but time does not run against the landlord and the reversion remains intact until the lease expires.[101] But while the tenant's title to an unregistered lease is extinguished in favour of the squatter at the expiration of the period of limitation, the tenant remains liable to pay rent and to observe and perform his covenants under the lease.[102]

Where the tenant defaults in observing a covenant and the landlord sues for forfeiture of the lease, the squatter in possession cannot claim relief from forfeiture.[103] It follows therefore, that the squatter's title can be defeated by forfeiture or by forfeiture and re-grant.[104] It can also be defeated by surrender or by surrender and re-grant.[105]

A squatter holding adverse possession of an unregistered lease during the limitation period is not entitled to the benefit or subject to the burden of the covenants in the lease unless it is proven that a new lease had been created in his favour;[106] and a new lease would not have been created by mere payment of rent.[107] However, the squatter will be bound by any restrictive covenants contained in the lease notwithstanding that he has not acquired title to the lease.[108]

Where a squatter holds adverse possession of an unregistered lease of land for the limitation period, the tenant cannot evict him during

---

[100] ibid.

[101] *Fairweather v. St Marylebone Property Co. Ltd* [1963] AC 510 at 536, HL. But the statute of limitations both in England and Nigeria does not prevent time from running against a mortgagee of a reversion on a lease in the absence of payment of principal and interest, or written acknowledgement of the mortgagee's title even if no rent is payable under the lease: See *Wakefield and Barnsley Union Bank Ltd v. Yates* [1916]1 Ch 452.

[102] *Fair-weather v. St Marylebone Property Co. Ltd* supra (n 101).

[103] ibid, at 547; *Tickner v. Buzzacott* [1965] Ch 426 at 434E- 435A.

[104] *Fairweather v. St Marylebone Property Co. Ltd* supra (n 101) at 547.

[105] ibid.

[106] *Tichborne v. Weir* (1892) 67 LT 735 at 736.

[107] *Tickner v. Buzzacott* supra (n 103).

[108] *Re Nisbet and Potts' Contract* [1905] 1 Ch 391.

the lease, but if the lease is surrendered, the landlord or any one claiming under him will be able to evict the squatter.[109] If the landlord grants a new lease to the tenant, the tenant will be able to evict the squatter by dint of the new right to possession vested in him by the new lease.[110] If the tenant had the right to request a new lease under an option to renew in the original lease, the tenant cannot evict a squatter under the new lease.[111]

During adverse possession, an adverse possessor may create a possessory leasehold estate over the land, but the fact that he has the equivalent of a fee simple estate in England or a right of occupancy in Nigeria does not empower him to create a legal lease binding on the whole world.[112] Although any lease or tenancy created may give the lessee or tenant exclusive possession, but only as against the grantor; it does not bind the title holder.[113] Nevertheless, following a similar right of alienation of the adverse possessor-landlord, the possessory leasehold may assign his leasehold term to a third party or create a sub-lease from his term of years.[114]

5.4.2 Adverse Possession and Mortgages

The right to redeem whether legal or equitable is barred if the mortgagee remains in possession of the mortgaged land for 12 years without a

---

[109] S. Jourdan and O. Radley-Gardner, *Adverse Possession*, supra (n 7) at 533, para 24-88.

[110] ibid, at 534 para 24-88.

[111] *Chung v. Lam Island Development Co. Ltd* [1997] AC 38.

[112] M. Pawlowski & J. Brown, "Adverse Possession and the Transmissibility of Possessory Rights-The Dark Side of Land Registration?" Available online at www.https//research.aston.ac.uk 1 at 10.

[113] This is the same effect found by the House of Lords in respect of a tenancy created by a landlord without a legal estate in *Brunton v. London & Quadrant Housing Trust* [2000] 1 AC 405.

[114] This is unlike the consequence of the tenancy found by the House of Lords in *Brunton's case*, supra (n 113), the reason being that the adverse possessor, unlike the landlord in *Brunton's case* who is practically a licensee, is in the position of a holder of a fee simple estate in England or a right of occupancy in Nigeria.

written acknowledgment of the title of the mortgagee's or his equity of redemption, and without receiving any payment in respect of the principal or interest.[115] Although the mortgagee is liable to account for the rents and profits whilst in possession of the mortgaged property, such receipt does not count to defeat the claim of the mortgagee to adverse possession.[116] Where a second mortgagee's rights against the mortgagor are barred, he can no longer exercise his right to redeem the first mortgage, since his interest in the property is terminated.[117]

The mortgagee's right to enforce the mortgage - such as the right to sue for principal and interest, or for possession, or to exercise the right to foreclose – all become barred after 12 years from the date when repayment became due under the mortgage[118] and consequently, his title becomes extinguished.

Where there is a shortfall after the mortgagee enforces his security, the right to sue for the shortfall is subject to the limitation period which runs from the date when repayment became due and is unaffected by the sale.[119]

5.4.3 Adverse Possession, Equitable Titles, Trusts and Remedies

Although the limitation period for the recovery of land applies as much to equitable interests as to legal estates, adverse possession by a stranger does not bar the trustee's title to the property until all the beneficiaries have been barred.

---

[115] *Young v. Clarey* [1948] Ch. 191.

[116] *Harlock v. Ashberry* (1882) 19 Ch.D 539; *Re Lord Clifden* [1900] 1 Ch. 774. Query: whether this position holds where the mortgage was created by demise, since a lessee may not bar his lessor's title.

[117] *Catterell v. Price* [1960] 1 WLR 1097.

[118] *Lloyds Bank Ltd v. Margolis* [1954] 1 WLR 644.

[119] *West Brunwich BS V. Wilkinson* [2005] 1WLR 2303.

As a general rule, a trustee cannot obtain title by adverse possession against the beneficiaries.[120] The reason is that, being the holder of the legal estate of the trust property, he cannot, at the same time claim to be in adverse possession.[121] However, where the trustee is also one of the beneficiaries "and acted honestly and reasonably in distributing the property," upon the expiration of the limitations period, "his liability to restore either the property or its proceeds is limited to the excess over his own proper shares."[122]

Adverse possession by a third party for the period of limitation "will bar not only the trustee's action to recover the trust property, but also the equitable interests of the beneficiaries of the trust ['cestui que trust'], although the latter may be under a disability."[123]

Except the statute of limitation specifically imposes periods of limitation, there are no limitations for claims in specific performance, injunction, or other equitable reliefs. However, the equitable doctrine of laches requires that remedies be sought without unreasonable delay. In cases where the statute of limitation applies, the court will not refuse relief within the statutory period on the ground of delay alone,[124] unless the delay is coupled with circumstances indicating acquiescence or abandonment, and *ipso facto* making it inequitable to prosecute the claim.[125]

5.4.4 Adverse Possession by Co-Owners

As a general rule, possession of a co-owner may not be adverse in law to the title of the other co-owners. The rationale for this is that each co-owner

---

[120] *Agbah v. B.D.U Jos Branch* (2001) 3 NWLR (Pt. 701) 579 at 598 para. A

[121] *Akinkunmi v. Sadiq* (2001) 2 NWLR (Pt. 696) 101.

[122] ibid.

[123] W. Waller, "Adverse Possession of Trust Property" 2 Tenn L. Rev. 147 (1923-1924). The rationale for this lies in the fact that "a trustee represents the cestui que trust in all matters relating to the legal title of the trust property."(supra).

[124] *Re Pauling's S.T (No. 1)* [1964] Ch. 303.

[125] *Re Loftus, decd* [2007] 1 WLR 591 at 605.

has a right to occupy the entire property owned by co-tenants,[126] so that exclusive possession by one co-owner is not sufficient "to meet the threshold standard for adverse possession."[127]

However, for one co-owner to establish adverse possession against the other co-owners, he must show unequivocally that he intends to oust every other co-tenant from the property. To prove 'ouster' or exclusion of other co-owners from the property, he must either give notice of the denial of others' right directly in writing or demonstrate this by necessary implication "such as claiming the whole property by himself, denying title of his companion(s), or refusing to permit him/them to enter."[128]

5.5 Transmission of Possessory Title

A claim to adverse possession may be "founded on successive adverse possessors who may each be claiming title based on their own occupation of the land."[129] The question is whether such possessory title is capable of transmission from one possessor to another on death, or by sale or gift during the lifetime of the adverse possessor?[130]

5.5.1 Transmission by Will or on Intestacy

A possessory title is capable of transmission on death by will or on intestacy.[131] The rationale lies in the fact that adverse possession "gives all the rights and powers of ownership" by virtue of which "the possessor acquires to all intents and purposes, a legal estate in fee simple absolute in

---

126 R.L. Richman, "Adverse possession by a co-owner: Intent to oust co-owner must be clear and unequivocal." Bullivant/Houser/Bailey (2012). Available online at www.bullivant.com, accessed on 4/11/2019.

127 ibid.

128 ibid.

129 See generally, M. Pawlowski & J. Brown, supra (n 112) at 3, 7.

130 ibid at 4-7.

131 ibid at 4,5. See also the old case of *Asher v. Whitlock* (1865) L.R. 1 QB, 1 at 6.

possession…"[132] The facts and decision in the English case of *Asher v. Whitlock*[133] is instructive. In that case, T.W had enclosed a piece of manorial waste, built a cottage on it and occupied the land until his death in 1860. By his Will, he devised the cottage and garden to his wife for life or until remarriage, and the remainder to his daughter in fee simple. After his death, the widow remained in possession with her daughter and a year later, married the defendant. The three of them lived at the property until the daughter's death in February 1863. On her death, the widow and the defendant continued to reside in the property until the widow's death in May 1863. The daughter's heir subsequently brought an action seeking to eject the defendant and the court held that he was entitled to recover the whole property on the ground that as between these two rival claimants, the land belonged to the heir who could lay claim to the earlier and therefore, better right to possession. It is said that "in this case, there were two stages of devolution. First, the possessory right passed to the widow under the testator's will and, secondly, it passed to the daughter's heir upon an intestacy."[134]

5.5.2 Transmission by Sale or Gift

An adverse possessory right in land can be sold or gifted.[135] In *Buckinghamshire County Council v. Moran,*[136] a plot of land owned by the

---

[132] M. Pawlowski & J. Brown, supra (n 112) at 4. See the English case of *Perry v. Clissold* (1907) AC 73. In the Australian case of *Wheeler v. Baldwin* (1934) 52 C.L.R 609, the court "acknowledged that adverse possessory right in land is akin to an estate in fee simple capable of inheritance by heirs."

[133] Supra (n 131) above.

[134] M. Pawlowski & J. Brown, supra (n 112).

[135] ibid, at 6, relying on Cheshire and Burn, *Modern Law of Real Property,* 18th ed. 2011 at 1133-1134; Ruoff and Roper, *Registered Conveyancing,* Loose-leaf, December 2014at para. 33.018; and *Simpson v. The Council of North West County District* (1978) 4 B.P.R. 97, 267 (Supreme Court of New South Wales); *Mount Camel Investments Ltd v. Peter Thurlow Ltd* (1988) 1 WLR 1078 (CA); *Treloar v. Nute* (1976) 1 WLR 1295 (CA).

[136] Supra (n 8).

Council had been in the occupation of a couple for four years since 1967. The house was subsequently conveyed to the defendant by a conveyance which was expressed to include not only the land comprised in the paper title, but also "all such rights, estate, title and interests as the vendors may have in or over….."the plot of land. The defendant deliberately arranged for a statutory declaration of use and occupation of the Council plot since 1967. The Council failed to repossess the land upon the defendant showing that it had been dispossessed of the plot for more than 12 years by relying ,on its own exclusive possession since 1973. This case "illustrates the possibility of a sale of possessory right taking place informally between successive possessors under the auspices of a formal transfer of property."[137]

5.6 Running of Time Under the Statute of Limitations

In cases of adverse possession, the title of the real owner is not extinguished and title is not vested in the squatter until the expiration of the period of limitation prescribed by the statute of limitations. Before time runs out under the statute of limitations, the real owner may evict the squatter using due process and re-take possession.

The Limitation Act 1966 applicable in the Federal Capital Territory of Nigeria[138] and the corresponding statute of limitations applicable in the various states of the federation, are similar in material particulars to the English Limitation Act 1980,[139] but far from being identical.[140] Relevant provisions of the Limitation Act of Nigeria are reproduced below for purposes of analysis:

---

[137] M. Pawlowski & J. Brown, supra (n 112) at 7.

[138] Limitations Act Cap 522 Laws of the Federal Capital Territory, 2007.

[139] For discussion on the relevant provisions of the English Limitation Act 1980, see chapter 2 *ante*.

[140] In Nigeria, the period of limitation regarding State land is 20 years as opposed to 30 years applicable to the Crown land in England and Wales. Whereas actions to recover possession of the foreshore by the Crown in England and Wales is 60 years, the statutes of limitations in Nigeria contain no limitation period in this

Section 16 provides:

> "(1) Subject to the provisions of subsection (2) and (3) of this section, no action will be brought by a State authority to recover any land after the expiration of twenty (20) years from the date on which the right of action accrued to the State authority, or if it first accrued to some person through whom the State authority claims, to that person.
>
> (2) The following provisions will apply to an action by a person to recover land-
>
> (a) subject to paragraph (b) of this subsection, no such action will be brought after the expiration of twelve (12) years from the date on which the right of action accrued to the person bringing it or, if it first accrued to some person through whom there are claims, to that person;

---

regard. While the English Limitation Act in relation to land applies to successive and future interests which are features of the English land tenure, the Nigerian Land Use Act 1978 (Cap L5 2010) allows only "a plain transfer of the whole of the rights of occupation over the whole of the land" (See s.25 of the Act) thereby jettisoning the common law tenure of successive and future interests. This obviously obviates the possibility of creating interests in succession or future interests in Nigeria sequel to the enactment of the Land Use Act. It would therefore be out of context in Nigeria to consider the implications of the running of time under the limitation statutes on future interests such as entailed interest, settlement made by person out of possession, entitlement to successive interests; settled land and land held on trust. The basis for non recognition of lesser estates and beneficial, successive and future interests by the Act lies in the distinction between proprietary freehold interests which is tantamount to absolute ownership at common law applicable in England and Wales, and a non proprietary interest in the form of a right of occupancy created by grant, under the Nigerian Land Use Act, 1978.

(b) if the right of action first accrued to a State authority, the action may be brought at any time before the expiration of the period during which the action could have been brought by the State authority or of twelve (12) years from the date on which the right of action accrued to some person other than the State authority, whichever period first expires.

(3) For the purpose of this Law, a right of action to recover any land which accrued to the Republic...before the commencement of this Law will be deemed to have become exercisable by an appropriate State authority on the date on which it first accrued to the Republic..."

As to when the right of action accrues for the purpose of the application of the Limitation Act, section 17 provides:

> "Where the person bringing an action to recover land, or some person through whom he claims, has been in possession thereof and has while entitled to it been dispossessed or has discontinued the possession, the right of action will be deemed to have accrued on the date of the dispossession or discontinuance."[141]

Section 19 of the Act makes adverse possession a pre-requisite for the application of the limitation period. The section provides:

"(1) A right of action to recover land will not be deemed to accrue unless the land is in possession (in this section

---

[141] Where a person brings an action to recover land of a deceased person under a will or an intestacy and the deceased person was, on the date of death entitled to the land in possession and was the last person entitled to the land in possession, the right of action shall accrue on the date of the death: See section 18 (1) (2) of the Act.

referred to as adverse possession) of some person in whose favour the period of limitation can run.

(2) Where-

(a) under the provisions of this Act a right of action to recover land is deemed to accrue on a certain date; and

(b) no person is in adverse possession of the land on that date;

the right of action will not be deemed to accrue unless and until adverse possession is taken of the land.

(3) Where a right of action to recover land has accrued, after and before the right of action is barred, the land ceases to be in adverse possession, the right of possession will no longer be deemed to have accrued and no fresh right of action will be deemed to accrue unless and until the land is again taken into adverse possession.''

By virtue of the provision of section 20 of the Act, ''no person will be deemed to be in possession of any or adverse land by reason only of having made a formal entry on it;''[142] and ''no continual or other claim upon or near any land will preserve any right of action to recover the land.''[143]

Section 21 of the Act provides that ''on the expiration of the period fixed by this Law for any person to bring an action to recover land, the title of that person to the land will be extinguished.''

The law will not apply to actions in respect of any matter which, immediately before the commencement of the Act was regulated by customary law.[144]

---

[142] Limitations Act Laws of the Federation of Nigeria 2004, s. 20(a)

[143] ibid, s. 20(b).

[144] ibid, s. 68.

5.6.1 Judicial Interpretation of the Nigerian Statutes of Limitations in Relation to Adverse Possession

It has been held that time begins to run under the statute of limitation when possession is lost save where there is fraudulent concealment[145]; in other words, the period of limitation begins to run from the date of adverse possession of the land by another person[146]. The effect of the operation of the statute of limitations is, like the position at common law, not merely to deny the right of action; it completely extinguishes an existing right at the expiration of the limitation period[147] so that the adverse possessor acquires rights to the land which are enforceable against the real owner of the land. In the words of Uwaifo J.S.C in *Majekodunmi v. Abina*[148]:

> Although sections 17 and 21 of the Limitation Law…are about the person bringing an action to recover land, the manner in which they can possibly, in their effect, provide an estate in favour of an adverse possessor is somehow reflected in the observation of Cozens-Hardy M.R in *In re Atkinson and Horsell's Contract* (1912) 2 Ch. 1 at page 9 as follows:
>
> "We have had a great deal of discussion as to the effect of the Statute of Limitation in a matter of this kind. As I indicated in the course of Mr Macnaghten's reply, my present view is that the phrase 'statutory conveyance' and so on, is a loose metaphorical term, and that the true view is this, that whenever you find a person in possession of property that possession is prima facie evidence of ownership in fee, and that prima facie evidence becomes absolute when once you have extinguished the right of every other person to challenge it. That is the effect of s.34 of the Real Property Limitation Act, and that explains how the person

---

[145] *Kasandubu v. Ultimate Petroleum Ltd* (2008) 7 NWLR (Pt. 1086) 274.

[146] *Eresia-Eke v. Orikoa* (2010) 8 NWLR (Pt. 1197) 421.

[147] *Odekilekun v. Hassan* (1997) 12 NWLR (Pt. 531) 56 at 76-77 paras G-A.

[148] (2002) 3 NWLR (Pt 755) 720.

> who has been in possession for more than the statutory period does get an absolute legal estate in the fee, and there is nobody who can challenge the presumption which his possession of the property gives''.

It follows therefore that adverse possession may be used as a sword and a person in adverse possession can, upon the extinction of the title of the former owner following the expiration of the limitation period, maintain an action in trespass against the former owner or any person purporting to have acquired interest in the land through him[149].

However, it is incumbent on the claimant to show not only that he has been in possession for the requisite number of years, but also that the title holder has been dispossessed or has discontinued his possession[150]. Mere non user does not amount to discontinuance of possession[151]; ''there must be something in the nature of an ouster of the true owner by the wrongful possessor''[152]. Also, there is no abandonment unless there is abandonment of the actual and legal possession of the land[153]. In the words of Uwaifo J.S.C in *Majekodunmi v. Abina*[154]:

> ...the fact of legal estate in fee being obtained through possession is subject to the adverse possessor proving that the title holder has been dispossessed, or has discontinued possession and that he has extinguished the right of every other person to challenge his having become the absolute owner in fee.

---

[149] *Odubeko v. Fowler* (1993) 7 NWLR (Pt. 308) 637.

[150] *Majekodunmi v. Abina,* supra (n 148)

[151] ibid, per Uwaifo JSC, relying on the English case of *Littledale v. Liverpool College* (1900) 1 Ch. 19 at 22.

[152] ibid, per Uwaifo JSC relying on Lord Denning M.R in the English case of *Wallis Ltd v. Shell-Mexand BP* (1974) 3 All ER 575 at 580.

[153] *Majekodunmi v. Abina,* supra (n 148) relying on the English case of *Norton v. London and North Western Railway Co.* (1879-1880) 13 Ch.D 268 at 273.

[154] supra (n 148).

For a claim of adverse possession to succeed, such possession must be adequate in continuity, in publicity and in extent to show that possession was adverse to the competitors[155]; it must be one which derogates from, and inconsistent with the ownership title of a person who claims to be the true owner of the land[156]. Knowledge of the actual owner of the land is irrelevant for the commencement of the running of the limitation period[157].

The Statute of Limitations does not apply to land held under customary land tenure; no matter how long an adverse possessor remained on land under customary tenure, his possession cannot ripen into rights of ownership in the land against the original owner. In the words of Dongban-Mensem, J.C.A in *Ogunlana v. Dada*[158]:

> "Land possession and ownership is a customary practice which is jealously guarded in different forms by different communities in Nigeria. One common denominator in all these practices is the perpetuity of land ownership by its original owners. In the instant case, it would therefore be importing an alien customary law into the Yoruba customary land holding to apply the Statutes of Limitation to divest the Itire people[159] of their customary law title".

While the above pronouncement is a re-statement of the provision of the Limitation statutes on the non applicability of the statutes to customary land tenure[160], it is necessary to clarify its scope. Contrary to the pronouncement, the provision of the limitation statutes is not limited to 'Yoruba customary land holding' as erroneously suggested, but applies to all customary land tenure systems across Nigeria. The provision of

---

155 *Adejumo v. Olawaiye* (1996) 1 NWLR (Pt 425) 436.

156 *Adedeji v. Oloso* (2007) 5 NWLR (Pt 1026) 133.

157 *Ajibona v. Kolawole* (1996) 10 NWLR (Pt. 467) 22; *Akibu v. Azeez* (2003) 5 NWLR (Pt. 814) 643; *Elabanjo v. Dawodu* (2006) 15 NWLR (Pt. 1001) 76.

158 (2010) 1 NWLR (Pt.1176) 534 at 564 paras C-D.

159 'Itire people' are indigenous people located in a geographical enclave in Lagos state, Nigeria.

160 See the Limitation Act 1966, s. 68.

statute of limitations excluding customary law from its ambit is not only unequivocal, judicial authorities emanating from the Supreme Court of Nigeria[161] and other appellate courts[162] suggest that the statutory provision applies to customary land tenure generally.

Islamic law of land tenure is not specifically exempted from the application of the Statute of limitations. However, considering the fact that the reception statutes transplanted the English common law subject to local circumstances, and to the extent that the Islamic principle of *hauzi* provides a parallel method of dealing with prescriptive right consequent upon stale claims in land[163] while customary law is treated as including Islamic law by statutes applicable in Northern Nigeria[164], it cannot be said that the statutes of limitations apply to holders of title under Islamic law.

5.7 Postponement of the Period of Limitation

The running of the period of limitations in cases of adverse possession may be postponed on account of *disability* of the title holder, or on account of *fraud, concealment* or *mistake*.

5.7.1 Disability

Disability in this case relates to legal incompetence such as infancy or unsound mind existing at the time when the cause of action accrued.[165] This is imperative as a result of the incompetence legally of these categories of people.[166] However, this provision of the law does not apply

---

161 See *Majekodunmi v. Abina* supra (n 148).

162 See *Holloway v. Jimoh* (2020) 2 NWLR (Pt 1707) 27; *Adetula v. Akinyosoye* (2017) 16 NWLR (Pt. 1592). 492.

163 See chapter 6 *infra*.

164 See e.g. District Court Law of Niger State of Nigeria Cap 37 vol.1 1992, s.2; High Court Law of Katsina State of Nigeria Cap 59 1991, s.2.

165 *Ogoh v. ENPEE Industries Ltd* (2004) 17 NWLR (Pt. 903) 449 at 462 paras D-E.

166 But query, whether it would not have been sufficient for the *guardian ad litem* or next of kin to bring an action on behalf of the infant or the person of unsound mind respectively.

to disability occurring after the cause of action arose, as for example, when the person becomes mentally disabled after dispossession[167] in which case, time continues to run against the title holder.

5.7.2 Fraud, Concealment and Mistake

Also, the period of limitations may be postponed on the grounds of fraud, deliberate concealment of facts relevant to the true owner's right of action, or mistake.[168] In the case of fraud or deliberate concealment of relevant facts, time does not run until the claimant discovers the fraud or concealment or could have, with reasonable diligence discovered it.[169] The requirement of reasonable diligence is met where he has taken steps which a reasonable person would have taken in the circumstances.[170]

In the case of mistake, the mistake itself must have given a right to apply to the court for relief on equitable grounds such as a relief to set aside a conveyance executed under a misapprehension, or by way of rectification or rescission - factors which are ordinarily not subject to any period of limitation. Outside those situations, there is no general rule that mistake stops time from running, and permission to a neighbour to take adverse possession owing to a mistake about boundary, does not stop time from running.[171]

In the absence of disability, fraud, deliberate concealment of facts, or mistake therefore, time runs under the limitation law against the true owner and the right to land is extinguished at the expiration of the period of limitation, notwithstanding that the true owner had no knowledge of dispossession by the adverse possessor.[172]

---

[167] *Goodhall v. Skerratt* (1855) 3 Drew. 216

[168] *Ogoh v. EMPEE Industries Ltd*, supra (n 165).

[169] See the English Limitation Act 1980; s. 32(1).

[170] *Peco Arts Inc. v. Hazlitt Gallery Ltd.* [1983] 1 WLR 1315 at 1323.

[171] *Phillips-Higgins v. Harper* [1954] 1 QB 411; *Cartledge v. Joplin & Sons Ltd* [1963] AC 758.

[172] *Davies v. Ajibona* (1994) 5 NWLR (Pt. 343) 234.

5.8 Starting Time Running Afresh

Time may start running afresh under the limitations statute where the adverse possessor or his representative either acknowledges the claimant's title in writing signed by him,[173] or makes a part payment of the principal or interest due in respect of a debt.[174] To constitute a sufficient acknowledgement of title "all that is required is that, as between himself and the owner of the paper title, the person in possession acknowledges that the paper title owner has better title to the land."[175]

5.9 Effect of Lapse of Time

Upon the expiration of the limitation period, both the right of action to recover the land and the claimant's title to it are extinguished.[176] Also extinguished are the rights appertaining to the right of the true owner, such as the right to sue a squatter for rent or damages for trespass.[177]

The adverse possessor in his own right holds a new estate founded on his adverse possession which dates back to the date of his initial entry thereby making it lawful. But the new title of the adverse possessor is subject to any third party rights such as existing easements and restrictive covenants legal or equitable, in existence at the time of dispossession of the title holder.[178] The squatter is also bound by a

---

[173] See the English Limitation Act 1980, s.29(1) (2), 30,

[174] ibid, s. 29(3)-(6).

[175] *Allen v. Mathews* [2007] EWCA Civ. 216 at para 75. This may be demonstrated in various ways, e.g. a letter by the squatter to the owner to buy the land, having realised the owner has a better title, as in *Edginton v. Clark* [1964] 1 QB 367; a letter by the squatter to the owner intimating the latter of his application for funding to refurbish the property, as in *Lambeth LBC v. Archangel* (2001) 33 HLR 490; a petition from the squatter to the owner not to sell the property to a third party, as in *Lambeth LBD v. Bigden* (2001) 33 HLR 478; or a recital in the counterpart of a void lease as in *Rehman v. Benfield* ([2006] EWCA Civ. 1392.

[176] See the English Limitation Act 1980, s. 17.

[177] *Re Jolly* [1900] 2 Ch. 616; *Mount Carmel Investments Ltd v. Thurlow Ltd* [1988] 1 WLR 1078.

[178] *Re Nisbet & Potts' Contract* [1906] 1 Ch 386.

mortgage created prior to the commencement of his adverse possession,[179] but not bound by a charge created after the commencement of his adverse possession.[180]

[179] *Ludbrook v. Ludbrook* [1901] 2 KB 96; *Carroll v. Manek* (1999) 79 P. & C.R 173.

[180] The reason is that once adverse possession has commenced, it is unaffected by any disposition which the true owner may make: See the English Limitation Act 1980, s. 15(4).

CHAPTER 6
APPLICATION OF THE DOCTRINE OF ADVERSE POSSESSION IN NIGERIA

6.1 Introduction

This chapter examines the background to the reception and application of the doctrine of adverse possession in Nigeria under a plural legal system. This requires an analysis of the historical background of the Nigerian land tenure systems portrayed by the indigenous customary land tenure, and the Islamic law of land tenure before the advent of British rule in the second half of the 19th Century, and the intervention of local statutes thereafter.

The reception of English law inclusive of the doctrine of adverse possession created a parallel system of land holding with implications for the pre-existing land tenure systems in Nigeria, and informed the enactment of the Statutes of limitations (following similar enactments in England) in different parts of the country. The advent of the Land Use Act with peculiar land holding features and the dual system of land registration are features unknown to the English land tenure system with implications for the application of the doctrine of adverse possession.

The Federal Capital Territory (FCT) of Nigeria which was created pursuant to the FCT Act 1976[1] particularly created a neutral system of land tenure which is essentially statute based vesting all lands there in the Federal Government of Nigeria exclusively. The non-recognition of the customary or Islamic land tenure and non-susceptibility to the provisions of the Land Use Act make the system of land tenure in the FCT unique with implications for the application of the doctrine of adverse possession therein.

[1] Federal Capital Territory Act Cap 503 Laws of the Federation of Nigeria 2007.

6.2 Background to the Nigerian Land Tenure System

An exploration of the political structure of Nigeria would explain the basis for the existence of the plural legal system applicable in the country and lay a foundation for the understanding of the hierarchy of laws which may not be familiar to the English legal system (applicable in Wales).

Nigeria operates a Presidential system of government with a Federal structure under a written Constitution[2] ('the Constitution').[3] The federation of Nigeria consists of thirty six States and a Federal Capital Territory.[4] This federal structure is reflected in the legislative, executive and judicial arms of government.[5] There are three tiers of government namely, the federal, the state and the local government.[6]

The Constitution which is the *grundnorm* (the basic law of the land) established inter alia, a Presidential system of government with a federal bicameral legislature and the state legislature. The Constitution is the supreme law, and any other law inconsistent with any of its

[2] See the Constitution of the Federal Republic of Nigeria 1999 as amended ('the Constitution').

[3] Nigeria attained independence from Britain on October 1, 1960. The country passed through Constitutional changes since the independence Constitution in 1960; amongst these were the 1963 Republican Constitution, the 1979 Constitution with amendments up to 1999 when the extant constitution came into force. The current 1999 Constitution is patterned, like the 1979 Constitution before it, and took after the Constitution of the United States of America: For further reading, see C. Nwalimu, 'The Nigerian Legal System' vol 1 Public Law 2005, New York. It is worthy of note that Nigeria experienced some periods of Military Rule between 1966 and 1979; and 1983 to 1999. The Supreme Law then was Decree No. 1 enacted by the Supreme Military Council or the Armed Forces Ruling Council as opposed to the Constitution. The Land Use Act 1978 the 1979 Constitution and, indeed, the 1999 Constitution, were legacies of the Military.

[4] ibid, s. 2(2) and (3). The Federal Capital was moved from Lagos to Abuja on December 12, 1991.

[5] ibid, Parts IV, V. and VI.

[6] For the establishment of the Local Government system, see section 7 of the Constitution.

provisions is void to the extent of its inconsistency.[7] Apart from its provisions on separation of powers, rule of law and fundamental rights and freedoms including the right to property, it entrenched certain enactments[8] including the Land Use Act[9] in the Constitution to ''continue to apply and have full effect in accordance with their tenor and to the like extent as any other provisions forming part of this Constitution.''[10] Section 315(6) of the Constitution provides that such enactments including the Land Use Act ''shall continue to have effect as Federal enactments and as if they related to matters included in the Exclusive Legislative List set out in Part I of the Second Schedule to this Constitution''. It is by virtue of this provision that the Land Use Act qualifies as an Act of the National Assembly despite the fact that land, the subject matter of the Act, is a residual matter which should ordinarily be within the powers of the State Houses of Assembly.

International treaties such as the African Charter on Human and Peoples' Rights (which is of relevance to this work) are binding on Nigeria only to the extent that it is domesticated as an Act of the National Assembly[11] – a federal legislature created by the Constitution. Although it is an Act of the National Assembly known as 'The African Charter on Human and Peoples' Rights (Ratification and Enforcement) Act'[12] it is a statute with international flavour. Consequently, if there is a conflict between it and another statute, its provisions will prevail over those of other statutes for the reason that it is presumed that the legislature does not intend to breach an international obligation.[13] Nigerian courts not only have jurisdiction to enforce the provisions of the Charter, there is also an

[7] ibid, s.1(3).

[8] These are the National Youth Service Corps Cap N84 Laws of the Federation of Nigeria 2010; the Public Complaints Commission Act Cap P37 Laws of the Federation of Nigeria, 2010; the National Security Agencies Act Cap N74 Laws of the Federation of Nigeria, 2010.

[9] Land Use Act 1978 Cap L5 Laws of the Federation of Nigeria 2010.

[10] ibid, s.315 (5).

[11] ibid, s. 12(1).

[12] Cap A9 Laws of the Federation of Nigeria, 2010.

[13] *Abacha v. Fawehinmi* (2000) 6 NWLR 228.

avenue for enforcement at the African Court on Human and Peoples' Rights established pursuant to Article 1 of the Protocol to the African Charter. According to the Protocol[14] and the Rules,[15] the Court may receive complaints and/or applications submitted to it by the African Commission on Human and Peoples' Rights, State parties to the Protocol, Africa Intergovernmental Organisations, Non-governmental organisations with observer status, and individuals from states which have made a Declaration accepting the jurisdiction of the Court. As of this date, only nine States have made such a declaration, and Nigeria is not one of them.

The federal legislature known as the National Assembly[16] makes laws "for the peace, order and good government of the federation or any part thereof" in respect of matters within the exclusive legislative list,[17] and concurrently with the states with regard to matters on the concurrent list.[18] It also makes laws for the Federal Capital Territory (FCT) with regard to all matters in respect of which the states have power to make laws.[19]

The states may legislate "for the peace, order and good government" on "any matter not included in the exclusive legislative list,"[20] any matter within the concurrent legislative list[21] in respect of which the federal legislature has not made laws, and on all other matters not specified either in the exclusive or in the concurrent list, with respect to which it is empowered to make Laws[22] otherwise known as residual

---

[14] Article 5 of the Protocol

[15] Rule 33 of the Rules of Court.

[16] The National Assembly consists of the Senate and the House of Representatives: See s. 4(1) of the Constitution.

[17] Section 4(2)(3) and Part I of the Second Schedule to the Constitution.

[18] Section 4(4)(a) and first column of Part II of the Second Schedule to the Constitution.

[19] Section 4(4)(b) of the Constitution.

[20] Section 4(7)(a) of the Constitution.

[21] Section 4(7)(b) of the Constitution.

[22] Section 4(7)(c).

matters. Such residual matters, over which the States and the Federal Capital Territory have powers to make Laws pertain, among others, to limitation of actions, land matters, registration of land instruments or title to land - matters not covered by either the exclusive or the concurrent legislative list under the Constitution. As regards the Federal Capital Territory, the Limitations Act[23]- a federal legislation regulating limitation of actions, the Land Registration Law of the old Northern Nigeria,[24] and the Registration of Titles Act[25] which hitherto applied in the former Federal Territory of Lagos, apply.[26]

Although the Land Use Act 1978[27] was enacted by the then Federal Military Government and subsequently presumed to be an Act of the National Assembly (the federal legislature) by the Nigerian Constitution,[28] land titling and management of land have been made the prerogative of the State Governor[29] with the exceptions of federal lands within the states,[30] or lands within the Federal Capital Territory over which the President exercises powers of management and control through the Minister of the Federal Capital Territory.[31]

The legal system of Nigeria is based on customary law prevalent in Southern Nigeria, and in the Northern Nigeria before the introduction of Islamic law; Islamic law predominantly in the Northern part of Nigeria; the English law and a number of local legislation including the Land Use Act. Intertwined therefore with the political structure highlighted is the

---

[23] No. 88 1966 applicable in the Federal Capital Territory of Nigeria and incorporated into the Laws of Nigeria by Cap 522 Laws of the Federation of Nigeria, 2004.

[24] This is due to the fact that the Federal Capital Territory was created on the area formerly belonging to the old Northern Nigeria with her existing Laws: See Land Registration Law, Laws of Northern Nigeria Cap 97 1958.

[25] Registration of Titles Act Cap 181 Laws of Nigeria 1958.

[26] See Second Schedule to the FCT Act 1976.

[27] Cap L5 Laws of the Federation of Nigeria, 2010.

[28] ibid, s. 315(5)(d).

[29] Land Use Act 1978, supra (n 9) ss.1, 5, 9, 34 and 36.

[30] ibid, s.49(1).

[31] ibid, s. 51(2).

evolution of the multiple system of land tenure discussed in the next section.

6.3 The Nigerian Land Tenure Systems and Adverse Possession

Before the advent of the Land Use Act[32] (LUA) in Nigeria, there were multiple land tenure systems applicable in the country depending on the status of the land,[33] the law of the place where the land is situated (the *lex situs*)[34] and the law applicable to the propositus.[35] Generally in Nigeria before colonisation by the British with effect from 1861 following the cession of Lagos by the then monarch of the island to the British,[36] title to land was predominantly governed by the customary land tenure systems

[32] Cap L5 Laws of the Federation of Nigeria, 2010.

[33] The land could be subject matter of customary, Islamic or English law.

[34] For example, while the common law and the Conveyancing Act 1881 applied to transactions on land in many parts of the country excluding the old Western and mid-western Nigeria, the Property and Conveyancing Law Cap 100 Laws of Western Nigeria applied in those parts of the country.

[35] Personal law applied and still applies in succession matters relating to land except where English law or statute applies. Personal law could be the customary or Islamic law applicable to the propositus: See *Zaidhan v. Mohssen* (1973) 11 S.C 1.

[36] In 1861, King Dosumu of Lagos (the 13th in succession) signed the Treaty of Cession dated 6 August 1861 purportedly on behalf of himself and the Chiefs, ceding to the British Crown "the Port and Island of Lagos with all the rights, profits and territories and appurtenances whatsoever thereunto belonging". The legal effect of the Treaty of Cession from the standpoint of judicial authorities is that general words of the Cession construed as having related primarily to Sovereign rights only, had nothing to do with the proprietary rights of the various landowning families in Lagos. See *Onisiwo v. Attorney General of Southern Provinces* (1912) 2 N.L.R 77; *Attorney General of Southern Nigeria v. John Holt & Ors* (1910) 2 N.L.R 1 at 6and 7.

applicable in Southern Nigeria,[37] and predominantly by Islamic law applicable in the Northern Nigeria.[38]

The original state of the tenurial system in Nigeria intertwined with her political history as captured by the Nigerian Supreme Court in the case of *Attorney General of the Federation v. Attorney General of Abia State & 35 Ors*[39] in the following words:

> Until the advent of the British colonial rule in what is now known as the Federal Republic of Nigeria...there existed at various times various sovereign states known as emirates, kingdoms and empires made up of ethnic groups in Nigeria. Each was independent of the other with its mode of government indigenous to it. At one time or another, these sovereign states were either making wars with each other or making alliances, on equal terms. This position existed throughout the land known as Nigeria...

The foregoing observation depicts the significance of ethnicity, tribal and religious groupings indigenous to Nigeria, and explains the background to the pre-existing land tenure systems before the advent of colonial rule.

6.3.1 Customary Land Tenure System

During the period dominated by these ethnic groupings, land tenure system was communal in nature and land was held by the community and later the family, under the control and management of the head chief,

---

[37] See for example, s.26 of the High Court of Lagos State, Cap H3 Laws of Lagos State 2003. The provision is basically the same in the High Court Laws of other states of the federation of Nigeria.

[38] See for example, s. 22 of Cap 49 Laws of Northern Nigeria, 1963 applicable in the various Northern States. Also s. 12(c) of the Sharia Court of Appeal Law 1960 which directs the Sharia Court of Appeal to hear any matter where all parties to the proceedings have requested the court of first instance in writing to hear the case under Islamic law.

[39] (2006) 1 FWLR (Pt. 298) 480 at 511.

the Oba, the Emir, the head of the family etc.,[40] who held the land as trustees for the community or family. This position characterises the customary law perspective of land ownership in Nigeria. In the words of the Nigerian Supreme Court in *Adejumo v. Ayantegbe*[41]: "At customary law, ownership of family [and communal land] is vested in the past, existing and future members of the family [or community]. Thus, communal or family land belongs to all members of the society or family"[42] to be preserved by generations as communal inheritance.

Customary land tenure system is the system of landholding indigenous to Nigeria and made applicable by the various High Court Laws meant to "observe and enforce the observance of customary law which is applicable and not repugnant to natural justice, equity and good conscience nor incompatible either directly or by implication with any law for the time being in force."[43] Customary law is a "mirror of accepted usage;"[44] it represents the customs and usages of the indigenous people within a geographical area from time immemorial which the people regard as binding on them, and which the court would apply as law upon proof of same[45] or upon judicial notice being taken of such custom.[46] One significant feature of this system of law is its flexibility and gradual response to changes in modern times.[47]

Members of the community or family under customary law are allocated land to occupy and use, by the head who is a *primus inter pares* (first among equals).[48] This allocation does not confer any form of

---

[40] I.O.Smith, *Practical Approach to Law of Real Property in Nigeria* (Revised edition) 2013 Ecowatch Publications (Nig) Ltd at 25.

[41] (1989) 3 N.W.L.R (Pt 110) 417.

[42] ibid, at 444 paras C-D

[43] See n 37.

[44] *Owoniyi v. Omotosho* (1961) All N.L.R 304

[45] Proof may be through witnesses, books or by calling assessors: See Evidence Act 2011, s.14(3).

[46] A judicially noticed custom requires no proof: ibid, s. 14(1) (2).

[47] *Lewis v. Bankole* (1908) 1 N.L.R 82.

[48] *Lewis v. Bankole* supra (n 47).

proprietary interest on the allottee, although the right of user automatically passes to his heirs in accordance with customary law.[49] Title to communal or family land cannot be transferred in any form to a third party without the consent of the family[50] and it cannot be devised by Will. Communal or family grant of right of use to third parties takes the form of customary tenancy to be enjoyed in perpetuity subject to good behaviour including acknowledgement of the overlord's title and payment of tribute to him.[51]

The Nigerian customary law does not permit acquisition of title to land by adverse possession.[52] As the Supreme Court pointed out in *Agboola v. Abimbola*:[53]

> "Assuming-and this fact was not proved and was in fact later jettisoned-that Kanyinde was an Egba refugee at the time that he purported to sell the land, he had no more than an interest under native law and custom. *We do not consider that any authorities are now needed to show the inapplicability of Statutes of Limitation to such tenures.*"[54] (Italics supplied).

The Limitation Act 1966[55] (which supersedes the English Statute of Limitation) - a Federal legislation adopted in the FCT[56] with

[49] ibid.

[50] *Ekpendu v. Erika* (1959) 4 FSC 79; *Alao v. Ajani* (1989) 4 N.W.L.R (Pt 113) 1.

[51] *Aghenghen & Ors v. Waghoregor & Ors* (1974) 1 SC 1; *Abioye v. Yakubu* (1991) 5 NWLR (Pt. 190) 130.

[52] See McCarthy, Ag. CJ in *Fiscian v. Nelson* (1946) 12 W.A.C.A 21, 22. The customary land tenure system is preserved under the Land Use Act 1978 Cap L5 2010, and the occupier of land under customary law is said to have a customary right of occupancy either by way of an actual grant under section 6(1) of the Act or by way of deemed grant under section 36 of the Act.

[53] SC.336/67 of 4/7/69 (Unreported) 1; *Mora v. Nwalusi* (1962) 1 All N.L.R 681.

[54] ibid, at 7.

[55] This Act which was enacted under the Military regime as a Decree became an existing law by virtue of section 315 of the Constitution of the Federal Republic of Nigeria 1999, and deemed to be an Act of the National Assembly. This Federal

corresponding Limitation Law applicable in the thirty six states of Nigeria- excludes customary law from the ambit of its application.[57]

However, where a party intending to rely on the exclusion under customary law is 'guilty' of laches and acquiescence in equity in circumstances paving way for the application of the principle of proprietary estoppel, he may lose his customary title to the adverse possessor.[58] As the court noted in *Nwakobi v. Nzekwu:*[59]

> If a stranger begins to build on my land supposing it to be his own, and I, perceiving his mistake, abstain from setting him right, and leave him to persevere in his error, a court of equity will not allow me to afterwards assert my title to the land on which he had expended money on the supposition that the land was his own...But it will be observed that to raise such an equity, two things are required first, that the person expending money suppose himself to be building on his own land; and secondly, that the real owner at the time of expenditure knows that the land belongs to

---

Legislation was later adopted and re-enacted in the various States of Nigeria as Limitations Law. The Act however applies to the Federal Capital Territory, Abuja.

[56] This is made applicable pursuant to the power of the National Assembly to make Laws for the FCT on residual matters, including limitation of actions

[57] See section 67(1) of the Act.

[58] See *Awo v. Cookey Gam* (1913) 2 NWLR 100. This rule known as the rule in *Akpan Awo v. Cookey-Gam* (supra) applies only upon fulfilment of certain conditions by the party relying on it to defeat a claim under customary law namely: 1. that he (the defendant) is an adverse possessor strictly speaking in law as opposed to a tenant, licensee or a person enjoying an occupational right within the title of the plaintiff; 2. that he took possession of the land under a mistaken belief that he had title to it; 3. that the plaintiff had knowledge of the adverse possession but acquiesced in it; 4. that as a result of this reliance on the plaintiff's acquiescence, the defendant has been led to expend money or otherwise alter his position; 5. that there exists no extenuating circumstances negativing acquiescence; 6. that the length of time is fairly long enough to establish a prima facie evidence of acquiescence on the part of the plaintiff.

[59] (1961) 1 All N.L.R 445.

> him and not to the person expending money in the belief that he is the owner.[60]

Clarifying this position earlier in *Akpan Awo v. Cookey-Gam,*[61] the court said:

> "We do not decide this point in accordance with any provision of English law as to the limitation of actions but simply on the grounds of equity, on the ground that the court will not allow a party to call in aid principles, which, as in this case, were developed in and are applicable to a state of society vastly different from that now existing merely for the purpose of bolstering up a stale claim."[62]

The above dictum demonstrates one of the characteristics of customary law which is flexibility and adaptation to changing circumstances. It also demonstrates the application of the rule of equity embellished in the rule of validity contained in the various High Court Laws across the various states in Southern Nigeria which provides that the court will apply a rule of customary law only where it is "not repugnant to natural justice, equity and good conscience or incompatible with any Law for the time being in force".

The rationale for the rule of equity which bars the application of the customary rule of land tenure was laid down by the court in *Akpan Awo v. Cookey Gam.*[63]In that case, the plaintiff's claim to the land in dispute failed because the defendants, under a mistaken belief that they were the owners of the land in dispute, had exercised acts of ownership by making agreements with strangers, granting leases and receiving rents for many years without interference or action taken by the plaintiffs to assert their rights under native law and custom. Formulating the rule in equity, Webber J. explained as follows:

---

[60] ibid, at 450.

[61] Supra (n 59).

[62] ibid, 101.

[63] Supra n 58.

> It would be wholly inequitable to deprive the defendants of property of which they have held undisturbed possession and in respect of which they have collected rents for so long a term of years with the knowledge and acquiescence of those who now dispute their title, even if it were...clear...that they entered into possession contrary to the principles of native law...

The rule in *Akpan Awo v. Cookey Gam* cannot be invoked unless the defendant relying on it is able to show by evidence: that his possession is adverse[64] to that of the customary land owner as he is not a tenant, a licensee or a person enjoying an occupational right within the title of the plaintiff;[65] that he took possession of the land under a mistaken belief that he had title to it;[66] that the plaintiff had knowledge of the adverse possession but acquiesced in it;[67] that as a result of this reliance on the plaintiff's acquiescence, the defendant has been led to expend money or otherwise alter his position;[68] that there exists no extenuating circumstances negativing acquiescence;[69] and that the length of time is fairly long enough to establish a prima facie evidence of acquiescence on the part of the plaintiff[70]. The defendant will succeed in invoking the rule

[64] The word 'adverse' is used in the ordinary grammatical sense as opposed to the technical legal sense.

[65] *Epelle v. Ojo* (1926) 1 N.L.R 96. See also *Chairman L.E.D.B v. Sunmonu & Ors* (1961) L.L.R 20; *Nezianya v. Okagbue* (1963) 1 All N.L.R 352.

[66] *Akpan Awo v. Cookey Gam,* supra (n 59).

[67] *Nwakobi v. Nzekwu* (1961) 1 All N.L.R 445 at 450. Knowledge may be presumed not only from the overt acts of the defendant such as expenditure of money on improvements on land, but also from long possession sufficient to impute knowledge to the plaintiff. In the case of family or community, knowledge by all members is unnecessary; it suffices that important members had knowledge: See *Saidi v. Akinwunmi* (1956) 1 FSC 107.

[68] *Suleman v. Johnson* (1951) 13 WACA 213.

[69] Such extenuating circumstances include intimacy, blood ties or family relationship existing between the parties which motivated moves towards settlement thereby causing delay in bringing the action in court.

[70] There is no hard and fast rule as to the length of time required. Although a period of twenty one years was held in *Akpan Awo v. Cookey Gam* as sufficient, five

in *Akpan Awo v. Cookey Gam* only where the foregoing requirements are met in their totality and fails where any one of those requirements is lacking.

The question whether land ceases to be regulated by customary law so as to be a subject of adverse possession and application of the statute of limitation is a question of fact depending on the nature of transaction and the evidence of it. For example, where the claimant relies on documents couched in English form *and it is not suggested that any reliance is placed on customary law,* any title covered by the documents is subject to the application of the doctrine of adverse possession and the provisions of the relevant statute of limitation. As the court observed in *Green v. Owo:*[71]

> Now what is the plaintiff's position in this case? He has in his possession documents in English Conveyancers' jargon, and plans attached to them. He has nothing but these documents. There is no evidence except the documents as to the title of the grantees to grant them. There is no evidence of possession under them. These documents profess to give to the plaintiff a right to the land in dispute which the defendant and his predecessors have occupied without interference for over twenty years, and which so far as the evidence before me goes -none of the plaintiff's predecessors has ever occupied...The Statute of Limitations in such circumstances in England would certainly bar the plaintiff's present claim. Where is the existing native custom to the contrary? There is, so far as I

---

years was considered as sufficient in *Okiade v. Morayo* (1940) 15 N.L.R 131. The true rule appears to be that the length of time required where the adverse possessor developed the land is shorter than in cases of undeveloped land since the former situation constitutes an overt act of which the plaintiff ought to have taken cognisance: See for example, *Yaro Ningi v. Dan Katsina* (1991) 3 NWLR (Pt. 177) 76.

[71] (1936) 13 N.L.R 43.

> know, no native custom as regards the effect of documentary titles in English conveyance form. How would there be?[72]

It is instructive to note that in cases in which the English type conveyance is involved, it is not the fact of the existence of the conveyance in English form that matters, it is the act of relying on the document to the exclusion of customary law relating to land. This is because customary law recognises the use of writing and, *ipso facto*, the use of Conveyance in English form.[73]

6.3.2 Islamic Land Tenure System

The indigenous land tenure system discussed above applied to both the Northern and Southern Nigeria until the advent of Islamic law. Unlike customary law which developed amongst, and applies generally to the indigenous people, Islamic law like the English common law is foreign to Nigeria. It originated in Saudi Arabia and through Egypt in North Africa, it came into West Africa through Mali from where it was introduced into Nigeria and subsequently imposed on the people of Northern Nigeria through conquest by the Islamic jihadists led by Usman dan Fodio sometime in the 19th Century.[74] Consequent upon the conquest, the Fulani conquerors took over all parcels of land in the conquered territories in conformity with the Maliki law of Islam which stipulates that "all lands which come into the possession of the faithful through conquests become wakhf, that is, tied up immediately after conquest."[75] The concept of Wakhf in Islamic law is that land, being public property, is vested in Allah, and no individual has radical title to it.[76] Different places were placed under the control of the Emir with the land held in trust for the people.[77] The people had land allocated to them for use by the Emir in

---

[72] ibid, at 45. See also *Agboola v. Abimbola* supra (n 53).

[73] *Rotibi v. Savage* (1944) 17 N.L.R 77; *Balogun v. Oshodi* (1929) 10 N.L.R 36.

[74] See generally, C. Nwalimu, *Nigerian Legal System* 2005, New York at 158-161.

[75] F.H Ruxton, Maliki Law (1916) OUP 1976.

[76] I.O. Smith, supra (n 40).

[77] F.D Lugard, Political Memoranda, No. 10 Lands, para 7.

return for their payment of tribute. This is in contrast to the customary land tenure system where land is communally owned and the individual members of the community or family is entitled to be allocated land by the head chief or the head of the family without payment of tribute or furnishing of any form of consideration.

Islamic land tenure system is an independent system applicable predominantly in the Northern States of Nigeria. In its classical form, Islamic law derives from the *Qur'an*, the *Sunna of Prophet Muhammad*, the consensus of Islamic scholars known as *Ijma*, and reasoning by analogy known as *Kiyas*. It is made applicable by the High Court Laws and the Sharia Court of Appeal Law of the Northern States of Nigeria.[78]

Existing literature have shown that despite the introduction of Islamic law in Northern Nigeria, the court system in that region favours enforcement of both Islamic and customary law.[79] By virtue of section 13 of the Sharia Court of Appeal Law applicable in the Northern States,[80] "Islamic law courts in Nigeria recognise and enforce not only Maliki law, but also customary law of the various indigenous tribal groups of Nigeria and "common law" to the extent it is the system of law that stipulates application of laws that are consistent with natural justice, equity and good conscience."[81] Also, both the District Court under the District Court Law[82] and the High Court under the various High Court Laws[83] define Customary law to include Islamic law.[84]

---

[78] See e.g. s.22 of Cap 49 Laws of Northern Nigeria, 1963 applicable in the various Northern States. Also s. 12(e) of the Sharia Court of Appeal Law, 1960 which directs the Sharia Court of Appeal to hear any matter where all parties to the proceedings have requested the court of first instance in writing to hear the case under Islamic law.

[79] C. Nwalimu, supra (n 74) at 174.

[80] See e.g. Sharia Court of Appeal Law, of Kano State 1960 as amended; Sharia Court of Appeal of Niger State 1992.

[81] C. Nwalimu, supra (n 74) at 174.

[82] See District Courts Law of Niger State Ch 37 vol. 1 1992 and District Court Law of Katsina State of Nigeria Ch. 39 1991 as amended, s.2.

The choice of Islamic law on land tenure is optional and depends on the consensus of the parties in the determination of any question. Although there are different schools of thought on Islamic law, only the Maliki School of thought is of relevance in Nigeria as it is the case in other West African countries.[85]

Islamic law recognises the principle of long possession known as *hauzi* as a mode of acquisition of title. *Hauzi* is the equivalent of the right of prescription under Roman as opposed to English law. It is rooted in Islamic jurisprudence to protect long possession and ensure that land is put to productive use. It is said that the effect of prescription known as *usucapio* in Roman law is:

> to confer a positive title to the land upon a person who had remained in possession for a certain time…[it] exemplified what is sometimes called acquisitive prescription in the sense that possession of another's land for a given period conferred a positive title upon the occupier, but English law has never adopted this theory in its treatment of corporeal hereditaments and chattels though it has done so in the case of easements and profits[86]

In the *Hadith* (one of the sources of Islamic law) however, the principle of *hauzi* as interpreted by scholars of Islamic Law[87] is as follows:

> He who sees somebody in possession of his (claimant's) property and claiming and using the same as his own over a long period [10 years] without any objection from him, the person in possession becomes the owner. If the original owner later brings an action to recover it neither the complaint nor evidence in support thereof will be listened to. But there are exceptions to this principle: 1.

---

[83] See e.g. High Court Law of Katsina State of Nigeria, Laws of Katsina State of Nigeria Ch 59, 1991.

[84] ibid, s.2.

[85] See Zaidhan v. Mohseen (1973) N.S.C.C 516.

[86] See Cheshire and Burn & Cartwright, 18th ed. O.U.P at 1127-1128.

[87] Ashalul Madarik vol. 3 at 236.

> cogent reason for not complaining in time e.g. blood relationship or fear of harm from authority; 2. minorship; 3. the person in possession is put there by the claimant either as a free or paying tenant; 4. the person in possession is put in there as a trustee; 5. the claimant is a partner or co-proprietor to the person in possession.[88]

The essence of bringing the principle of *hauzi* and its exceptions to the fore is to appreciate the fact that its rule of prescription and the exceptions to it keep the concept of prescription strictly within the ambit of Islamic law as an in-built machinery for dealing with stale claims.

The principle of *hauzi* in Islamic law has peculiar requirements which do not coincide with those of the doctrine of adverse possession or the provisions of the statutes of limitation. The right of *hauzi* accrues to a party who has been in undisturbed possession of the land of another for a period of ten years or more while the true owner stood by and did nothing to claim his property, and the parties are not related by blood or marriage.[89] In *hauzi,* knowledge actual or constructive on the part of the claimant is required; the defendant must have had a mistaken belief that the land belonged to him; the inaction of the claimant must have led the defendant to expend money or to take some steps to his detriment; and the relationship by blood or marriage of the parties is a factor to be taken into consideration – factors which are of no moment in adverse possession cases. Also, whereas, under the Limitation Act, the period of limitation in the case of individual parties is twelve years from the date the right of action accrues,[90] the period of undisturbed possession in the case of *hauzi* is between ten and forty years depending on whether there exists or not between the parties, the relationship by marriage or by blood.[91]

---

[88] Mayyarah Vol. II 164; Maliki Law (Summary Translation of Mukhtasha Khalil by Ruxton) 309 para 1698

[89] See *Yaro Ningi v. Dan Katsina* (1991) 3 NWLR (Pt 177) 76; *Gunku v. Doro* (1992) 3 NWLR (Pt. 228) 190.

[90] See the Limitation Act No.88 1966, s.16(2). It is twenty years in the case of a State authority: See s.16(1).

[91] *Gunku v. Doro* supra (n 89).

6.3.3 The Received English Land Tenure

As a result of the contact of the indigenous people of Nigeria with the British during colonisation, and following the advent of trade and commerce and the recognition of the use of writing by customary law,[92] the use of the English mode of conveyancing was embraced.[93] The application of the English land tenure system was facilitated by the reception statutes[94] making the common law of England, the doctrines of equity and certain English statutes of general application applicable in England on January 1, 1900 applicable to transactions including land matters generally in Nigeria,[95] alongside the existing Customary and Islamic law of land tenure. Consequently, the common law doctrine of adverse possession and the successive English statutes of limitation up to 1874 were generally made part of Nigerian law. The colonial regime also facilitated the emergence of Crown grants of land in some specific areas in the cities[96] later culminating in the designation of State land governed by the State Lands Law.[97] Also, English law as defined applies in the FCT pursuant to section 13 of the FCT Act 1976.

It is pertinent to note that the application of the English law of land tenure depends on local circumstances and application of local legislation on land tenure.[98] It does not apply where the customary or Islamic law of land tenure applies, and applies subject to local legislation.

---

[92] *Rotibi v. Savage* supra (n 73).

[93] *Oshodi v. Balogun* (1936) 2 All E.R 1632

[94] See e.g. Law (Miscellaneous Provisions) Act Cap 89 Laws of Nigeria 1958.

[95] ibid, s.45(1). Application is however subject to local circumstances: See s. 45(3).

[96] See e.g. the Crown Grants (Township of Lagos) Act No. 18 1947; The Arotas (Crown Grants) Act No. 19 1947; The Epetedo Land Act No. 20 1947; and the Glover Settlement Act No. 21 1947.

[97] See e.g. State Lands Law Cap S11 Laws of Lagos State, 2003.

[98] Law (Miscellaneous Provisions) Act 1964, s.45(3).

6.3.4 The Land Tenure Law 1962

In 1962, the Northern Nigeria enacted the Land Tenure Law[99] subjecting land ownership in that region to state grants, imposing state control and management of land, streamlining unlimited interests in land such as the fee simple estate, and converting same and other indigenous rights to rights of occupancy.[100] The right of occupancy can only be alienated with the consent of the Minister.[101] Such rights can be revoked by the Minister for public purpose[102] with the holder of the right of occupancy entitled to compensation.[103]

The Land Tenure Law is the precursor of the Land Use Act 1978 (LUA) which now applies to all parcels of land within the territory of a state in Nigeria. Although the Land Tenure Law is preserved by the LUA[104] - the principal legislation on land titles, control and management of land in Nigeria, it "shall have effect with such modification as would bring those laws into conformity with this Act or its general intendment."[105]

Since the provisions of the LUA supersede those of the Land Tenure Law, the provisions of the LUA are discussed below.

6.3.5 The Land Use Act Regime

The Nigerian Land Use Act 1978 (LUA) is the principal legislation on title to land in Nigeria. Section 1 of the Act vests radical title of all lands within the territory of each state of the federation in the Governor of the State to be held in trust for the citizens. Unlimited land rights in the form of the English fee simple absolute in possession were abolished and substituted

---

99 Land Tenure Law Cap 59 Laws of Northern Nigeria 1963.

100 ibid, ss.4, 5, 10(1).

101 ibid, ss.27, 28.

102 ibid, s.34.

103 ibid.

104 ibid, s. 4(a).

105 ibid, s.4(b).

with a right of occupancy. In the words of Kawu J.S.C in *Safuratu Salami v. Sunmonu Oke*[106]:

> "Absolute ownership of land is no longer possible since according to the provisions of section 1 of the Act all land comprised in the territory of each state in the federation are hereby vested in the governor of the state and such land shall be held in trust and administered for the use and common benefit of all Nigerians in accordance with the provisions of the Decree."[107]

The only land not affected by section 1 of the Act which vested all land in the state in the Governor, is the land which is vested in the Federal Government of Nigeria or any of its agencies at the commencement of the Act under section 49 thereof.[108]

Whilst it abolished all unlimited rights existing on land such as the English freehold estates and converted same to rights of occupancy, it preserved pre-existing rights including customary land rights in land subject to the provisions of the Act.[109] In the words of Nnaemeka-Agu J.S.C in *Ogunleye v. Oni*[110]:

> ...the Land Use Act never set out to abolish all existing titles and rights to possession of land. Rather, when such rights or titles relate to developed lands in urban areas, the possessor or owner of that right or title is deemed to be a statutory grantee of a right of occupancy under section 34(2) of the Act. Where it is non-urban land, the holder or owner under Customary [and Islamic] law or otherwise is deemed to be a deemed grantee of a right of occupancy by the appropriate Local Government under section 36(2).

---

[106] (1987) 9-11 S.C. 43.

[107] ibid, at 63.

[108] ibid.

[109] ibid, ss. 34, 36 and 48.

[110] (1990) 2 N.W.L.R (Pt 135) 745 at 784. See also *Ogunola v. Eiyekole & Ors* (1990) 4 N.W.L.R (Pt 146) 632, on the preservation of the customary land tenure system by the Act.

Furthermore, in *Ogunola v. Eiyekole*,[111] the Supreme Court held regarding pre-existing customary land rights that:

> Land is still held under customary tenure even though dominium is in the Governor. The most pervasive effect of the Land Use Act is the diminution of the plenitude of the powers of the holder of the land. The character in which they hold remain substantially the same

Also, Section 48 of the Act which preserves:

> All existing laws relating to the registration of title to, or interest in, land or the transfer of title to or any interest in land shall have effect subject to such modification (whether by way of addition, alteration or omission) as will bring those laws into conformity with this Act or its general intendment.

It follows therefore that the Act did not abolish pre-existing titles and rights to possession on land in favour of the State and it would be wrong to describe the Act's intervention on 29 March 1978 as nationalisation of land.[112] The Act preserves customary and Islamic law, the common law of England and statutes of general application as at January 1 1900 and pieces of local legislation – all predating the Act, "subject to such modifications as will bring those laws into conformity with this Act or its general intendment". Although section 1 of the Land Use Act which vests radical title in the governor of the state[113] is tantamount to an expropriation of absolute ownership, this provision is

---

111 (1990) 4 NWLR (Pt 146) 632 at 653.

112 An opinion to that effect expressed by Eso J.S.C obiter in *Nkwocha v. Governor of Anambra State* (1984) 6 S.C 362 was dismissed subsequently by the Supreme Court in *Salami v. Oke* (1987) 4 NWLR (Pt 63) 1.

113 In the case of the Federal Capital Territory (FCT), radical title is vested in the Federal Government of the Federal Republic of Nigeria while powers of control and Management is exercisable by the President or any Minister designated by him in that behalf: See s.51 of the Land Use Act 1978; and s.1(1) of the FCT Act No.6 of 1976.

subject to the other provisions of the Act especially sections 34 and 36, which preserve pre-existing rights in land.

A right of occupancy unlike a fee simple estate is by way of state grant actual or deemed, mainly. Section 5(1) of the Act makes it lawful for the Governor of the State "in respect of land whether or not in an urban area, to grant a statutory right of occupancy to any person for all purposes," while section 6(1) makes it lawful for a Local Government "in respect of land not in an urban area, to grant customary rights of occupancy to any person or organisation for the use of land in the Local Government Area for agricultural, residential and other purposes."

A holder of a right of occupancy statutory[114] or customary[115] lacks the form of proprietary rights associated with the holder of a fee simple estate absolute in possession known to English law.[116] The holder has no absolute title to the land, only to the un-exhausted improvements made thereon;[117] lacks the form of exclusive possession known to English law;[118]

---

[114] A statutory right of occupancy is a grant made by the Governor on land in urban and non-urban area pursuant to the power vested in him by section 5(1) of the Act.

[115] A customary right of occupancy is one granted by the Local Government over land in a non urban area exclusively pursuant to the power vested in it by section 6(1) of the Act.

[116] It is said that "the right is less than ownership and therefore cannot amount to a proprietary right over land. It is essentially and inextricably the right to use and occupy land:" See I.A Umezulike, *A B C of contemporary land law in Nigeria,* First ed. (2013) Snaap Press Nigeria Ltd. at 81.

[117] Section 15 of the Act.

[118] Section 11 of the Act provides that "[t]he Governor or any public officer duly authorised by the Governor in that behalf, shall have the power to enter upon and inspect the land comprised in any statutory right of occupancy or any improvements effected thereon, at any reasonable hours in the day time and the occupier shall permit and give free access to the Governor or any such officer to enter and inspect." Also, section 14 of the Act provides that: "...the occupier shall have exclusive possession to the land the subject of the statutory right of occupancy against all persons **other than the Governor**."

and is bereft of freedom of alienation of his right or part thereof.[119] The holder or occupier may have his right revoked with or without compensation by the Governor.[120] Where compensation is payable upon revocation of a right of occupancy, the holder of a right of occupancy is compensated for his un-exhausted improvements on the land mainly,[121] as radical title is vested in the Governor.

A right of occupancy is said to be "highly inferior to a leasehold interest...but similar to a license in many respects."[122] It is said that "it is only when the holder of right of occupancy is issued with a state backed certificate of occupancy that the licence becomes supported with interest by virtue of the contractual obligations of the state under the holder's certificate of occupancy."[123]

The assertion that a right of occupancy is not a lease is said to be potent notwithstanding the references to the granting of sublease or sub-underlease pursuant to certain provisions of the Act[124] for the following

---

[119] The holder of a right of occupancy cannot alienate his interest in the land without the consent of the Governor or Local Government being sought and granted: See ss. 21 and 22 of the Act.

[120] See s. 28 of the Act. For provision relating to revocation without compensation, see s.9(3) of the Act.

[121] See s. 29 of the Act.

[122] Umezulike (n 116) at 81, 82.

[123] ibid, at 82. This view appears to be supported by Balogun J. when he said that: "The holder of right of occupancy under the Act is strictly speaking not a free-holder nor a leaseholder, but he is not a mere licensee." See Balogun J. in the text of a paper delivered at the Faculty of Law, University of Lagos 1982 Lectures.

[124] As Okuniga warned: "Hence one must be wary: First against rashly inferring that a statutory right of occupancy is a leasehold interest simply because there are references to the grant of sub-lease or sub-underleases. The Act is no doubt sufficiently confusing in its provisions in this regard, but that does not entitle one to adopt the Humpty-Dumpty type of definition. The lease is a concept of English law and has its own characteristics and incidents unknown to our own indigenous system of landholding. The statutory right of occupancy does share with the English leasehold the quality of certainty of duration but that is about all that is invariably common to both." See A.O Okuniga, "The Land Use Act 1978 and

reasons: Unlike a lessee under English law, a holder of a right of occupancy has no exclusive possession for, by virtue of section 14 of the Act, "the occupier shall have exclusive rights to the land the subject of the statutory right of occupancy against all persons other than the Governor."[125] Whereas, a lease cannot be revoked either by the lessor[126] or by the state, a right of occupancy introduced under the Act is revocable for overriding public interest by the governor under section 28 thereof.[127] A right of occupancy, unlike the English type lease, is inalienable[128] without the consent of the Governor[129] or the Local Government[130]

Private Ownership of land in Nigeria" being text of a paper delivered at the Law Teachers Conference at the University of Ife, 1979.

[125] A licensee is not given and is not expected to have or exercise exclusive possession over land subject matter of the license: See *Mobil Oil Nigeria Ltd v. Johnson* (1961) 1 All NLR 93.

[126] Whilst it may be tempting to equate revocation to a right of re-entry for forfeiture under English law, reasons have been adduced for non-equation of the two concepts. According to Umezulike: "In the first place whilst revocability like inalienability is an inexorable component of a right of occupancy under the Act, the liability of forfeiture is however not inherent in a lease. It arises only from express stipulation in the instrument creating the lease and cannot be exerted in the absence of a forfeiture clause except where the tenant denies the lessor's title, or is in breach of an obligation which is expressly stated to be a condition of the lease." It is also said that while revocation is peremptory and automatic upon service of the notice of revocation, forfeiture of a lease is not automatic or self operating; it can only be ordered by the court, and the court may even refuse to grant it if there are grounds to grant the tenant relief against forfeiture: See I.A Umezulike, note 110 at 86.

[127] In *Premchand Nathu and Co. Ltd v. Land officer*(1963) A.C 177 at 189, the Privy Council held that: "The right of revocation conferred upon the Governor is a right which is quite unknown in the law of England and bears little resemblance to a lessor's right of re-entry or forfeiture."

[128] For the right of the lessee to alienate his interest to be streamlined or prohibited, the lease agreement must so stipulate. Thus, unlike the English lease, the requirement of consent is not an element superimposed on the right of occupancy but is an intrinsic component of it.

[129] Land Use Act 1978 Cap L5 Laws of the Federation of Nigeria, 2004, s. 22 (1).

[130] ibid, s. 21.

otherwise, such alienation is void[131] and in certain circumstances, illegal with penalty imposed in the form of fine or imprisonment.[132]

Summarising the incidents of a right of occupancy which makes it different from the proprietary land rights under English law, Umezulike observes that:

> "(a) The right cannot be alienated without the consent of the Governor first had and obtained.
>
> (b) The Governor can enter upon the land for inspection without the consent of the holder of statutory right of occupancy free from any civil or criminal sanctions.
>
> (c) The holder's right is subject to the Governor's wide and uncertain powers of revocation which are free from judicial control [once due process is followed].
>
> (d) Upon revocation by the state, compensation is not payable to the holder for the land *per se* but for the un-exhausted improvements on the land.
>
> (e) Devolution upon heirs of a holder under a will or intestate is no longer automatic. The consent of the Governor is necessary for its legal validity."[133]

While the Act preserves pre-existing laws on land rights and land transactions including the statutes of limitations and land registration laws, application of these laws is subject to its provisions.[134] Any acquisition of title or transactions on land not in accordance with its

---

[131] ibid, s. 26.

[132] ibid, s.36(6). This is a situation where there is a total bar on alienation with regard to agricultural land in non-urban areas and in respect of which there is a total bar on alienation and therefore, the land cannot be sub-divided or laid out in plots: See s.36(5) of the Act.

[133] I.A Umezulike, n.116 at 82.

[134] Land Use Act 1978 Cap L5 Laws of the Federation of Nigeria, 2010, s.48.

provisions is null and void.[135] The root of title by transferees of rights of occupancy relates to the initial grant actual or deemed by the Governor, and that is the rationale behind the requirement of requisite consent by the transferor.

How does a squatter's possession qualify as adverse possession under the dispensation of the LUA, for the limitation period to run in his favour? In the first place, no right or interest in land exists or cognisable under the Act unless it is the subject of a grant by either the Governor or the Local Government, or traceable to that grant; it cannot exist outside a grant. Thus while the basis of adverse possession at common law is the possession of the squatter as opposed to the title of the dispossessed owner, the Act recognises no such exercise of possession that is not tied to a grant by the Governor or the Local Government.

Secondly, the question whether a squatter is in exclusive possession so as to satisfy the requirement of law for him to dispossess the actual owner, is a question of law dictated by sections 11 and 14 of the Act. As an occupier, the squatter ''shall have exclusive rights to the land subject of the statutory right of occupancy against all persons *other than the Governor.*''[136] In this regard, the Governor on his behalf, or through a public officer duly authorised by him, ''shall have the power to enter upon and inspect the land comprised in any statutory right of occupancy or any improvements effected thereon...and the occupier [the squatter] shall permit and give free access...''[137] Thus, the outward exercise of possession by the squatter is understood or taken as exclusive against all but the Governor who retains the residual legal right to enter into possession at any reasonable hour in the day time.

Thirdly, section 37 of the Act frowns against illegitimate claims to land and prescribes penalty there for. The section provides:

---

135 ibid, s.26.

136 ibid, s.14.

137 ibid, s. 11.

> If any person other than one in whom any land was lawfully vested immediately before the commencement of this Act enters any land in purported exercise of any right in relation to possession of the land or makes any false claim in respect of the land to the Governor or any Local Government for any purpose under this section he shall be guilty of an offence and liable on conviction to imprisonment for one year or to a fine of N5,000.

The effect of the foregoing provision is to make any claim by a squatter after the coming into effect of the Act on March 29 1978 not merely wrongful or unlawful, but illegal.[138] The essence is to discourage any person in whom the land was not lawfully vested by a grant; actual or deemed, from entering any land in purported exercise of any right of possession, and the squatter or trespasser is such a person. If a statute has declared initial entry by an adverse possessor illegal, it is difficult to see the basis for the recognition of such adverse possession in law for, the rule is, *ex turpi causa non oritur actio.*[139]

Section 48 of the Act which preserves pre-existing laws provides that "all existing laws relating to the registration of title to, or interest in, land or the transfer of title to or any interest in land shall have effect subject to such modifications... as will bring those laws into conformity with this Act or its general intendment." The literal interpretation of this provision is that the Act preserves all pre-existing laws on *land registration* or *transfer of title to, or interest in land.* If that is the case, it could be argued that the doctrine of adverse possession is not preserved by the Act since it is not a *transfer of title to, or interest in land.*[140] Technically, at common law,

---

[138] This is so because it runs counter to the provisions of statute and carries penalty.

[139] "From the dishonourable cause, an action does not arise". It is a legal doctrine which states that a claimant will be unable to pursue legal remedy if it arises in connection with his own illegal act.

[140] Perhaps this is a proper situation where the courts are obligated to discard the strict literal constructionist interpretation and apply a purposive interpretation in a situation such as this, where this approach will lead to absurdity. Such interpretation, if adopted by the court, could interpret the provision of section 48

an adverse possessor gets title at the expiration of the limitation period not by virtue of any transfer of title, not even by the operation of the obsolete concept of statutory conveyance upon the extinguishment of the owner's title, but by virtue of his own possession of land; his title is not derivable from the extinguished title of the owner, but consequent upon and rooted in his own possession.[141] This interpretation accords with the various provisions of the Act which actually frustrate the application of the doctrine, as discussed hereafter. The fact that the common law of England had been received into the Nigerian legal system through the local reception statute[142] is of no moment since the received common law is subject to the Nigerian local circumstances and local legislation, and the Nigerian LUA is one of such local statutes.

Under the Limitation Laws applicable in Nigeria, "a right of action to recover land will not be deemed to accrue unless the land is in possession [referred to as adverse possession] of some person in whose favour the period of limitation can run."[143] For the purpose of accrual of right of action to the person entitled to possession, the right of action will be deemed to have accrued on the date of dispossession by the adverse possessor or on the date when the person entitled to possession discontinued with possession accordingly.[144]

However, section 37 of the Act makes it impossible for a holder of a right of occupancy, actual or deemed to be dispossessed by a squatter. That would suggest entry on land by the squatter "in purported exercise of a right in relation to possession of the land", contrary to the provision of that section, and where he seeks consent of the Governor to alienate his right in furtherance of his right of possession, it would amount to making

---

to cover the doctrine of adverse possession: See *Escoigne Properties Ltd v. IRC* (1958) AC 549, per Lord Denning at 565; *Nigerian Army v. Aminu Kano* (2010) 5 NWLR (Pt 1188) 429.

[141] See *Gatward v. Alley* (1940) 40SR NSW) 174 at 196.

[142] See the Law (Miscellaneous Provisions) Act Cap 89 Laws of Nigeria, 1958, s.45(2).

[143] ibid, s. 19(1).

[144] ibid, s. 16.

a false claim in respect of the land for that purpose in violation of the provision. Also, it would appear that entry into possession by a squatter following the discontinuance of possession by a person entitled to possession, is also a violation of the provision of section 37, and an attempt to obtain Governor's consent to validate any form of alienation thereafter amounts to making a false claim.

Assuming *arguendo*,that the limitation period runs in favour of the squatter consequent upon dispossession of, or discontinuance of possession by a person entitled to possession resulting in extinguishment of right of occupancy of the person entitled to possession, the purported title acquired by the adverse possessor is precarious in view of section 27 of the Act which allows the Governor to "accept ...the surrender of any statutory right of occupancy granted under this Act". Thus, where the holder of the statutory right of occupancy against whom time has run under the statute of limitation surrenders the right of occupancy to the Governor who accepts same, the possessory title obtained by the squatter although good against the whole world including the holder of the right of occupancy, is not, against the Governor who can exercise the right of re-entry and eject the adverse possessor.[145] The cause of action will not arise for the purpose of time running under the statute of limitations until the term of the right of occupancy has lapsed.

Also, relevant acts of exclusive possession exercised by any person which is not supported by a right of occupancy or licence is illegal, and penalty imposed for unauthorised use of land. Section 43 of the Act provides:

> "(1) Save as permitted under section 34 of this Act,[146] as from the commencement of this Act, no person shall in an urban area –

[145] This tallies with the position of the reversioner *vis a vis* the adverse possessor in cases of leaseholds under English law: See *Fairweather v. St Marylebone Property Co. Ltd* [1963] A.C 510.

[146] Section 34 deals with deemed grants by the Governor in respect of title existing prior to the enactment of the Land Use Act, 1978.

(a) erect any building, wall, fence or other structure upon; or

(b) enclose, obstruct, cultivate or do any act on or in relation to, any land which is not the subject of a right of occupancy or licence lawfully held by him or in respect of which he has not received the permission of the Governor to enter and to erect improvement prior to the grant to him of a right of occupancy.

(2) Any person who contravenes any of the provisions of subsection (1) of this section shall on being required by the Governor so to do and within the period of time fixed by the Governor, remove any building, wall, fence, obstruction, structure or thing which he may have caused to be placed on the land and he shall put the land in the same condition as nearly as may be in which it was before such contravention.

(3) Any person who contravenes any of the provisions of subsection (1) of the section shall be guilty of an offence and liable on conviction to imprisonment for one year or to a fine of =N=5000.

(4) Any person who fails or refuses to comply with a requirement made by the Governor under subsection (2) of this section shall be guilty of an offence and liable on conviction to a fine of =N= 100 for each day during which he makes default in complying with the requirement of the Governor".

The foregoing provisions have made it clear that acts of exclusive possession which is necessary to be exhibited to qualify a squatter for adverse possession in order for time to run in his favour under the limitation law are not only prohibited under the Act, but are also made illegal with penal consequences. The provisions buttress the fact that unless land is the subject matter of a grant of a right of occupancy or a licence, any form of occupation under whatever motive or mistaken belief as to legitimate entitlement, is unlawful.

It is the position of this work therefore that all Nigerian cases on adverse possession decided post March 29 1978 when the Land Use Act was enacted without taking cognisance of the relevant provisions discussed above would have been decided *per incuriam* and may very likely be upturned by an appellate court on appeal. The application of the doctrine of adverse possession is indeed, negated by the provisions of the Land Use Act.

6.3.6 The State Land Laws

Apart from the Land Tenure Law applicable in the Northern States of Nigeria, the Land Use Actretains the application of the State Lands Lawapplicable in each state of the federation "until other provisions are made in that behalf and subject to the provisions of the Act."[147]

The State Lands Law applicable in the various states of the federation[148] does not recognise the interest of the adverse possessor, and excludes the application of the Statute of limitation from its ambit. Section 32 of that Law provides that "no action or other remedy by or on behalf of the State for recovery of possession of State land shall be barred or affected by any statute, ordinance or other law of limitation". In addition, "any person who shall unlawfully occupy State land, in any manner whatsoever, shall be liable to a fine of =N=100." The claim of adverse possession on State land is undoubtedly an offence and cannot extinguish the title of the State at any point in time. The position of this work therefore is that the State Lands Law applicable in the various states

[147] Land Use Act 1978 supra (n 134), s.4.

[148] See for example, State Lands Law of Lagos State, Law No. 8 2015, s. 100.

within the Nigerian federation makes the common law doctrine of adverse possession inapplicable.

6.3.7 Federal Government Ownership of Land in the Federal Capital Territory (FCT)

The Land Use Act does not apply in the Nigeria Federal Capital Territory, Abuja.[149] However, section 13 of the Federal Capital Territory Act 1976 (FCT Act) provides that:

> In addition to any law having effect or made applicable throughout the federation, the laws set out in the Second Schedule to this Act shall as from the 9th May 1984 apply in the Federal Capital Territory

Two categories of laws are applicable in the FCT pursuant to the foregoing provision of the FCT Act. The first is any law having effect or made applicable throughout the federation of Nigeria. This covers the received English law discussed in the last chapter which includes the doctrine of adverse possession; and laws set out in the Second Schedule to the Act. Amongst other local statutes listed under the Second Schedule to the Act , item 53 listed the Limitation Act 1966, while item 85 listed the State Lands Act. Whilst the common law of adverse possession applies alongside the Limitation Act 1966 to enable the application of the doctrine in the FCT, the provisions of the State Lands Act with similar provisions with other states counterpart, render the doctrine inapplicable to State Land. Consequently, since parcels of land in the FCT are being allocated and statutory right of occupancy granted accordingly, State land can only refer to any unallocated land. Entry into such land is not only an offence as earlier discussed, it does not pave way for the application of the common law doctrine of adverse possession applicable in England and Wales.

---

[149] *Ona v. Atenda* (2000) 5 NWLR (Pt 656) 244.

6.4 Adverse Possession and Statutes of Limitation in Nigeria

The statute of limitation applicable in the Federal Capital Territory of Nigeria known as the Limitation Act with corresponding statutes of limitation applicable in the various states of the federation (Statute of Limitations Law) are similar in material particulars to the English Limitation Act, 1980, but far from being identical. Relevant provisions of the Limitations Act of Nigeria are reproduced below for purposes of analysis:

Section 16 provides:

> "(1) Subject to the provisions of subsection (2) and (3) of this section, no action will be brought by a State authority to recover any land after the expiration of twenty (20) years from the date on which the right of action accrued to the State authority, or if it first accrued to some person through whom the State authority claims, to that person.
>
> (2) The following provisions will apply to an action by a person to recover land-
>
> (a) subject to paragraph (b) of this subsection, no such action will be brought after the expiration of twelve (12) years from the date on which the right of action accrued to the person bringing it or, if it first accrued to some person through whom there are claims, to that person;
>
> (b) if the right of action first accrued to a State authority, the action may be brought at any time before the expiration of the period during which the action could have been brought by the State authority or of twelve (12) years from the date on which the right of action accrued

to some person other than the State authority, whichever period first expires.

(3) For the purpose of this Law, a right of action to recover any land which accrued to the Republic...before the commencement of this Law will be deemed to have become exercisable by an appropriate State authority on the date on which it first accrued to the Republic..."

As to when the right of action accrues for the purpose of application of the Limitation Act, section 17 provides:

> "Where the person bringing an action to recover land, or some person through whom he claims, has been in possession thereof and has while entitled to it been dispossessed or has discontinued the possession, the right of action will be deemed to have accrued on the date of the dispossession or discontinuance."[150]

Section 19 of the Act makes adverse possession a pre-requisite for the application of the limitation period. The section provides:

"(1) A right of action to recover land will not be deemed to accrue unless the land is in possession (in this section referred to as adverse possession) of some person in whose favour the period of limitation can run.

(2) Where-

(a) under the provisions of this Act a right of action to recover land is deemed to accrue on a certain date; and

[150] Where a person brings an action to recover land of a deceased person under a will or an intestacy and the deceased person was, on the date of death entitled to the land in possession and was the last person entitled to the land in possession, the right of action shall accrue on the date of the death: See section 18 (1) (2) of the Act.

(b) no person is in adverse possession of the land on that date;

the right of action will not be deemed to accrue unless and until adverse possession is taken of the land.

(3) Where a right of action to recover land has accrued, after and before the right of action is barred, the land ceases to be in adverse possession, the right of possession will no longer be deemed to have accrued and no fresh right of action will be deemed to accrue unless and until the land is again taken into adverse possession."

By virtue of the provision of section 20 of the Act, "no person will be deemed to be in possession of any or adverse land by reason only of having made a formal entry on it;"[151] and "no continual or other claim upon or near any land will preserve any right of action to recover the land."[152]

Section 21 of the Act provides that "on the expiration of the period fixed by this Law for any person to bring an action to recover land, the title of that person to the land will be extinguished."

The law will not apply to actions in respect of any matter which, immediately before the commencement of the Act was regulated by customary law.[153]

6.4.1 Judicial Interpretation of the Nigerian Statutes of Limitations in Relation to Adverse Possession

It has been held that time begins to run under the Statute of limitations when possession is lost save where there is fraudulent concealment;[154] in

---

[151] Limitations Act 1966 Laws of the Federation of Nigeria 2004, s. 20(a)

[152] ibid, s. 20(b).

[153] ibid, s. 68.

[154] *Kasandubu v. Ultimate Petroleum Ltd* (2008) 7 NWLR (Pt. 1086) 274.

other words, the period of limitation begins to run from the date of adverse possession of the land by another person.[155] The effect of the operation of the Statute of limitations is, like the position at common law, not merely to deny the right of action; it completely extinguishes an existing right at the expiration of the limitation period[156] so that the adverse possessor acquires rights to the land which are enforceable against the real owner of the land. In the words of Uwaifo J.S.C in *Majekodunmi v. Abina*[157]:

> Although sections 17 and 21 of the Limitation Law…are about the person bringing an action to recover land, the manner in which they can possibly, in their effect, provide an estate in favour of an adverse possessor is somehow reflected in the observation of Cozens-Hardy M.R in *In re Atkinson and Horsell's Contract* (1912) 2 Ch. 1 at page 9 as follows:
>
> > "We have had a great deal of discussion as to the effect of the Statute of Limitation in a matter of this kind. As I indicated in the course of Mr Macnaghten's reply, my present view is that the phrase 'statutory conveyance' and so on, is a loose metaphorical term, and that the true view is this, that whenever you find a person in possession of property that possession is prima facie evidence of ownership in fee, and that prima facie evidence becomes absolute when once you have extinguished the right of every other person to challenge it. That is the effect of s.34 of the Real Property Limitation Act, and that explains how the person who has been in possession for more than the statutory period does get an absolute legal estate in the fee, and there is nobody who can challenge the presumption which his possession of the property gives".

[155] See pp. 132-133 ante.

[156] *Odekilekun v. Hassan* (1997) 12 NWLR (Pt. 531) 56 at 76-77 paras G-A.

[157] (2002) 3 NWLR (Pt 755) 720 at 746.

It follows therefore that adverse possession may be used as a sword and a person in adverse possession can, upon the extinction of the title of the former owner following the expiration of the limitation period, maintain an action in trespass against the former owner or any person purporting to have acquired interest in the land through him.[158]

However, it is incumbent on the claimant to show not only that he has been in possession for the requisite number of years, but also that the title holder has been dispossessed or has discontinued his possession.[159] Mere non user does not amount to discontinuance of possession;[160] "there must be something in the nature of an ouster of the true owner by the wrongful possessor."[161] Also, there is no abandonment unless there is abandonment of the actual and legal possession of the land.[162] In the words of Uwaifo J.S.C in Majekodunmi v. Abina:[163]

> ...the fact of legal estate in fee being obtained through possession is subject to the adverse possessor proving that the title holder has been dispossessed, or has discontinued possession and that he has extinguished the right of every other person to challenge his having become the absolute owner in fee.

For a claim of adverse possession to succeed, such possession must be adequate in continuity, in publicity and in extent to show that possession was adverse to the competitors;[164] it must be one which derogates from, and inconsistent with the ownership title of a person who

---

[158] *Odubeko v. Fowler* (1993) 7 NWLR (Pt. 308) 637.

[159] *Majekodunmi v. Abina,* supra (n 157) 746-747.

[160] ibid, per Uwaifo JSC, relying on the English case of *Littledale v. Liverpool College* (1900) 1 Ch. 19 at 22.

[161] ibid, per Uwaifo JSC supra, 748 relying on Lord Denning M.R in the English case of *Wallis Ltd v. Shell-Mexand BP* (1974) 3 All ER 575 at 580.

[162] *Majekodunmi v. Abina,* supra (n 157) relying on the English case of *Norton v. London and North Western Railway Co.* (1879-1880) 13 Ch.D 268 at 273.

[163] Supra, (n 157).

[164] *Adejumo v. Olawaiye* (1996) 1 NWLR (Pt 425) 436.

claims to be the true owner of the land.[165] Knowledge of the actual owner of the land is irrelevant for the commencement of the running of the limitation period.[166]

The statute of limitations does not apply to land held under customary land tenure. No matter how long an adverse possessor remained on land under customary tenure, his possession cannot ripen into rights of ownership in the land against the original owner. In the words of Dongban-Mensem, J.C.A in *Ogunlana v. Dada*[167]:

> "Land possession and ownership is a customary practice which is jealously guarded in different forms by different communities in Nigeria. One common denominator in all these practices is the perpetuity of land ownership by its original owners. In the instant case, it would therefore be importing an alien customary law into the Yoruba customary land holding to apply the Statutes of Limitation to divest the Itire people[168] of their customary law title".

Whilst the above pronouncement is a re-statement of the provision of the Limitation statutes on the non applicability of the statutes to customary land tenure,[169] it is necessary to clarify its scope. Contrary to the pronouncement, the provision of the limitation statutes is not limited to 'Yoruba customary law holding' as erroneously suggested, but applies to all customary land tenure systems across Nigeria. The provision of statute is not only unequivocal, judicial authorities emanating from the Supreme Court of Nigeria[170] and other appellate courts[171] suggest that the statutory provision applies to customary land tenure generally.

---

[165] *Adedeji v. Oloso* (2007) 5 NWLR (Pt 1026) 133.

[166] *Ajibona v. Kolawole* (1996) 10 NWLR (Pt. 467) 22; *Akibu v. Azeez* (2003) 5 NWLR (Pt. 814) 643; *Elabanjo v. Dawodu* (2006) 15 NWLR (Pt. 1001) 76.

[167] (2010) 1 NWLR (Pt.1176) 534 at 564 paras C-D.

[168] 'Itire people' are indigenous people located in a geographical enclave in Lagos state, Nigeria.

[169] See the Limitation Act 1966, s. 68.

[170] See *Majekodunmi v. Abina* (supra) n.72.

Islamic law of land tenure is not specifically exempted from the application of the Statute of limitation. However, considering the fact that the reception statutes transplanted the English common law subject to local circumstances, and to the extent that the Islamic principle of *hauzi* provides a parallel method of dealing with prescriptive right consequent upon stale claims in land[172] while customary law is treated as including Islamic law by statutes applicable in Northern Nigeria,[173] it cannot be said that the statutes of limitation apply to holders of title under Islamic law.

6.5 Adverse Possession of Unregistered Land

The position at common law applicable in England and Wales is that a squatter on unregistered land is not regarded as the successor or transferee of the person barred by the statute of limitations.[174] It is said that "the squatter enters and acquires a title by virtue of his possession."[175] The title acquired is a fee simple absolute in possession, and this is so "notwithstanding the possibility of determination by ejection by title paramount."[176]

However, the time-barred owner's title is extinguished as against the squatter but not as against interested third parties such as a lessor when time has run against the lessee.[177] This position would ordinarily apply in Nigeria under the received English law and it is buttressed by

[171] See *Holloway v. Jimoh* (2020) 2 NWLR (Pt 1707) 27; *Adetula v. Akinyosoye* (2017) 16 NWLR (Pt. 1592). 492.

[172] See pp. 110-111 *infra*.

[173] See e.g. District Court Law of Niger State of Nigeria Cap 37 vol.1 1992, s.2; High Court Law of Katsina State of Nigeria Cap 59 1991, s.2.

[174]M.S. Dockray: 'Adverse Possession and the Limitation of Actions to Recover land.' Thesis submitted for the degree of Ph.D in Laws of the University of London, 1984 at 414. Available online at https://kclpure.kcl.ac.uk/portal/ visited on 11/8/2020

[175] ibid.

[176] *ibid.*

[177] *Fairweather v, St Marylebone Property Co. Ltd* [1963] A.C 510.

the Statute of Limitations applicable in the federating states and the Federal Capital Territory.[178]

In the case of customary law and by extension Islamic Law,[179] the running out of the limitation period by an adverse possessor does not extinguish customary or Islamic title on land. However, it is said that "where the claimant relies solely on documents couched in English form and it is not suggested that any reliance is placed on customary law, such claimant has excluded the application of customary law and cannot be heard to say that there cannot be adverse possession of the land."[180] This position is explicated in the words of Graham Paul J. in the Nigerian case of *Green v. Owo*[181] as follows:

> Now what is the plaintiff's position in this case? He has in his possession documents in English Conveyancers' jargon, and Plans attached to them. He has nothing but these documents. There is no evidence except the documents as to the title of the grantees to grant them. There is no evidence of possession under them. These documents profess to give to the plaintiff a right to the land in dispute which the defendant and his predecessors have occupied without interference for over twenty years and which so far as the evidence before me goes-none of the plaintiff's predecessors has ever occupied...The Statute of Limitations in such circumstances in England would certainly bar the plaintiff's present claim. Where is the existing native custom to the contrary? There is, so far as I know, no native custom as regards the effect of documentary titles in English Conveyancer form . How would there be?

In such cases the statute of limitations extinguishes the title of the claimant at the expiration of the limitation period under the general law.

---

[178] See e.g. Limitation Act 1966, s. 30.

[179] See s.2 of both the various District Court Laws and the various High Court Laws of Northern Nigeria which define customary law to include Islamic law.

[180] J. A Omotola: 'The Adverse Possessor of Registered Land'. Nig Law Journal vol. 7, 38 at 39.

[181] (1936) 13 N.L.R 43 at 45.

This position of the law has been replicated by the courts in subsequent cases.[182]

[182] See Coker Ag. C.J in *Agboola v. Abimbola* (Unreported) SC.336/67 OF 4/7/69; *Oyedele v. Ogun* (Unreported) LD/40A/69 of 14/8/71.

CHAPTER 7
ADVERSE POSSESSION AND LAND REGISTRATION

7.1 Introduction

The position at common law applicable in England and Wales is that a squatter on unregistered land is not regarded as the successor or transferee of the person barred by the statute of limitation.[1] It is said that "the squatter enters and acquires a title by virtue of his possession."[2] The title acquired is a fee simple absolute in possession, and this is so "notwithstanding the possibility of determination by ejection by the title paramount."[3] However, the time-barred owner's title is extinguished as against the squatter but not as against interested third parties such as a lessor when time has run against the lessee.[4] This position would ordinarily apply in Nigeria under the received English law and it is buttressed by the Statutes of Limitation applicable in the federating states and the Federal Capital Territory.[5]

Some of the arguments often canvassed against the efficacy of adverse possession revolve around the emergence of title registration in contemporary times,[6] with reliance on the register as the mirror of title. This is in accordance with the theory of indefeasibility of registered title.[7] The transformation of adverse possession from being an overriding interest to the status of a registrable title, it is argued, has rendered the

---

[1] M.S. Dockray: 'Adverse Possession and the Limitation of Actions to Recover land.' Thesis submitted for the degree of Ph.D in Laws of the University of London, 1984 at 414. Available online at https://kclpure.kcl.ac.uk/portal/ visited on 11/8/2020

[2] ibid.

[3] ibid.

[4] *Fairweather v, St Marylebone Property Co. Ltd* [1963] A.C 510.

[5] See e.g. Limitation Act 1966, s. 30.

[6] JE Stake, 'The Uneasy Case for Adverse Possession.' 89 Geo. L.J 2419.

[7] See Chapter 3 *ante* for discussion on this.

application of the doctrine unnecessary[8] and making it more relevant, if at all, to the regime of unregistered titles.

This chapter examines the doctrine of adverse possession under the land registration regime applicable under the English and Nigerian law.

7.2 Effect of Adverse Possession on Registered Land in England and Wales

7.2.1 The System of Land Registration in England and Wales

In England and Wales, there is a single and uniform land registration system known as title registration. Within this system, the Land Registry keeps a register of title and records thereon the particulars of the land, the details of the land owner, and the title transferred. The effect of adverse possession on the registered title of the proprietor under the repealed Land Registration Act 1925 differs from the position under the extant law put in place in 2002.

7.2.2 The Regime of Title Registration Under the English Land Registration Act 1925

The old English Land Registration Act of 1925 made first registration of a freehold or leasehold title subject to overriding interests, and one of such overriding interests was right acquired or in the course of being acquired under the Limitation Acts.[9]

Where the squatter was in adverse possession of unregistered land which title was subsequently registered, the registered title was made subject to the squatter's possessory title. If the registered proprietor subsequently made a disposition of the land in respect of which a squatter

[8] JE Stake, supra (n 6).

[9] See the Land Registration Act 1925, s. 70(1) (f).

was an adverse possessor, the disposition was made subject to the squatter's right,[10] and where the limitation period is still running, it continues to run against the disponee.[11]

As to the effect of the squatter's rights at the expiration of the limitation period, section 75 of the Registration Act 1925 provided that the title of the proprietor 'shall not be extinguished,' but the proprietor was said to hold such title in trust for the squatter in favour of whom time had run under the limitation statute, 'but without prejudice to the estates and interests of any other person interested in the land whose estate or interests in the land is not extinguished by those Acts.'[12]

Any person claiming to have acquired title under the Limitation Act to a registered estate in the land may apply to be registered as proprietor,[13] and where the registrar is satisfied as to the applicant's title, he shall enter the applicant as proprietor either with absolute, good leasehold, qualified or possessory title, as the case may require. This is without prejudice to any estate or interest protected by any entry on the register which may not have been extinguished under the Limitation Act, and such registration shall, subject as aforesaid, have the same effect as the registration of a first proprietor.[14]

Notwithstanding that the proprietor's title was not extinguished in favour of the squatter upon the expiration of the limitation period but was said to be held on trust for the squatter, initial judicial authorities suggested no difference in substance between adverse possession of

---

[10] ibid, ss. 5(b) and 9(c).

[11] *Charwood v Lyall* (No.2) [1930] 2 Ch 156.

[12] ibid, s.75(1). It was observed that were it not for this provision, the title of the registered proprietor would have been extinguished: See *Belize Estate and Produce Co. Ltd v Quilter* [1897] AC 367; *Brogden v Brogden* (1920) 53 DLR 362.

[13] ibid s. 75(2).

[14] ibid s. 75(3). The applicant and any other person may apply to the court for the determination of any question arising under the relevant section of the law.

registered and unregistered land.[15] The trust mechanism employed by the provision of section 75(1) was said to be ''wholly inconsistent with the conceptions of the Limitation Acts as previously understood''[16] but had the effect of a ''parliamentary conveyance'' (through the medium of trustee and cestui que trust)'.[17] The trust mechanism was also said to be inconsistent with the provision of section 75(2) which allows the squatter to register 'his independent possessory title acquired by adverse possession.'[18] However, later judicial authorities support the 'parliamentary conveyance' principle.[19] It was held, for example, that a squatter in adverse possession of land under an unregistered lease beyond the limitation period was entitled to be registered as proprietor of the registered lease,[20] and that the registered proprietor could not effect a surrender of the lease.[21]

7.2.3 The English Land Registration Act 2002

The Land Registration Act (LRA) 2002, the extant Law which came into effect on 13 October 2003, repealed the statutory trust imposed under the old Law and provides in Schedule 12, paragraph 18(1) that where a registered estate in land was held in trust for a person by virtue of section 75(1) of the 1925 Act immediately after 13 October 2003, that person 'is entitled to be registered as proprietor of the estate' not with a new title, but as the new registered owner of the existing registered estate. He has a defence to any action for the possession of the land, and the court shall

---

[15] per Lord Denning in *Fairweather v St Marylebone Property Co. Ltd* supra (n 4) at 514. See also, *Jessamine Investment Co. v Schwartz* [1978] QB 264 at 275A; *Mount Carmel Investments Ltd v. Peter Thurlow Ltd* [1988] 1 WLR 1078.

[16] per Lord Radcliffe in *Fairweather v. Marylebone* supra (n 15) at 542.

[17] ibid.

[18] ibid.

[19] See *Spectrum Investment Co. v. Holmes* [1981] 1 WLR 221; *Central London Commercial Estates Ltd. v. Kato Kagaku Ltd* [1998] 4 All ER 948.

[20] See *Spectrum Investment Co. v. Holmes* supra, (n 19).

[21] Surrender of the lease was initially made possible by the court in *Fairweather v. Marylebone* supra (n 15).

order the registrar to register him as the proprietor of the estate where the court determines that such a person is entitled to such a defence.

The LRA 2002 has made inapplicable to registered land, the provision of section 15 of the Limitation Act 1980 which automatically extinguishes the title of the original title holder after the limitation period,[22] but instead, entitles a squatter in adverse possession for a minimum of ten years to apply to be registered as the proprietor of the land.[23]

The squatter may apply for first registration of title to the land.[24] Upon registration of a freehold estate, the estate is vested in the proprietor subject to interests the subject of an entry in the register in relation to the estate;[25] unregistered interests falling within any of the paragraphs of Schedule 1,[26] in particular, any interest belonging to a squatter in adverse possession for the limitation period;[27] and interests acquired under the Limitation Act 1980 of which the proprietor has notice.[28]

Where a squatter has been in adverse possession of land with a registered title for more than ten years, he may apply to be registered as proprietor of that land.[29] The registrar shall, upon receipt of the

---

[22] See s. 96 of the Land Registration Act 2002.

[23] ibid Sch 6 para 1.

[24] ibid s. 3(2).

[25] ibid s. 11(4)(a).

[26] ibid s. 11(4)(b).

[27] See Sch 1, para 2.

[28] LRA 2002, s. 11(4)(c). However, where the squatter is not in actual occupation at that date, his rights bind the registered proprietor only if the latter has notice of those rights.

[29] ibid Sch 6, para. 1. Application can also be made under sub-paragraph 2 if the squatter "(a) has in the period of six months ending on the date of the application ceased to be in adverse possession of the estate because of eviction by the registered proprietor, or a person claiming under the registered proprietor, (b) on the day before his eviction he was entitled to make an application under sub-paragraph (1), and the eviction was not pursuant to a judgment for possession." Sub-paragraph 3 prohibits a person from making an application "if-(a) he is a defendant in proceedings which involve asserting a right to possession of the

application, serve a notice of it on the registered proprietor and other interested persons.[30] The notice shall warn that 'failure to serve a counter notice in time will lead to the squatter being registered.'[31] Where the person served fails to object by filing a counter notice within sixty five (65) business days, the squatter will be registered as proprietor.[32] The effect of registration consequent upon failure to file a counter notice is that the squatter becomes the successor in title of the previous registered proprietor by virtue of a statutory assignment, and if the title is leasehold, the squatter becomes the lessee under the lease from the date of registration.[33] However, the squatter takes the estate subject to interests affecting it other than any registered charge.[34]

Where a counter-notice is served by any of the persons served with the notice of application, the application will be dismissed unless the squatter can satisfy one of three conditions namely: that it would be unconscionable because of an equity by estoppel for the registered proprietor to seek to dispossess the applicant, and the circumstances are such that the applicant ought to be registered as the proprietor;[35] or that the applicant is for some other reason entitled to be registered as the proprietor of the estate;[36] or that the land to which the application relates is adjacent to the land belonging to the applicant, and the exact line of the boundary between the two has not been determined under rules provided in section 60[37] for at least ten years of the period of adverse possession ending on the date of the application; or that the applicant (or any

---

land, or (b) judgment for possession of the land has been given against him in the last two years." Sub-paragraph 4 provides that, "for the purposes of sub-paragraph 1, the estate need not have been registered throughout the period of adverse possession."

30 Sch. 6 para 2 (1).

31 Sch.6 para 2(2).

32 Land Registration Rules 2003.

33 Sch. 6 para 9.

34 Sch. 6 para 9(2) and (3).

35 Sch 6 para 5(2).

36 Sch 6 para5(3).

37 Sch 6 para5(4).

predecessor in title) reasonably believed that the land to which the application relates belonged to him, and the estate to which the application relates was registered more than one year prior to the date of the application.[38]

The squatter succeeds to the registered title sequel to non-service of the counter-notice, but may be subject to any registered charge affecting the estate immediately before his registration, with provision for the apportionment of such charges.[39] However, where the squatter's application is rejected and he subsequently remains in adverse possession for two years from the date of that rejection, he acquires the right to be registered as proprietor of the land.[40] A successful application made under paragraph 6 of Schedule 6 aforesaid entitles the squatter to be entered on the register as the new proprietor of the estate.

The certainty provided by the register of titles and the indefeasibility of title registration as opposed to reliance on possessory title were the underlying rationale of the LRA 2002. Making the register a mirror of title entails encouraging the adverse possessor to apply for registration as a proprietor in deserving cases without prejudicing the right of an existing proprietor to the protection afforded by law. Thus, landowners are now better placed to resist adverse possession claims while landowner's title assures him of notice of any adverse possession on the land, and enables him to resist by way of counter-notice when notice of adverse possession is served on him upon the squatter's application to be registered.

Clear cases of proprietor's discontinuance of possession or prevailing circumstances showing that it would be inequitable or unconscionable to refuse the adverse possessor access to registration, especially when it is apparent that the registered proprietor is no longer protective of his title, are acknowledged and considered by the registrar in taking a decision to register the adverse possessor. This reasoning

[38] Sch 6 para 5(4).

[39] Sch 6 para 9

[40] Sch 6 paras 6 and 7.

accords with one of the underlying objectives of the 2002 Act, namely that:

> The title that registration confers should be capable of being overridden by adverse possession only where it is essential to ensure the marketability of land or to prevent unfairness.[41]

It is therefore apt to say that 'the land registry's adverse possession regime is based on the principles of neutrality and fairness to both parties'.[42]

However, considering the limited grounds under which the adverse possessor may be registered as proprietor in the event of an objection, it is said that the adverse possessor is more likely to avoid the risk of alerting the registered proprietor of his existence and thereby prompt opposition to the application for registration.[43] In the words of Pawlowski and Brown:

> The incentive to stay quiet is made even more attractive given the principle of relativity of title in English property law and the possibility of transmission of possessory rights between possessors creating in effect a dark market.[44]

The Law Reform Consultation Paper[45] reveals that the past 8 years indicated a steady drop in the number of such application brought under the 2002 Act.

---

41 See Law Commission/H.M. Land Registry, Land Registration for the Twenty-First Century : Consultative Document, (1998) No. 254, at para. 1043.

42 ibid.

43 M Pawlowski and J Brown, 'Adverse Possession and the Transmissibility of Possessory Rights – The Dark Side of Land Registration?'[2017] (2) Conv. 116 at 117.

44 ibid.

45 See Law Commission Consultation Paper, *Updating the Land Registration Act 2002*, No. 227, (2016). at para 17.66.

In a recent study by Pawlowski and Brown[46] using questionnaire sent to 200 conveyancing solicitors throughout England and Wales, it was revealed that:

> …as many as 67 percent of solicitors who responded indicated that they had advised clients who had been in adverse possession of land not to apply for registration because of the risk of alerting the registered proprietor to the adverse possession and prompting opposition to the application.

The result has been a proliferation of a 'dark market' in possessory estates "given that such estates may pass through a succession of possessors and endure indefinitely off the register"[47] in the absence of any compulsion on the part of the possessor to apply for registration as proprietor in place of the registered proprietor of the land. Consequently, an amendment to the 2002 Act has been suggested which would require the squatter to bring his application to be registered as a proprietor during a stated period following his adverse possession of the land for ten years.[48] It is said that failure in this regard "would have the effect of automatically extinguishing the squatter's possessory title in respect of the land, so that it would cease to exist for all purposes".[49]

7.3 Effect of Adverse Possession on Registered Land in Nigeria

Apart from the land instrument registration system which applies in the various states of the federation and the Federal Capital Territory[50] under

[46] Supra (n 43) at 127-128.

[47] M Pawlowski and J Brown, supra (n 43) at 131.

[48] ibid.

[49] ibid at 130.

[50] See Land Registration Law Cap 97 Laws of Northern Nigeria 1958, applicable in the Federal Capital Territory of Nigeria.

different nomenclature,[51] the Registration of Title system existed in Lagos State,[52]and still exist in the Federal Capital Territory[53] mainly. The extant Land Registration Law of Lagos State 2015 is an amalgam of the two systems of land registration, theState having repealed the earlier Laws on land registration.

7.3.1 Land Instruments Registration

The history of the Land Instruments Registration Law in Nigeria dates back to 1883 when compulsory registration of title deeds was introduced first in the colony of Lagos[54] by the Registration Ordinance of 1883.[55] Subsequently, the Land Registry Proclamation No. 16 of 1900 introduced the Registration of instruments in the protectorate of Southern Nigeria.[56] An amalgamation of the two areas in 1906 resulted in the introduction of a unified system of registration under the Land Registration Ordinance of

[51] The precursor of the State Laws was the Land Registration Act No. 36 of 1924 which was enacted for the whole country and later adopted and re-enacted in the various states under different nomenclature. See Cap 56(W/N) 1959 adopted as Cap 70 Laws of Oyo State of Nigeria 2000, Cap 64 Laws of Osun State of Nigeria 2002, Cap 74 Laws of Ondo State of Nigeria 2006, Cap L54 Laws of Ogun State of Nigeria 2006; Cap 72 (E/N) 1963 adopted for example, as Cap 75 Laws of Anambra State of Nigeria 1991; Cap 58 (N/N) 1963 adopted for example as Cap 83 Laws of Kwara State of Nigeria 2007, Cap 75 Laws of Taraba State of Nigeria 1997, Cap 82 Laws of Jigawa State of Nigeria 1998, Cap 77 Laws of Bornu State of Nigeria 1994, Cap 85 Laws of Kaduna State of Nigeria 1991, Cap 74 Laws of Katsina State of Nigeria 1991, Laws of Niger State of Nigeria 1992, Cap 77 Laws of Kano State of Nigeria 1991; and Cap L58 Laws of Lagos State of Nigeria

[52] See the Repealed Registration of Title Law Cap R4 Laws of Lagos State 2003

[53] Cap 546 Laws of the Federation of Nigeria (Abuja) 1990.

[54] At that time, the Colony of Lagos was administered as part of the Gold Coast, and the main objective of the Ordinance was to regulate registration of title instruments in the Gold Coast from where the Colony of Lagos was being administered: See O.W. Igwe, *Land Instruments and Registration and Practice in Nigeria* (2014) Lap Lambert Academic Publishing, 14

[55] O.W. Igwe, supra (n 54) at 13-14.

[56] ibid, at 14.

1907, which amended the existing laws on registration of instruments.[57] An enactment similar to this was in force in the Protectorate of Northern Nigeria under the Land Instrument Proclamation No. 10 of 1901; a law which was repealed by the Land and Native Rights Proclamation of 1910 (Part 2).[58]

The unification of the Northern and Southern Protectorates in 1914 resulted in the re-enactment of the pieces of legislation into a single legislation known as the Land Registration Ordinance No. 12 of 1915 applicable throughout the country.[59] This Law was subsequently amended and became known as the Land Registration Ordinance No. 36 of 1924, which remained the principal legislation regulating land instrument registration in Nigeria.[60] Consequent upon the creation of States in Nigeria in 1967, each of the states had since re-enacted the 1924 Act with similar provisions, but under slightly varying titles.[61] The recognition of the Federal Government land under the provisions of the Land Use Act[62] necessitated the enactment of the Federal Lands Registry (Miscellaneous Provisions) Decree No. 7 1992 (now re-designated as Act) 1992.A registered title deed under the Land Instrument Registration Law is not a guarantee of the validity of the title covered by it, and *ipso facto,* does not cure any defect in it.[63] Its main objective is to evidence transfer of title or dealing in the land shown on the registered Survey Plan and

---

[57] ibid.

[58] ibid.

[59] ibid.

[60] ibid. This legislation is preserved under section 48 of the Land Use Act 1978 Cap L5 Laws of the Federation of Nigeria, 2010.

[61] See n 51.

[62] See s.47 of the Land Use Act 1978.

[63] See for example, s.24 of Cap 75 Laws of Anambra State of Nigeria 1991, and corresponding provision in other states. See also *Onasanya v. Anifowose* 4FSC 94; *Folashade v. Duroshola* (1951) 1 All N.L.R 87.

assure priority of interest as against subsequent but not prior registered instrument[64] or any existing overriding interest.[65]

A registered title deed under the Land Instrument Registration Law is not a guarantee of the validity of the title covered by it, and *ipso facto,* does not cure any defect in it.[66]Its main objective is to evidence transfer of title or dealing in the land shown on the registered Survey Plan and assure priority of interest as against subsequent but not prior registered instrument[67]

Registration of land instrument without possession by the land owner could be defeated by the statute of limitation in favour of an adverse possessor. Consequently, adverse possession of land by a party for the duration of the limitation period without eviction by the owner extinguishes the title of the latter against the adverse possessor notwithstanding registration of title documents by the owner.

7.3.2 Registration of Titles

The system of title registration under the Registration of Titles Act 1935[68] (RTA) was first applicable in the Southern Provinces, and subsequently adopted by the Federal Territory of Lagos in 1935 as the Registration of

---

[64] See s. 23 Cap 75 Laws of Anambra state of Nigeria 1991 and corresponding provision in the Law of other states. See also *Amankara v. Zankley* (1963) 1 All N.L.R 304.

[65] Overriding interests are interests or rights of every person in possession or actual occupation of the land to which he may be entitled in right of such possession or occupation except where the rights are not disclosed upon inquiry.

[66] See for example, s.24 of Cap 75 Laws of Anambra State of Nigeria 1991, and corresponding provision in Law of the other states of the federation. See also*Onasanya v. Anifowose* 4 FSC 94; *Folashade v. Duroshola* (1951) 1 All N.L.R 87

[67] See s. 23 Cap 75 Laws of Anambra State of Nigeria 1991, and corresponding provision in the Law of the other states of the federation. See also *Amankara v. Zankley* (1963) 1 All N.L.R 304.

[68] Registration of Titles Act, Cap 181 1935.

Titles Law. This Law as amended was adopted by Lagos State,[69] but was subsequently repealed and replaced by the Land Registration Law in 2015.[70]Also, the Federal Capital Territory had adopted the Registration of Titles Act 1935 as part of its Laws.[71]

The aim of the 1935 Act was 'to make conveyancing simple, cheap, speedy and reliable by obviating most of the difficulties and hazards to which a purchase of land is exposed…'[72] It is said that 'once the title has been investigated and put on the register, proof of title becomes easier as the register becomes an evidence of title.'[73]

Section 52(h) of the RTA makes all registered land subject to certain overriding interests including *rights acquired or in the process of being acquired by virtue of any enactment relating to the limitation of actions or by prescription*. The effect of this provision is to recognize the potency of interests which do not appear on the register but which are binding on the registered proprietor,such as adverse possession. Consequently, the interest of the registered proprietor may be defeated by such interests thereby contradicting the theory of indefeasibility of registered title.However, the prevalence of overriding interests can only be raised as a defence and not as a cause of action against the land owner.

7.3.3 The Lagos State Land Registration Law 2015

The Lagos State Lands Registration Law No. 1 of 2015 ("LRL") is, indeed, a milestone in the history of land registration in the State.[74] The Law harmonised the provisions of the Land Instruments Registration Law,[75]

---

[69] See Cap R4 Laws of Lagos State 2003.

[70] Land Registration Law No. 8 2015.

[71] See Cap 546 Laws of the Federation of Nigeria (Abuja) 1990.

[72] CO Olawoye, *Title to Land in Nigeria,* 2nd ed. Evans, 132

[73] ibid. See also *Onagoruwa v. Aderemi* (2001) 13 NWLR (Pt 721) 38 at 56, 63.

[74] The Law harmonised the law and practice of registration of document and title registration to reflect the dynamics of e-commerce and modern Conveyancing practice.

[75] Cap 58 Laws of Lagos State, 2003, now repealed: See the LRL No. 8 2015, s.122

the Registration of Titles Law[76]and the Electronic Documents Management System Law[77] towards meeting the reasonable expectations of Conveyancers, holders of interests in land and their successors in title, assignors, lessors, investors and creditors and other vested interests in land. The main objective is an assurance of security of title and interests in land and the enhancement of the register as a mirror of title. It accommodates not only registration of 'paper title' and other registrable instruments, but also possessory interests including adverse possession cognisable in law.

One of the areas of focus of the LRL for registration purposes, is adverse possession. The express inclusion of adverse possession as a registrable title under the LRL is novel.[78] An assumption of its application from the provision of section 6(1)(a) of the repealed Registration of Titles Law[79] failed, as the investigative duty of the Registrar of Titles before first registration[80] was construed by the Supreme Court in *Majekodunmi v. Abina*[81] as limited to instruments in the form of ascertained muniments of title verifiable without going outside "legal evidence or evidence ordinarily required by Conveyancers".[82]Indeed, the existence of adverse possession, the court said,would have to be determined by the regular court sequel to parties' callingevidence, and the Registrar of Titles had no jurisdiction to entertain such disputes and lacked the powers to make a decision in this regard. However, the judgment of a court of competent jurisdiction in favour of an adverse possessor would provide satisfactory evidence of proof of title and could form the basis for the decision of the Registrar of title to register the interest of the adverse possessor.

---

[76] Cap R4 Laws of Lagos State 2003 (repealed).

[77] This Law was made in 2007.

[78] Neither of the repealed registration Laws expressly provided for registration of an adverse possessor.

[79] Cap R4 Laws of Lagos State 2003.

[80] For the duty of the Registrar in this regard, see Cap R4 Laws of Lagos State 2003; s. 9.

[81] (2002) 3 NWLR (Pt. 755) 720.

[82] See Cap R4 Laws of Lagos State 2003; s.9(1) cited per Uwaifo JSC in *Majekodunmi v. Abina* supra(n 81) at 748 paras E-G.

The provisions of the LRL on registration of adverse possession as an interest in land has given legislative approval to the Supreme Court pronouncements in *Majekodunmi v.Abina*[83] with the additional requirement of notice supposedly meant to give efficacy to the registered title of the adverse possessor. But while the LRL contains express provisions on the registrability of adverse possession and guarantees its efficacy as against an accurate and definitive record of 'estate ownership', it poses challenges to the indefeasibility of registered title and raises fundamental issues of fairness and expropriation of property rights without compensation.

7.4 An Overview

No system of registration in Nigeria could overreach adverse possession which is regarded as an overriding interest constituting an impediment to the acquisition of clean title to land, and the statutes of limitation applicable fortify this position. A registered title deed under the Land Instrument Registration Law may be defeated by adverse possession of the land beyond the limitation period. The 'paper owner' dispossessed by an adverse possessor or who discontinued possession allowing time to run in favour of a squatter, would have his title defeated and extinguished under the limitation statute, notwithstanding registration of his title deed.[84] The same is the position of an adverse possessor vis-a-vis a registered proprietor whose title is bound by overriding interests of which adverse possession is one.[85]

Also, the title of the registered owner may be extinguished under the Limitation Law. Section 62 of the Registration of Titles Act (RTA) applicable in the FCT provides:

---

[83] Supra (n 81).

[84] *Majekodunmi v. Abina,* supra (n 81) .

[85] Registration of Titles Act Cap 181 Laws of Nigeria 1958, s.52(h); Land Registration Law of Lagos State 2015, s.66(f). See *Onagoruwa v. Aderemi,* supra (n 73).

> "Where it is shown to the satisfaction of the court that the title of the registered owner of any land or charge has been extinguished under the provisions of the Limitation Law, the court may order the register to be rectified accordingly and the person suffering loss by such rectification shall not receive any compensation."

In the same vein, the provision of section 100 of the Land Registration Law (LRL) of Lagos state which is *in pari materia* with that of the RTA above provides:

> "Where the court is satisfied that the title of the registered holder of any land or any mortgage has been extinguished under the Limitation Law, the Court may order the register to be rectified accordingly, and the person aggrieved by such a rectification shall not receive any compensation."

Thus, apart from the fact that the title of an adverse possessor constitutes an overriding interest to which any registered land is subject, the adverse possessor may register such title after rectification of the register pursuant to an order of court upon satisfactory proof that the title of the registered owner has been extinguished under the Limitation Law. It follows therefore that the adverse possessor of registered land has no obligation to register his title since same constitutes an overriding interest binding on the registered proprietor and any person deriving title from such registered proprietor; although he is also at liberty to register same as he may wish.

However, while the title of the adverse possessor may be registered after rectification of the register pursuant to a court order, this procedure for registration is affected by delays experienced in courts as the title of the adverse possessor remains inchoate until the court exercises its discretion in his favour. That the Registrar of titles is incapacitated to facilitate the registration of an adverse possessor without a court order is very clear from the observation of the Supreme Court of Nigeria in *Majekodunmi v. Abina* ,[86] regarding the RTA that:

> "The duty of the Registrar is to investigate the title of an applicant; he is required to act strictly on legal evidence or evidence ordinarily required by conveyancers. His power is confined to acceptance or refusal of the application for registration and he cannot be expected to decide the question as to ownership of land arising from long possession which is a decision on the Limitation Law."[87]

Thus, in the absence of evidence of adverse possession such as the judgment and order of a court of competent jurisdiction, it would appear that there is no avenue for the adverse possessor to seek to register his title under the RTA applicable in the FCT, or the LRL of Lagos State.

Furthermore, the provision of section 112(2) of the LRL requires the adverse possessor prior to application to court for an order, to advertise or give notice in a manner as the Registrar may require. Such a notice may prompt the registered proprietor to oppose the application of the adverse possessor, but failure to do so may be fatal as this might result in the adverse possessor having his way. It is expected however, that the adverse possessor would join the registered proprietor as a party whose interest would be affected by the order of court as required by the Rules of court.[88]

Upon rectification of the register and registration of the adverse possessor, no compensation is payable to the 'aggrieved person' or 'the person suffering loss' as a result of such rectification. The rationale for non-payment of compensation after rectification is that since the

---

[86] supra (n 81).

[87] ibid.

[88] It is trite that an order of court is binding only on parties before it. For provisions relating to joinder of parties under the High Court Civil Procedure Rules, see for example, *Order 15 Rule 17 of the High Court of Lagos State (Civil Procedure) Rules 2019,* and corresponding provisions in the High Court Rules of other states and the Federal Capital Territory, Abuja.

registered owner has always held the land subject to the title of the adverse possessor which constitutes an overriding interest, the registered owner cannot be said to have suffered any loss.[89]Also, section 44 (1) of the Constitution of the Federal Republic of Nigeria 1999 (as amended) which prohibits acquisition of interest in an immovable property without prompt payment of compensation does not apply in cases where such interest is extinguished under the provisions of any general law relating to limitation of actions.[90]

[89] That was the construction ascribed to s.83(1) of the English Land Registration Act 1925 per Clauston J. in *Re Chowood Registered Land* [1933] Ch 574 at 580, 582.
[90] See s. 44(2) (i) of the Constitution.

CHAPTER 8
ADVERSE POSSESSION WITHIN THE CONTEXT OF THE HUMAN RIGHTS REGIME

8.1 Introduction

The doctrine of adverse possession is associated with property right.[1] However, the struggle towards the recognition of property right as human right over time has been a tortuous one.[2] Its evolution has been coloured by a combination of political, socio-cultural and economic considerations, and the reasoning of scholars sometimes polarised by the East-West dichotomy.[3] Before the advent of the United Nations Universal Declaration on the subject in 1948,[4] and later, the Regional Conventions subsequently domesticated by member states,[5] property right was hardly regarded universally as human right.[6]

One of the scepticism about qualification of property right as human right is the fact that right to property "does not derive from the human condition, but rather from the mere material fact that someone has

---

[1] See generally, J. Gilbert, "Land Rights as Human Rights: The Case for a Specific Right to Land." International Journal of Human Rights (2013) vol. 10 No. 18 at 114; J.E. Alvarez, "The Human Rights of Property." University of Miami Law Review (2018) 580.

[2] For a full account, see J. Gilbert, J.E. Alvarez, supra (n 1).

[3] ibid.

[4] Universal Declaration of Human Rights (UDHR), Art. 17, December 10, 1948. Art. 17 of the UDHR provides that: "1. Everyone has the right to own property alone as well as in association with others. 2. No one shall be arbitrarily deprived of his property." G.A. Res. 217 (III) A.

[5] Amongst these are the European Convention on Human Rights domesticated in the United Kingdom as Human Rights Act 1998 (Art. 1 Protocol No.1); and the African Charter on Human and Peoples' Rights domesticated in Nigeria as Cap A9 Laws of the Federation of Nigeria 2010 (Art 14).

[6] J. Gilbert, supra (n 1).

managed to secure first possession."[7] This view is buttressed by the fact that property right "diminishes the right of other persons by excluding them from possession since the right to property largelyconsists…in the right to exclude others from enjoying one's property."[8] Even philosophers such as Locke[9] and Rousseau[10] who were proponents of private property, conceded the significance of private property subject to limitations.[11] Others have treated property as a form of theft;[12] "a manifestation of pernicious possessive individualism,"[13] and sometimes associating it with violence required for dispossession. The idea of territorial sovereignty strengthened the view that the decision of governments on how to treat the property of citizens should be the exclusive preserve of States in line with the provisions of the United Nations Charter on prohibition of interference with States' domestic jurisdictions, in recognition of the right to self determination.[14]

While land rights may be seen as a subject of complex focus, "the claim that land rights are human rights has been a common denominator

---

[7] M. Monteagudo, "The Right to Property in Human Right and Investment Laws: A Latin American Perspective of an Unavoidable Connection." (SECO/WTI Academic Co-operation Project Working Paper Series No. 2013/06/2013.

[8] J.E. Alvarez, supra (n 1) at 592.

[9] J.Locke, *Two Treatises of Government,* 308 (Peter Laslettv ed., (Cambridge University Press 1960) (1690).

[10] J. Rosseau, *The Social Contract and Discourses* 221 (G.D.H Cole ed. , J.M Dent& Sons (1913) (1755).

[11] For example, Locke argued that persons should not possess property than they could use, while Rosseau believed that the right to one's personal property does not include the right to make profit therefrom: See Howard-Hassmann, "Reconsidering the Right to own Property." 12 Journal of Human Rights 180, 182 (2013)

[12] "Property is theft" says Pierre-Joseph Prodhon in *What is Property? An inquiry into the Principle of Right and Government.* First written in French in 1840, later translated into English by Benjamin R. Tucker. Humboldt Publishing Co. c.1890. See University of Virginia Library Electronic Text Centre, http://etext.lib.virginia.edu/; Accessed on 01/05/2020.

[13] Howard-Hassmann, supra (n 11) at 182, cited inJ.E. Alvarez, supra (n 1) at 594.

[14] J.E. Alvarez, supra (n 1) at 596.

to movements in many parts of the world,"[15] and today, a number of widely ratified international Treaties and prominent regional human rights regimes have entrenched property right as basic human right.[16] Consequently, Constitutions of most countries of the world have entrenched guarantee of this right in response to the domesticated international obligations, and in recent times, Constitutions of some countries, Nigeria inclusive,[17] have equally addressed in addition, the right to acquire possessions in land.

8.2 Adverse Possession and Human Rights Instruments

The application of the doctrine of adverse possession within the context of human right is best appreciated through international and regional instruments as they affect domestic law of adverse possession. In particular, it would be helpful to see how the European Convention on Human Rights (ECHR) applicable in the United Kingdom and the African Charter on Human and Peoples' rights domesticated in Nigeria have impacted, if at all, on the doctrine of adverse possession. This is important in view of the land mark decisions in England and Nigeria which have impacted on the efficacy of the doctrine under English and Nigerian law. Consequently, the application of these important regional instruments is appraised through the window of domestic law in England and Nigeria. While the *ECHR* is not applicable in Nigeria, it provides the lenses through which the efficacy of the doctrine of adverse possession is gleaned from different perspectives.

---

[15] J. Gilbert, supra (n 1) at 116.

[16] See e.g. Art 1, Protocol No. 1 of the European Convention on Human Rights domesticated in the U.K as Human Rights Act 1998; and Art. 14 of the African Charter on Human and Peoples' Rights domesticated in Nigeria as Cap A9 Laws of the Federation of Nigeria, 2010.

[17] See for example, s. 44 of the Constitution of the Federal Republic of Nigeria, 1999 as amended.

8.3 Appraisal of the Application of the European Convention on Human Rights (ECHR) in the United Kingdom

The right to property is a concept cherished by many common law jurisdictions.[18] In the United Kingdom –a country without a written constitution, the domestic sources of rights are the common law, and the Human Rights Act of 1998 (HRA)[19] which incorporates into UK law, the rights contained in the European Convention on the Protection of Human Rights and Fundamental Freedoms also known as the *European Human Rights Convention* (EHRC),[20] consequent upon her membership of the Council of Europe.[21] The *European Commission on Human Rights* was established in 1954 while the *European Court of Human Rights* was established in 1959.[22]

The HRA (UK) 1998 provides that so far as possible, domestic legislation shall be read and given effect in a way which is compatible with Convention Rights.[23] Where a provision of the domestic legislation is found to be incompatible with a Convention right, the court may make a

[18] This is demonstrated by the Constitution in many African countries.

[19] *Human Rights Act 1998* (UK).

[20] *European Human Rights Convention* (213 U.N.T.S 221, E.T.S 5). It was signed in 1950 and came into effect in 1953.

[21] The Council of Europe was created in 1949 with the initial membership of ten. Today, the membership has gone up to almost fifty (50) member states with Headquarters at Strasbourg, France. Its main purpose is to foster European unity and facilitate economic and social progress. Its main concern is the issue of human rights amongst others. Although it has a close relationship with the European Union (EU), it is not part of the EU. It is not affiliated with the "European Council" which is a special meeting of the EU's Council of Ministers. See generally, *Theory and Practice of the European Convention on Human Rights*, 4th ed. (KJC5132.A4195 V36 2006) and *Practitioner's Guide to the European Convention on Human Rights*, 3rd ed. (KJC5132.R45 2008).

[22] See generally, *Short Guide to the European Convention on Human Rights*, 3rd ed. (KJC5132.G66 2005).

[23] *HRA*, 1998(UK), s.3.

declaration of incompatibility under the HRA;[24] and this may necessitate amending legislation by statutory instrument under the Act.[25]

One of the rights protected under the Convention is the protection of property under the EHRC. Article 1 of Protocol No. 1 provides:

> "Every natural or legal person is entitled to the peaceful enjoyment of his possessions. No one shall be deprived of his possessions except in the public interest and subject to the conditions provided for by law and by the general principles of international law.
>
> The preceding provisions shall not, however, in any way impair the right of a State to enforce such laws as it deems necessary to control the use of property in accordance with the general interest or to secure the payment of taxes or other contributions or penalties."

Another provision meant to protect the right of property is Article 8 which provides:

> "1. Everyone has the right to respect for his private and family life, his home and his correspondence.
>
> 2. There shall be no interference by a public authority with the exercise of this right except such as is in accordance with the law and is necessary in a democratic society in the interests of national security, public safety or the economic well being of the country, for the prevention of disorder or crime, for the protection of health or morals, or for the protection of the rights and freedoms of others."

The two provisions are germane to a determination whether the efficacy of the doctrine of adverse possession in the U.K is affected by the regime of human rights. Whilst Article 1 of Protocol 1 to the EHRC may

---

[24] ibid, s.4.

[25] ibid, s.10.

be invoked generally by a paper owner of unregistered land and a registered proprietor of registered land against the adverse possessor, the adverse possessor who has been putting property to use particularly where the property is his home, may generally be entitled to protection under Article 8.

The connections between Article 8 on the one hand and Article 1 of Protocol No.1 on the other hand, have been highlighted in the *European Court of Human Rights Guide on Article 8 of the European Convention on Human Rights,*[26]under 'Right to respect for private and family life'[27] as follows:

1. There may be an overlap between the concept of home in Article 8 and that of property under Article 1 Protocol No. 1, but the existence of a "home" is not dependent on the existence of a right or interest in respect of real property.[28]Thus an adverse possessor in occupation of residential accommodation is entitled to protection under Article 8 notwithstanding lack of interest in the property itself. This principle supports the occupation theory, the labour theory and the utilitarian theory.[29]

2. An individual may have a property right over a particular building or land for the purpose of Article 1 of Protocol 1 without having sufficient ties with the property for it to constitute his or her "home" within the meaning of Article 8.[30] This principle complements the first one in that the owner of an abandoned property may not have sufficient ties to property for it to constitute a home. Following the personhood theory,[31] this

[26] Available online at www.echr.coe.int/Documents/Guide_Art_8_ENG.pdf updated on 31 August 2019, Accessed on 18 April 2020. However, these Guides are not binding on the court and may be subject to review from time to time.
[27] ibid, paras 60-62.
[28] ibid, para 60. See *Surugiu v. Romania* no. 48995/99 of 20 April 2004.
[29] See Chapter 3 ante for the exposition of these theories.
[30] ibid. See *Khamidon v. Russia* no. 72118/01 of 15 November 2007
[31] For an exposition of the personhood theory, see Chapter 3 ante.

principle justifies the right of the adverse possessor under Article 8.

3. In view of the crucial importance of the rights secured under Article 8 to the individual's identity, self determination, physical and mental integrity, the margin of appreciation afforded to states in housing matters is narrower in relation to the rights guaranteed by Article 8 than to those protected by Article 1 of Protocol 1.[32]

4. A violation of Article 8 may result from a finding of a violation of Article 1 of Protocol 1. Some measures that constitute a violation of Article 8 will not necessarily lead to a finding of a violation of Article 1 of Protocol 1.[33]

5. There is a significant mark of difference between the interests protected by the two Articles and hence, the disparity in the extent of the protection they can afford, particularly when it comes to applying the proportionality requirements to the facts of a particular case.[34]

The operation and interaction of the doctrine of adverse possession with human rights in the U.K is demonstrated by the decision of the Grand Chamber of the European Court of Human Rights in *JA Pye (Oxford) Ltd & Ors v. United Kingdom*.[35] It was a decision which followed an appeal from the judgment of the House of Lords[36] by *Pye* against the U.K Government, and the question for determination was whether the law of adverse possession in relation to registered land infringed Article 1 of Protocol 1 of the European Convention on Human Rights.

---

[32] ibid, para 61: See *Gladysheva v. Russia* n. 7097/10 of 6 December 2011.

[33] ibid, para 62. See *Ivanova and Chakezor v. Bulgaria* n. 467577/15 of 21 April, 2016.

[34] ibid, para 62. See *Ivanova and Chakezor v. Bulgaria* supra(n 33).

[35] (2008) 46 EHRR 1083.

[36] The title of the case up to the House of Lords was *JA Pye (Oxford) Ltd & Ors v. Graham & Ors* [2002] 3 WLR 221; [2002] UKHL 30 (House of Lords).

8.3.1 The *Pye* Case

In 1983, JA Pye (Oxford) Ltd, a professional real estate developers and the registered proprietor of land which it intended to develop, entered into a contract with Graham, allowing him the use of a portion of the land adjacent to Graham's farm for grazing purposes. The only access to the land was through a gate, for which Graham had a key. At the expiration of the agreement which lasted for 11 months, parties were unable to re-negotiate a new agreement, but Graham and his family continued to use the land from September 1984, without permission. In 1985, Graham sought to contact *Pye* about an agreement, but *Pye* refused to respond. In 1997, Graham lodged cautions with the Land Registry claiming to be entitled to the land based on adverse possession. *Pye* sought to challenge those cautions and when Graham died, his wife and estate lodged further cautions against the land. In 1999, *Pye* began proceedings to seek possession of the disputed land.

Facts before the court showed that from the period 1984 to 1997, Graham had tilled the lands, fertilised and limed it, and never vacated the land during that period. The land was used primarily for grazing though in 1994 parts of the land became arable.

The House of Lords, reversing the decision of the Court of Appeal and restoring the decision of Neuberger J., held that Graham had factually possessed the land coupled with an intention to possess it, and had therefore acquired beneficial ownership of it by adverse possession under the Limitation Act 1980, section 15(1), Schedule 1, paragraphs 1, 8(1),[37] and entitled to be registered as the owner under section 75 of the Land Registration Act 1925. However, in the House of Lords, no argument was canvassed based on human rights as the matter arose prior to the

[37] Its decision notwithstanding, the House of Lords passed critical comments. Lord Bingham of Cornhill, quoting from the trial judge Neuberger J., said that the decision was arrived at "with no enthusiasm;" and in the words of Lord Hope of Craighead, it was unfair, not "in the absence of compensation, although that is an important factor, but in the lack of safeguards against oversight or inadvertence on the part of the registered proprietor."

enactment of the Human Rights Act 1998 in the U.K.[38] Dissatisfied with the House of Lord's decision, *Pye* took the matter to the European Court of Human Rights arguing that it had lost its property as a result of a law that was inconsistent with Article 1 of Protocol No.1 referred to above.

Before the first Chamber of the European Court of Human Rights, the U.K government canvassed four arguments why the Limitation Act of 1980 did not breach human rights. In the first place, that the acquisition of land by the owner became subject to the limitation as an integral component of ownership after registration.[39] Secondly, that what was deprived was *Pye's* right of access to court, not their property.[40] Thirdly, that the State through its limitation provisions was controlling use rather than removing the proprietary or possessory rights of *Pye*.[41] Finally, that given that government had recognised the inadequacies of the law through amendments of the Land Registration Act 2002, a fair balance was struck between the demands of the public and protection of the individual's fundamental rights.[42]

These arguments were rejected by the majority of the court who held that the registered title was absolute and not subject to any limitation or restriction;[43] that the legislation for which the State was responsible alone, operated to deny the registered proprietor (*Pye*) of its title which

---

[38] But passing comments were made by two judges of the Court of Appeal. For example, Mummery LJ framed the matter as involving blocking access to court after limitation periods as opposed to a deprivation of property, and more so, that the limitation period "was reasonable and did not impose undue burden on the landowner." Also, Keene J. regarded the matter as one "concerning limitation rights, and as these were not incompatible with the Convention, no breach had occurred." See L. Griggs, "Possession, Indefeasibility and Human Rights" vol 8 No. 2 QUT Law Journal at 289.

[39] *J.A Pye (Oxford)Ltd & Ors v. Graham & Ors* [2005] EGLR I, para 49.

[40] ibid, at para 53.

[41] ibid, para 58.

[42] ibid, para 60.

[43] In the words of the court, "[i]t was the operation of the [legislation] which brought to an end ...the applicant's title and not any inherent defect or limitation in that title:" ibid, at para 50.

was transferred to the Grahams;[44] that the fact that the land was transferred between individuals rather than to the State, led to the conclusion that this was a deprivation rather than a control;[45] and that given that government had recognised the inadequacies of the Law through an amendment of the LRA 2002 was suggestive of the conclusion that this upset the fair balance between the public interest and the individual's enjoyment of their own possessions.[46] Consequently, the court held that there had been a breach of Article 1 of Protocol No. 1 of the EHRC.

Upon appeal to the Grand Chamber, the court held by a majority of ten votes to seven that there had been no violation of Article 1 of Protocol No. 1.[47] The majority held that *Pye* did not lose its land because of a legislation permitting the State to transfer ownership in particular circumstances nor as a result of social policy, but "rather as a result of the operation of the applicable rules on limitation periods for actions for recovery of land."[48] Consequently, the statutory provisions which had eliminated *Pye's* title were "not intended to deprive paper owners of their title, but to regulate questions of title in a system"[49] in which 12 years of adverse possession extinguished title.

The court recognised that limitation periods were a common feature of domestic legal systems and "serve several important purposes namely: To ensure legal certainty and finality, protect potential defendants from stale claims which might be difficult to counter, and prevent the injustice which might arise if courts were required to decide upon events which took place in the distant past on the basis of evidence which might become unreliable and incomplete because of the passage of

[44] ibid, para 56.
[45] ibid, paras 58-62.
[46] ibid, at para 75.
[47] *J.A Pye (Oxford) Ltd &Anor v.The United Kingdom* [2008] EHRLR 132.
[48] ibid, para 65.
[49] ibid, para 66.

time."[50] Explaining the rationale behind limitation periods, the court observed that:[51]

> "It is a characteristic of property that different countries regulate its use and transfer in a variety of ways. The relevant rules reflect social policies against the background of the local conception of the importance and role of property. Even where title to real property is registered, it must be open to the legislature to attach more weight to lengthy unchallenged possession than to the formal fact of registration.[52] The court accepts that to extinguish title where the former owner is prevented as a consequence of the application of the law, from recovering possession of land cannot be said to be manifestly without reasonable foundation. There existed therefore a general interest in both the limitation period itself and the extinguishment of title at the end of the period."

The court reasoned that the operation of the doctrine of adverse possession leading to the extinction of registered title was not without foundation which was embellished in paragraph 2 of Article 1 of Protocol No. 1, enabling a fair balance to be struck within the legislation.[53]

The court held that whilst accepting that there must be a reasonable relationship of proportionality and that a fair balance must be struck, States are to enjoy a wide margin of appreciation, "with regard to both choosing the means of enforcement and to ascertaining whether the

---

[50] ibid, paras 68, 69.

[51] ibid, para 74.

[52] One of the strong arguments of the minority of the Grand Chamber was the distinction drawn between registered and unregistered land. They argued that while a system of limitation had good justification in the case of unregistered land which depends on possession, there is no justification for its application to registered land which depends not on possession, but on registration of the proprietor.

[53] ibid, para 75.

consequences of enforcement are justified in the general interest for the purpose of achieving the object in question."[54]

Addressing the issue of lack of compensation to *Pye*, the majority expressed the view that as the interference with *Pye's* possession was a control of use rather than a deprivation of possession, "the case-law on compensation for deprivations is not directly applicable."[55] The court reasoned that a requirement for compensation for the "situation brought about by a party failing to observe a limitation period would not sit easily alongside the very concept of limitation periods."[56]

The court further held that *Pye* was not denied procedural protection for, "while limitation period was running...it was open to them to remedy the position by bringing a court action for re-possession of the land," which "would have stopped time running."[57] It was the view of the majority that the law of adverse possession should not have come as a surprise to *Pye*, and despite amendments tightening the operation of the principle, the facts of the case must be considered in light of the law as it stood at the time.[58]

Finally, the court held that limitation periods must operate irrespective of the amount, adding that the value of the land lost by *Pye* was of no consequence.[59]

8.3.2 Rationale for the Decision of the Grand Chamber

Panesar and Wood[60] opine that the decision of the Grand Chamber "is to be welcomed on a number of grounds."[61] It is said to be in line with the

---

[54] ibid, para 75.
[55] ibid, para 79.
[56] ibid.
[57] ibid, para 80.
[58] ibid.
[59] ibid, para 84.
[60] S. Panesar, J. Wood (2007) Adverse Possession and the European Convention on Human Rights 1950 Protocol 1 art. 1. Coventry Law Journal, vol. 12(2), 41 at 54.

common law tradition in respect of ownership of land which is a question of fact based on the concept of seisin,[62] rather than the concept of right. In the words of Gray:[63]

> "[T]he pre-eminent position accorded to de facto position in English law ensures that there is no such thing as absolute title to land. All title is ultimately relative: the title of the present possessor will customarily be upheld unless and until a better claim is advanced on behalf of somebody else [and] sustained possession remains the basis of the right to challenge the title of both the registered and unregistered owner."

Apart from the legal justification underlying acquisition through adverse possession, "there are important social and economic justifications for the rules."[64] One of the social objectives behind the doctrine of adverse possession is said to be "certainty of title."[65] In the words of Panesar and Wood:[66]

> "[i]f claims to land that are based on long possession are nevertheless allowed to be defeated by others showing that they were the owner sometime in the past, it is inevitable that title to land becomes uncertain. Such titles are not conducive to a liberal market engaged in exchange and bargain. The basic premise must be that long unchallenged possession of land should not be disturbed...The resulting uncertainty over title has an impact not only on the person who has been in possession of the land, but also on third parties such as purchasers and mortgagees who may have

---

[61] ibid.

[62] The concept of *seisin* emphasises that proprietary rights in land are based on physical possession rather than on abstract title: See A.W.B Simpson, *An Introduction to the History of English Land Law* (1961) .

[63] K. Gray, Elements of Land Law (1989) at 64.

[64] S. Panesar, J. Wood, supra(n 60).

[65] ibid.

[66] ibid.

interests in the land. In other words, title in property law must be seen as operating in a multitude of transactions concerning the same piece of land. Uncertainty over title is undesirable because the effects are far reaching and they affect more than one transaction. It is only on reliance of title that some of these transactions are entered into; therefore subsequent uncertainty is a bad thing. In this sense the law of adverse possession pursues a legitimate objective and is proportional to it."

The foregoing considerations would always weigh more heavily in favour of adverse possession against the dispossession of the paper owner in the event of disputes following the expiration of the limitation period.

8.3.3 Effect of the ECHR Decision in *Pye* for the English Courts

Whilst some academic writers[67] are of the view that *Pye* has closed the doors on all human rights challenge against the legality of the system of adverse possession under domestic law, others[68] seem to tow the delicate path with caution against the backdrop of the contradictory case law sequel to the decision of the Grand Chamber in *Pye*,[69] and the statement from the Land Registry that *Pye v. United Kingdom*[70] "does not affect domestic case law."[71] It is therefore necessary to examine certain grey areas with a view to identifying the correct legal positions.

The contention that the *Pye v. U.K* has closed the door on a human rights challenge in the U.K may appear to be misplaced in view of the

---

[67] See for example, M Dixon, "Human rights and adverse possession: the final nail?" Conveyancer and Property Lawyer, (2008) 2, at 160-165.

[68] See for example, I Issaias, Property Law and Human Rights, available online at www.researchgate.net/publication/313869735_Property_Law_andHuman_Rights_of_2017/02/21, accessed on 8/6/2020.

[69] *J.A Pye (Oxford) Ltd and J.A Pye (Oxford) Land Ltd v. the United Kingdom.* Application no.44302/02 (ECHR) 30 August 2007).

[70] Supra (n 47).

[71] Additional Practice Guide LRPG005 of September 14, 2007.

truism that the European Court of Human Rights case law does not bind English courts,[72] and in light of the position in cases such as *Beaulane v. Palmer,*[73] lavishly relied on by the Practice Guidance issued by the Land Registry.

In *Beaulane,* the court held that the Limitation Act 1980 operated in such a way that the registered owner of land would be deprived of all of his rights to it, thus violating the European Human Rights Convention. However, the court acknowledged that the Land Registration Act "is not disproportionate unlike the 1980 Act, as it rightly places the burden on the adverse possessor."[74] This case was upturned by the Court of Appeal in *Ofulue and Anor v. Bossert.*[75]

In *Ofulue and Anor v. Bossert,* Mr Ofulue, who became the registered proprietor of the property known as 61, Coburn Road, Bow in 1976 had let the property to tenants. In 1981, a former tenant let Ms Bossert and her father into the property and both father and daughter remained in possession since then with Ms Bossert taking on the property when her father died in 1966. Although Mr Ofulue had visited the property during the intervening years and had negotiations for the grant of a lease to Ms Bossert, but this did not materialise, and the possession proceedings initiated by Mr Ofulue was not continued. All along, the Bosserts had improved the property by repairs and renovations, and when Mr Ofulue sought possession again, Ms Bossert claimed title by

---

[72] See *Kay v. Lambeth LBC* [2006] 2 AC 465 on how to approach inconsistencies between Strasbourg and House of Lords decisions.

[73] (2005) EWCA 817. This case requires an adverse possessor "to establish a degree of possession of the registered title that was inconsistent with the use of or intended use of the land by the registered proprietor" and "this was despite the fact that the House of Lords in *Pye v. Graham* had earlier described the *Beaulane* approach as a heresy": See M. Dixon, supra (n 67) at 1.

[74] This reasoning has been questioned on the ground that "if Beaulane is right, then even the process of the 2002 Act is open to human rights challenge." M. Dixon, "Adverse Possession and Human Rights." (2005) Conv. 160-165

[75] (2009) H.L 11.

adverse possession. The trial judge found for Ms Bossert and the Court of Appeal upheld the decision.

In upholding the decision of the lower court, the Court of Appeal considered first, whether *Pye v. U.K* should be followed and secondly, even if it should, whether it in fact decided that adverse possession principles as applied under the Land Registration Act 1925 were *per se* compatible with the European Convention on Human Rights. The Court held that every court should follow *Pye v. U.K* and other Strasbourg decisions that affect domestic law unless there were good reasons for not doing so.[76] Consequently, the court held that the adverse possession principles as applied under the Land Registration Act 1925 were compatible with the Convention. This is in line with section 2 of the Human Rights Act 1998 as applied by the House of Lords in *R (on the application of Ullah) v. Special Adjudicator*[77] which made it clear that English courts should not depart from Strasbourg on human right matters.

The court held further that the test of proportionality and legitimate aim within Article 1 Protocol No. 1 to the Convention at issue in *Pye* and in this case, for these matters had also been settled by the Strasburg Court claims under the Limitation Act 1980 as it applied to registered land governed by the Land Registration Act 1925; it was therefore not open to a litigant to challenge them in every dispute coming before the court.

It follows from the foregoing therefore, that the Land Registry Practice Statement supporting principles set out in *Beaulane*is *ultra vires* and contrary to the established principle as laid down by the House of Lords in *Kay v. Lambeth*[78]to the extent that "English Courts and national authorities (including in this context, the Land Registry) though not bound, must apply the principles expounded from Strasbourg and follow

[76] Per Arden L.J in *Pye* at 32. According to Dixon, "[t]his might be where the Strasbourg Court had misunderstood domestic law, or domestic law caused *(sic)* for the exercise of a discretion, and we might add, where there is a contrary House of Lords decision..." M. Dixon, (n 67).

[77] (2004) UKHL 26, 2 A.C 323, per Lord Bingham at para 20.

[78] (2006) UKHL 10.

precedent on human rights matters even if it might involve a conflict with the Convention."[79]

The next question is whether it is necessary to distinguish the impact of *Pye* on registered and unregistered land bearing in mind that the position taken was in respect of registered land, especially against the backdrop of the English doctrine of judicial precedent that 'like cases must be treated alike'. Also, since *Pye* directly concerns registered land under the Land Registration Act 1925, should it apply to cases of registered land under the extant Land Registration Act 2002 in view of the reform introduced into the UK land registration as earlier discussed in chapter 7?

Taking the second question first, it is of note that "in practical terms, the 2002 Act has brought several reforms to aid the fairness of adverse possession [which] significantly rules out the possibility of a human rights claim against the state on the claimants' part..."[80] It is therefore "likely that the law in the 2002 LRA will be compliant with the EHRC and its safeguards for the paper owner."[81] It is safe to therefore presume that "the Pye judgment still facilitates having closed the door on a human rights challenge for registered land despite the enactment of a new Act."[82]

In the case of unregistered land however, it cannot be said that *Pye* has drawn the curtain on human rights challenge. Unlike the case of

---

[79] *Kay & Ors v. Lambert London Borough Council* supra (n 78) para. 44. Consequently, it is said that it is "now time for the Land Registry to rescind its Guidance on this point:" M. Dixon, "Adverse Possession and Human Rights." supra (n 74).

[80] I. Issaias (n.68) at 5. Not only is the title of the registered owner protected against automatic extinction unlike the case of unregistered land, the registered proprietor is notified of the squatter's application for registration with the opportunity to oppose such application and also set the necessary legal machinery in motion to evict such applicant, the registered proprietor is encouraged to keep an eye on his land thereby obviating the possibility of losing title to the adverse possessor.

[81] J. Duddington, *Land Law*, Second ed. Pearson (2014) at 236.

[82] I. Issaias (n 68) at 5.

registered land where the LRA 2002 has introduced a number of provisions that exude fairness and are human right compliant, the unregistered system is governed by the hard core rule of the statute of limitation requiring 12 years of adverse possession for the title of the owner to be extinguished with no safeguards or protection whatsoever for the paper owner. For example, there is no notice of the adverse possessor's presence required, and there is naked deprivation of title without compensation, with the very high possibility of it being challenged under Article 1 Protocol 1 of the European Convention on Human Rights in future.

8.4 Adverse Possession and Human Rights in Nigeria

Nigeria operates a constitutional democracy, and successive written constitutions made provisions for the protection of right to property.[83] The extant constitution of the country guarantees right to property,[84] subject to a number of exceptions.[85] Section 44 of the Constitution of the Federal Republic of Nigeria 1999 as amended provides:

> "(1) No movable property or any interest in an immovable property shall be taken possession of compulsorily and no right over or interest in any such property shall be acquired compulsorily in any part of Nigeria except in the manner and for the purposes prescribed by a law that, among other things-
>
> (a) requires prompt payment of compensation therefore
>
> (b) gives any person claiming such compensation a right of access for the

---

[83] See e,g, The Nigerian Republican Constitution, 1963, s.31; The Constitution of the Federal Republic of Nigeria 1979, s. 40; The Constitution of the Federal Republic of Nigeria 1999 as amended, s. 44.

[84] See the Constitution of the Federal Republic of Nigeria, 1999 as amended, s. 44(1).

[85] ibid, s. 44(2).

determination of his interest in the property and the amount of compensation to a court of law or tribunal or body having jurisdiction in that part of Nigeria.

(2) Nothing in subsection 1 of this section shall be construed as affecting any general law:

...

(i) relating to limitation of actions.

The foregoing constitutional provisions protect property rights save in circumstances prescribed by a law which allows for prompt payment of compensation, and gives the owner of the right access to court for purposes of determining the extent of such right and the amount of compensation payable. However, the protection of this right shall not affect "any general law relating to limitation of actions;" in other words, the exercise of adverse possession by a squatter over the period stipulated under the limitation law shall not be affected by the constitutional protection of property right. The effect of section 44(2)(i) of the Nigerian Constitution therefore, is to make the enforcement of the limitation law non-susceptible to a human rights challenge.

On June 22 1983, Nigeria ratified the African Charter on Human and Peoples' Rights[86] and subsequently domesticated its content as part of Nigerian law,[87] pursuant to the provision of section 12(1) of the Nigerian Constitution 1979.[88] Article 14 of the African Charter provides that:

---

[86] The African Charter on Human and Peoples' Rights was adopted by member States of the then Organisation of African Unity (O.A.U) now known as the African Union (A.U) in 1981in Nairobi, Kenya and came into effect on 21 October 1986.

[87] The African Charter (Ratification and Enforcement) Act 1983. See Cap A9 Laws of the Federation of Nigeria 2010.

[88] Section 12(1) of the Constitution of the Federal Republic of Nigeria 1979 (the same provision in the extant Constitution of the Federal Republic of Nigeria 1999), provides that: "No treaty between the federation and any other country shall have

> "The right to property shall be guaranteed. It may only be encroached upon in the interest of public need or in the general interest of the community in accordance with the provisions of appropriate law."

Whilst the status of the provision of the above Article as a guarantee of right to property is not in doubt, the vagueness of the circumstances for derogation by the State betrays its effectiveness as an instrument meant to curb the despotism and flagrant violation of property rights by many governments in Africa prior to its coming into effect. It is said that "the provisions of the African Charter are [too] brief and vague and in some circumstances, allow national laws [which it was meant to check] to limit or derogate from these rights without setting any standard for such national law."[89] This is said to be contrary to the well defined clauses on circumstances for derogation from those rights by the State set out in many international instruments on human rights[90] including the EHRC. In particular, section 44 of the Nigerian Constitution on protection of property rights which the Charter was meant to compliment, contains a better and much more detailed provisions on circumstances under which the right may be derogated from by the State, than the Charter. For example, whilst the question whether the derogation clause in Article 14 of the Charter covers limitation of actions in relation to adverse possession would depend on the court's interpretation of the vague clause on derogation by the State from the property right guaranteed, section 44(2) of the Nigerian Constitution catalogued the various circumstances under which the right may be derogated from by the State which includes

---

the force of law except to the extent to which any such treaty has been enacted into law by the National Assembly."

[89] N. Ogbu, 'The African Charter on Human and Peoples' Rights as Incompatible with despotism: The Nigerian Experience (2005) 8 UBLJ 113 cited by E. Ekhator in "The impact of the African Charter on Human and Peoples' Rights on domestic law: A case study of Nigeria." (2015) Commonwealth Law Bulletin vol. 41, No. 2 253 at 255.

[90] Abdi Ali, "Derogation from Constitutional Rights and Its Implications under the African Charter on Human and Peoples' Rights (2013) 1 LDD 78.

the *general law on limitation of actions*. Consequently, section 44(2) of the Nigerian Constitution is a better protection and affords a better defence to an adverse possessor than the provision of Article 14 of the African Charter on Human and Peoples' Rights.

Also,the provision of Article 1, Protocol 1 of the EHRC contains a better and much more detailed provisions on circumstances under which the right may be derogated from by the State, than the Charter. For example, whilst the question whether the derogation clause in Article 14 of the Charter covers limitation of actions in relation to adverse possession would depend on the court's interpretation of the vague clause on derogation by the State from the property right guaranteed, the third leg (contained in the second paragraph) of Article 1, Protocol 1 of the ECHR contains a much more detailed and definitive provision on the subject. The second paragraph of the Article provides:

> "The preceding provisions shall not, however, in any way impair the right of a State to enforce such laws as it deems necessary to control the use of property in accordance with the general interest or to secure the payment of taxes or other contributions or penalties."

This provision therefore authorises the state to enforce "such laws as it deems necessary to control the use of property in accordance with the general interest;" which was one of the major reasons behind the decision of the Grand Chamber of the European Court in *Pye* that is, that the enforcement of the relevant provisions of the Limitation Act 1980 did not offend against the European Convention. The same cannot be said of Article 14 of the ACHPR which provides that right to property "may only be encroached upon in the interest of public need or in the general interest of the community in accordance with the provisions of appropriate law"- a provision too vague to be susceptible to definitive interpretation on the subject. Thus, unless the provision of Article 14 of the ACHPR is interpreted in light of section 44(2)(i) of the Nigerian Constitution, it may be difficult to take a definitive position as the Grand Chamber of the European Court on Human Rights did, in *Pye*.

Both the EHRC as domesticated in the Human Rights Act of the U.K, and the Nigerian Constitution protect the interest of the property owner from encroachment or acquisition except in prescribed circumstances. However, derogation from such protection by the State depends on varying circumstances as between the two jurisdictions: whereas in the U.K, derogation from protection shall be in the "public interest," in Nigeria, the constitutional provisions on protection of property right may be derogated from "for purposes prescribed by a law" that provides for compensation and access to court by the property owner, to determine the extent of interest and quantum of compensation. Thus, the scope of appreciation left to the State for the purpose of striking a fair balance between the individual property right and public interest in both jurisdictions differs. It would appear that whereas the parameters for derogation from the provision of the EHRC as domesticated by the Human Right Act is left entirely to the discretion of the State in the case of the U.K as to what constitutes "public interest," in Nigeria, such derogation is to be determined by a law which expressly provides for "purposes" of derogation, and which law is expected to pass the two tests of provision of compensation and access to court by the property owner.

Whereas, the requirement of prompt payment of compensation is a *sine qua non* for taking control or for acquiring such interest compulsorily under the Nigerian Constitution, this is not so provided under the HRA of the U.K. The issue of payment of compensation under the HRA depends on the prevailing circumstances by the State.

In Nigeria, the "general law relating to the limitation of actions" is an exception to the general provision on the protection of property right,[91] under the EHRC as domesticated by the U.K Human Rights Act 1998, protection of property right "shall not...in any way impair the right of a State to enforce such laws as it deems necessary to control the use of property in accordance with the general interest ..."[92] Thus, not only is the general law on adverse possession not affected by the EHRC as

[91] ibid.

[92] The second leg of the provision of Art. 1 of Protocol No. 1 to the Convention of Human Right domesticated as Human Rights Act in the U.K.

domesticated by the HRA of the U.K and the provision of section 44(1) of the Nigerian Constitution on the protection of property right, non-inclusion of the right to compensation by a landowner whose interest is extinguished in the case of unregistered title, or whose name is removed from the title register in the case of registered title, does not amount to a violation of property right in both jurisdictions.

In the case of *J.A Pye (Oxford) Ltd v. UK*,[93] the Grand Chamber of the European Court of Human Rights held that:

> "[a] requirement of compensation for the situation brought about by a party failing to observe a limitation period would sit uneasily alongside the very concept of limitation periods, whose aim was to further legal certainty by preventing a party from pursuing an action after a certain date. Even under the provisions of the Land Registration Act 2002, no compensation was payable by a person who was ultimately registered as a new owner of registered land on expiry of the limitation period."

The position in Nigeria cannot be different as neither the provisions of the various limitation statutes in Nigeria nor the Land Registration Law of Lagos State include the right to compensation.

Unlike the position in the United Kingdom where Pye has shed some light on the impact of the human rights regime on the doctrine of adverse possession, there are no judicial decisions in Nigeria on the point, and the tenacity of the doctrine without some palliatives for loss of title and in circumstances which may appear unfair or unconscionable due to absence of good faith, may open doors for human rights challenge in future. In the case of unregistered title or where only land instrument is registered, enforcement of the limitation law without compensation to the actual owner may work injustice particularly as the law does not take cognisance of the owner's lack of knowledge of the presence or the motive of the adverse possessor.

---

[93] Supra (n 47).

Also, unlike the LRA 2002 of the United Kingdom which provides some safety measures and protection to the registered proprietor against the adverse possessor-applicant for registration as a new proprietor of title,[94] the LRL of Lagos State[95] contains no such safeguards. The LRL which partly allows title registration through the use of the register, entitles an adverse possessor to apply for registration upon showing thatthe court is satisfied that the title of the registered holder of the land has been extinguished under the Limitation Law.The registered proprietor under the LRL has no opportunity of advance notification of an imminent loss of title, unlike the case under the English Land Registration Act 2002.[96]

8.5 Conclusion

The position in the U.K and other European countries is that the application of the doctrine of adverse possession is not a violation of the right to property. This is the position of the European Court on Human Rights in *Pye v. UK* and it is in tandem with the letters and spirit of the extant Land Registration Law 2002. Whatever impression formed by the Land Registry with regards to registered land has to change sequel to that decision. However, it cannot be said with certainty that the decision in *Pye* is authority for closing the door on human rights challenge to the system governing unregistered land and pending a resolution of this question by

[94] See Schedule 6 thereto.

[95] Land Registration Law of Lagos State, 2015.

[96] See Schedule 6 paragraph 2(1) thereto.This would have served as a warning to the registered owner who is expected to take appropriate legal steps to evict the squatter accordingly. The fact that the court is expected to pronounce on the fact of adverse possession under the LRLafter hearing both parties is of no moment, since the court's inquiry is as to the validity of the claim in adverse possession without affording the registered owner the opportunity of reversing the illegally acquired status of the adverse possessor by initiating legal proceedings for eviction.

the courts in the UK, it is inapt to extend the decision in *Pye* to unregistered land.

In Nigeria, the position is that the enjoyment of rights in land is subject, among other exceptions, to the law relating to limitation of actions and *ipso facto,* the law of adverse possession. Although there are no judicial decisions (unlike the situation in the United Kingdom) streamlining the parameters of application of the constitutional provisions to the registered or unregistered land, those provisions and the African Charter on Human and Peoples' Rights (ACHPR) would ordinarily apply to unregistered land. From the unambiguous provision of section 43(2) of the Constitution and, on the face of it, the provision of section 14 of the ACHPR, it may be impossible to impugn the application of the doctrine of adverse possession from the human rights perspective. But the same cannot be said of registered land in the Lagos State of Nigeria where the Land Registration Law of the State does not exude the kind of fairness and equity associated with the reform of the registration procedure under the LRA - a reform which makes vast concessions for registered land owners in the UK. Thus, the enforcement of the limitation law against registered proprietors in Nigeria may be subject of human rights challenge.

CHAPTER 9
ADVERSE POSSESSION AND SQUATTERS' RIGHT IN LAND

9.1 Introduction

This Chapter engages the dynamism of property concept within the parameters of the socio-legal construct of modern societies and against the backdrop of user rights cognisable under domestic and international legal regimes. The social malaise of homelessness culminating in squatting has resulted generally in forced evictions in many jurisdictions in the developing third world, and in the criminalisation of urban squatting in some others.

The focus is essentially on the aggregate effect of these on the basic rights of persons and the implications for state responsibility in the provision of housing around the world. How these play out both in the outlook of the various legal responses generated and in the way some jurisdictions managed to turn squatters' settlements around positively in the direction of socio-economic growth and the general welfare of the people, are critical areas of engagement.

The Chapter examines the efficacy of the application of the doctrine of adverse possession in light of the overbearing exercise of executive power of the State to overrun citizens' rights acquired by adverse possession, and in the legitimate exercise of basic fundamental rights as enshrined in the Constitution and the various international human rights instruments. It demonstrates how adverse possession may turn out to be an instrument of social emancipation, economic growth and community development.

In essence, the discourse provides a veritable window for appreciating the concept of 'property right' from the socio-legal perspectives in the contemporary world. Whilst the positivist's position of property right as an outcome of a strict legal construct[1] would explain its

---

[1] The positivists regard property as a positive right (as opposed to a natural right) created by the instrumentality of the law. In the words of Bentham, 'law and

existence and the parameters of its application within the legal context, it runs short of its dynamism in modern societies. Consequently, the absoluteness of its nature[2] and the individualistic outlook of its essence[3] in its pristine form may overshadow the evolutionary trend of its application and undermine the public good which it serves as human right, unless the social realities as encapsulated in the performance of its social functions are understood.

Since the decision of the English Court of Appeal in *McPhail v. Persons, Names Unknown,*[4]the position of the common law is that it would protect the property right of a land owner as against the occupation of a trespasser, and that the property right of the landowner is a strong factor in support of the proportionality required for eviction of the trespasser, and defeats his defence under Article 8 of the Human Rights Act 1998. This position which is the law in England and Wales takes no cognisance of the circumstances of the squatter and provides no remedy for his social predicament of homelessness as a result of failure of the State to ensure alternative accommodation or provide for the adequate housing need of the citizens – factors which are of concern to the international community and human rights law.In all of these, this Chapter explores the dynamism

---

private property are born together and die together'. 'Without laws' he says, 'there is no private property'. He argues that all laws flow from the state and deprecates the idea of natural rights as '…rhetorical nonsense - nonsense upon stilts.'See J Bentham, 'Anarchical Fallacies Nonsense upon stilts.' *Bentham, Burke, and Max on the rights of Man,* J Waldron ed., (London, Methuen, 1987) 53.

[2] In the words of Alston and Mueller, 'a full set of private rights in property consists of the following: 1) the right to use the asset in any manner that the user wishes, generally with the caveat that such use does not interfere with someone else's property right; 2) the right to exclude others from the use of the same asset; 3) the right to derive income from the asset; 4) the right to sell the asset; and 5) the right to bequeath to someone of your choice.' See L.J Alston and B. Mueller, 'Property Rights and the State' in *Handbook of New Institutional Economics*. C Menard, M. Shorley (eds), 2005 Springer Boston MA.

[3] L Lomansky, *Persons, Rights, and the Moral Community* 111-51 (1987) cited in Foster and Bonilla, 'The Social Function of Property: A comparative Law Perspective.' Fordham Law Review [2011] vol. 80, 218.

[4] [1973] Ch. 447.

of the concept of property right in the contemporary world with useful lessons drawn there from.

9.2 The Concept of Property Right

The traditional concept of property right is an aggregate of various rights referred to as a 'bundle of rights' which include the right to possess and use the property exclusively, and to alienate and destroy the property at will, limited by the rights of others and public interest. It is private and individualistic in nature and it is strictly regulated by law. It is said that property rights "are creations of law and may be extinguished only by law or in a manner authorised by it."[5]

However, modern development in the conception and use of property have resulted in a paradigm shift from the classical liberal conception of property as a subjective internalised rights in the occupation, use and disposition of an asset limited only by the rights of others and public interest, to a wider, externalised and functional conceptwhich demonstrates the social function of property with its fairness and redistributive ethos.The theory of social function of property is one of the notable challenges to the classical liberal concept of property and underpins what is known today as squatters' rights.

9.3 The Social Function of Property Theory

The idea behind the social function of property as discussed in Chapter 3 of this book is in creating an obligation on the part of the owner of property to put it at the service of the community.[6] It deprecates the idea of keeping property out of use without justification, and discourages speculation for selfish interest. It is therefore opposed to the classical

---

[5] I.O.Smith, *Practical Approach to Law of Real Property in Nigeria* (2013) Ecowatch Publications, Lagos-Nigeria at 38.

[6] L Duguit, *Las Transformaciones Del Derecho Publico Y Privado* (Editorial Heliasta 1975). See generally SR Foster & D Bonilla, 'The Social Function of Property: A Comparative Law Perspective.' Fordham Law Review [2011] vol. 80 101.

liberal conception of property as a mere "independent positive exercise of bundle of rights to private property."[7]The rationale for this theory lies in interdependence between people as the central element of social reality.

Property serves a social function to the extent that it serves the larger interest of the community which is tantamount to putting it into production. This function corroborates the justification advanced by proponents of the labour and utilitarian theories underlying the doctrine,[8] and gives impetus to the functional perspective of the doctrine of adverse possession as an instrument of economic growth, social cohesion and community development. It forms the basis for the peoples' right to housing andremains a potent justification for squatters' rights.

This theory underscores the extinction of title over unproductive land at the end of the limitation period in many jurisdictions[9] and informs constitutional provisions safeguarding public interest in the occupation and use of abandoned land.[10] Many international instruments[11] on the protection of right to private and family life, and the state obligation in making provision for adequate and affordable housing available for the homeless are reminiscent of the social function of property. This concept of the social function of property plays out in many parts of the world through the proliferation of squatting in urban centres including

---

[7] L. Lomansky, *Persons, Rights and Moral Community* 111-51 (1987) cited in Foster and Bonilla, supra (n 6).

[8] See Chapter 3 *ante*.

[9] See for example, the Limitation Act 1980 applicable in England and Wales and the Limitation Act 1966 applicable in Nigeria.

[10] See for example, s. 44(2)(i) of the Constitution of the Federal Republic of Nigeria 1999 as amended which excludes acquisition of land by the operation of the statute of limitation from the ambit of provision for compensation. See also s. 26 of the Constitution of the Republic of South Africa, 1996in balancing competing interests and, in particular sub section (3) on protection of squatters' rights.

[11] See for example, International Covenant on Civil and Political Rights (ICCPR), Art. 6 with a corresponding provision on Right to adequate standard of living including Housing as contained in the International Covenant on Social, Cultural and Economic Rights (ICSCER), Art. 11.

abandoned apartments by local authorities[12] and the growth of informal settlements especially in the developing world[13] consequent upon social discontent and economic distress.

9.4 Evolution of Squatting and Squatters' Rights

It is said that 'squatting' "is probably as old as history itself"[14]. An account has been given of the ancient Code of Hammurabi existing as far back as the 2250 B.C.[15] The Code abhors leaving vacant land to lie fallow[16], rewards long possession[17] while maximising user's land for productivity[18]. Squatting has also been 'influenced by the Roman property law tradition'[19]. It is said that '[i]n the agrarian tradition of ancient Rome, the goal of most property owners was not to increase their

[12] For example, the Department of the Environment in the U.K reported that in 1995, there were an estimated 864,000 empty homes in Britain, out of which 17,000 were reported by the 'Advisory Services for Squatters,' to contain squatters: See I. Hunter, *Streetwise Moves to Outsmart Squatters*, Guardian (London) March 26, 1995, available in 1995WL 7590927.

[13] This has been reported in different parts of Africa (such as Nigeria, Kenya, South Africa, etc.) and many parts of Latin America (such as Peru, Brazil, Mexico, etc.).

[14] B Gardiner, "Squatters Rights and Adverse Possession: A search for Equitable Application of Property Laws." [1997] Ind. International & Comparative Law Review, vol. 8:1, 119 at 123 citing Dukeminier & Krier, *PROPERTY* 112 (1981).

[15] RF Harper,*The Code of Hammurabi, King of Babylon* 23 (Robert Francis Harper trans., Univ. of Chicago Press 1904).

[16] Section 44 of the Code states that: 'If a man rents an unclaimed field for three years to develop it, and neglects it and do not develop the field, in the fourth year he shall break up the field with hoes, he shall hoe and harrow it and he shall return it to the owner of the field…' ibid, at 27.

[17] Section 60 of the Code states that: 'If a man gives a field to a gardener to plant as an orchard and the gardener plants the orchard and care for the orchard for four years, in the fifth year the owner of the orchard and the gardener shall share equally…' ibid, at 33

[18] Section 61 states that: 'If the gardener do not plant the whole field, but leave a space to waste, they shall assign the waste space to his portion.' ibid.

[19] B Gardiner, supra (n 14) at 124.

holdings.'[20] The 'Roman policy and tradition allowed a man only as much public land as he could cultivate himself'[21] thereby favouring the interests of the whole Empire over the interests of any individual land owner. Thus, the Roman property system 'did not allow a large landholder to waste potentially economically viable land'[22].

Following from the Roman law tradition, the root of English property ownership lies in possession. The law favours a party in possession and not necessarily a paper or absentee owner. Clothing the squatter in possession with a strong indicia of title which may ripen into a fee at the expiration of a period prescribed by law, became the essence of seisin. This strong property right has provided a useful tool for squatters in contemporary English land tenure system.

Whilst the traditional perception of the squatter by governments and citizens in many parts of the world is that of a criminal who takes advantage of 'neglectful municipalities and land owners'[23], the United Nation's Commission on Human Rights dispels this notion in a Report by the Sub-Commission on Prevention of Discrimination and Protection of Minorities[24]. It is however found as a fact that many squatters contribute to local economies,[25] and 'there are times when squatters and squatters'

---

[20] J Christman, *The Myth of Property* 17 (1994).

[21] A Lintott, *Judicial Reform and Land Reform in the Roman Republic* 34 (1992).

[22] B Gardiner, supra (n 14) 124.

[23] ibid, at 121.

[24] The Report illuminated the 'Twelve Misconceptions and Misrepresentations of the Right to Housing'. See Justice R. Sachar, Working Paper on Promoting the Realisation of the Right to Adequate Housing, at 4-11, U.N. Doc. E/CN.4/sub.2/1992/15 available online at http://www.undp.org/un/habitat/presskit/dpi1778e.htm. Accessed online on 25/06/2020.

[25] For example, "the Asian Coalition on Housing Rights found squatters who worked an average of 9.9 hours per day, compared to higher income groups who only worked 7.3 hours per day". See B. Gardiner, supra (n 14) at 121 relying on the United Nations Department of Public Information, *Is There a Right to Housing?* Available online at https://www.undp.org/un/habitat/presskit/dpi1778e.htm. Accessed on 25/06/2020.

movements must be recognised for their noble and courageous efforts in developing efficient uses of property and alleviating one of society's ills'[26].

The theoretical justification for protecting the squatters' right to respect for the home against the underlining factor of homelessness lends credence to the sanctity of squatters' right. The occupation theory,[27] the labour theory[28] and the utilitarian theory[29] would give priority to land use and prevention of waste and nuisance as against preservation of

[26] B Gardiner, supra (n 14) at 121.

[27] The occupation theory of private property suggests as a rule that 'objects become the private property of individuals when such individuals have taken occupation of them': See S. Panesar, (2000) 'Theories of Private Property,' Denning Law Journal, vol. 15, 113 at 118. This theory justifies the fulcrum of the doctrine of adverse possession which is the act of possession coupled with *animus possidendi*.

[28] John Locke, in his *Second Treatise on government*, finds justification for the rule of adverse possession in the old labour theory. He argues that the interest of a squatter who has improved the property through concerted labour has overriding interest in it over an owner who has abandoned it. The *raison d'etre* of this theory is that since labour belongs to the person performing it, exerting it in developing or cultivating the land brings the land out of the commons and makes it a subject matter of acquisition by the labourer to the exclusion of all claims by other persons: See J Locke, 'Two Treatises of Government' (1690, P Laslet ed. 1963) Oxford Blackwall (1966) para 25.

[29] J.S Mill in his *Principles of Political Economy*says that: "in the case of land, "no exclusive right should be permitted in any individual which cannot be shown to be productive of positive good." "When land is not intended to be cultivated," he says, "no good reason can in general be given for its being private property". He states that possession ought to be recognised as ownership if it has not been challenged within a moderate number of years, pointing out that "revival of a claim which had long been dormant, would generally be a greater injustice, and almost always [cause] a greater private and public mischief, than leaving the original wrong without atonement". This reasoning has its root in rule-utilitarianism which states that utility is maximized in a legal system by having a rule, namely, the acquisition of property through adverse possession, thereby resolving conflicting claims and promoting legal certainty: See JS Mill, *Principles of Political Economy* (1902), University of Chicago Press 1993 at 35.

innocuous title to land without productive use. The personhood theory[30] also provides the emotive underlining for the right to respect for the home. For example, the idea that an Englishman's home is his castle is deeply rooted in the English folklore, and if the homeless found a home in an abandoned property and made it an abode for long enough to establish a home, the personhood theory legitimises his use of the property as a home as against the title holder who abandoned the property to fall into disuse. What then is the attitude of the English common law in the evolution of squatters' rights?

9.5 Legal Status of Squatters Under English Law

The position of the law applicable in England and Wales could be examined from both the common law perspective as encapsulated in *McPhail v. Persons, Names Unknown,* and from the judicial interpretation of Article 8 of the ECHR.

9.5.1 The Position of Squatters Before October 2000 in England and Wales

The position of squatters in England and Wales before the coming into effect of the Human Rights Act 1998 is encapsulated in the decision of the Court of Appeal in *McPhail v. Persons, Names Unknown (McPhail).*[31] In that case, a leasehold property at Islington which had remained unoccupied all along was later put under lock and Key by the owner, Mr McPhail. Two days after, some persons unknown made entry, got in through the front door and changed the lock. The following day, McPhail went to the

---

[30] This theory recognises that a squatter in possession of land after a certain time, forms a personal attachment to it than the actual owner 'who has presumably become detached from the land'. In the words of Oliver Wendell Holmes: 'A thing which you have enjoyed and used as your own for a long time whether property or an opinion, takes root in your being and cannot be torn away without your resenting the act and trying to defend yourself, however you came by it': See O.W.Holmes, 'The Path of the Law,' 10 Harvard Law Review 457, 477 (1897).

[31] [1973] Ch. 447.

property in the company of a detective Inspector to ask the squatters for their names which they refused to furnish. Consequently McPhail brought an action in court against the squatters for possession of the property under R.S.C Order 113. The Writ was served on them. The squatters later gave their names and said they believed that the house had been empty for at least two years and as they had nowhere to live, they decided to make their home there. Philip J. made an order that McPhail do recover possession forthwith.

On Appeal, the squatters admitted that they had no defence in law (as they were trespassers), but asked that the court give them four weeks of grace. The court, did not recognise homelessness as a defence for occupying an empty premises[32] and held that the owner was entitled to obtain a court order, 'that the owner do recover the land and issue a writ of possession immediately' as the common law courts would not suspend the order for possession.[33] The court also recognised that a 'summons can be issued for possession against squatters even though they cannot be identified by name [as in this case]' and may be obtained after judgment to recover possession which 'can be enforced by a writ of possession immediately'; and 'there is no provision giving any time.'[34] Thus, the position of the law before 2000 in England and Wales was that the court would make an order for possession forthwith and had no powers to give the squatter time.

9.5.2 The Position in England and Wales After October 2nd 2000

The coming into effect of the Human Rights Act 1998 (HRA) made relevant provisions of the European Convention on Human Rights

---

[32] As Lord Denning said at 456-458: "What is a squatter? He is one who, without any colour of right , enters on an unoccupied house or land, intending to stay there as long as he can. He may seek to justify or excuse his conduct. He may say that he was homeless and that this house or land was standing empty, doing nothing. But this plea is of no avail in law."

[33] ibid.

[34] ibid.

(ECHR) part of the domestic law in England and Wales. Section 6(1) of the HRA makes it unlawful for a public authority to act in a way which is incompatible with a Convention right, while section 6(3) makes the court a public authority in this regard.

Where squatters have established their homes on the land of another, the prospect of eviction from their homes must engage the relevant rights under Article 8 of the ECHR[35], and in interpreting this Article, the court is obligated to act in a way that is compatible with a Convention right. Article 8 provides:

1. Everyone has the right to respect for his private and family life, his home and his correspondence.

2. There shall be no interference by a public authority with the exercise of this right except such as is in accordance with the law and is necessary in a democratic society in the interests of national security, public safety or the economic well-being of the country, for the prevention of disorder or crime, for the protection of health or morals, or for the protection of the rights and freedoms of others.

The purport of Article 8 as explained by the court in *McCann v. UK*[36] is for an independent tribunal to have the proportionality of an eviction determined in light of its provisions notwithstanding that, under domestic law, the right of occupation of the person evicted has come to an end. In view of the purport of Article 8, can it now be said that *McPhail* remains the law in England and Wales?

---

[35] The corresponding provisions of Article 1 of the first Protocol applies to owners of land.

[36] (2008) 47 EHRR 40 at 50.

9.5.3 Judicial Interpretation of Article 8 of the ECHR post *McPhail*

Judicial interpretation of Article 8 of the Convention is hinged on the common ground that where the squatter has established a home on the land, the prospect of eviction there from must engage Article 8. However the possibility of engagement of Article 8 in cases of homelessness involving public authority owners as demonstrated in a long line of judicial authorities[37] may not defeat contractual and proprietary rights to possession. It has been established by judicial authorities that:

> [I]n virtually every case where a residential occupier has no contractual or statutory protection, and the local authority is entitled to possession as a matter of domestic law, there will be a very strong case for saying that making an order for possession would be proportionate.[38]

This is especially the case where 'domestic law imposes no requirement of reasonableness and gives an unqualified right to possession'[39]. The right of the public authority to enforce a claim of possession under domestic law would generally be enough justification under Article 8(2) for interfering with the occupier's right to respect for his home,[40] but where Article 8(1) is raised as a defence against interference, such interference by a public authority is legitimate only if it is dependent on compliance with domestic law, responds to 'a pressing social need and be proportionate to the legitimate aim which it is sought to achieve'.[41] However, a defence

---

[37] See for example, *Harrow London Borough Council v. Qazi* [2004] 1 A.C 983; *Kay v. Lambert London Borough Council* [2006] UKHL 10; *Manchester City Council v. Pinnock* [2011] UKSC 6 at 54; *Hounslow London Borough Council v. Powell* [2011]UKSC 8; *Birmingham City Council v. Lloyd* [2012] EWCA Civ 969; *Thurrock Borough Council v. West* [2012] EWCA Civ 1437, to mention a few

[38] *Manchester City Council v. Pinnock*supra, (n 37) at 54.

[39] ibid, at 57.

[40] *Kay v. Lambert London Borough Council* supra,(n 37) at 28.

[41] ibid.

which does not challenge the law under which the possession order is sought as being incompatible with Article 8, but is based only on the occupier's personal circumstances is not valid under Article 8(1) unless there is to be applied a statutory test of reasonableness in making a possession order as required by the relevant law. In such cases, the occupier must be given the opportunity of presenting his case based on this[42].

While there is generally a consensus of judicial opinion on the possibility of engagement of Article 8(1) by the occupier of property owned by a local authority, this is not the case where the person seeking the order for possession is a private land owner. There was a divergent judicial opinion expressed domestically[43] and in Strasbourg[44] on the point until the Court of Appeal decision in *Malik v. Fassenfelt & Ors*[45].

In that case the respondent Mr Imran Malik (*Malik*) purchased land in 2003. He was refused planning permission to develop the land for office use. His subsequent intention to build Flats on the land was abandoned when he became aware of the potential development of the land as a third runway to the Heathrow Airport. Instead, he used the land for parking and storing cars and later let the land to car importers and subsequently to one Mr Asad (*Asad*) who used the land for unlawful purposes resulting in the prosecution and conviction of both Malik and Asad. The land was vacated by Asad and the key returned to Malik. Before Malik could implement his new plan to convert the land back to a garden centre and use it as a boxing club, unknown persons represented

[42] ibid, 110.

[43] In *Harrow London Borough Council v. Qazi,* supra (n 37), the views of Lord Bingham and Lord Steyn at paras 23 and 26, contrast with the view of Lord Hope at para.52.

[44] While the European Court (First Session) in *Belchikova v. Russia* (Application No. 2408/06 (Unreported) given 25 March 2010) considered Article 8 relevant even when the person seeking possession was a private sector land owner, in *Di Palma v. United Kingdom* (1986) 10 EHRR 149, 155-156, the European Human Rights Commission appeared to have taken a different view.

[45] [2013] EWCA Civ 798.

by the appellant Mr Joseph McGahan gained entry without Malik's permission and remained there as trespassers. The occupiers were part of a group known as 'Grow Heathrow'. They cleared the land which had become contaminated with spillage of car oils and fuels and restored it to its former attractiveness as a market garden centre with a range of glass houses which in time became their dwelling places and their homes. They consequently gained the admiration and support of the people of Sipson village.

When the claimants sued for possession of the land, the defendants raised a number of defences one of which was their enjoyment of the protection of Article 8 of the European Convention alleging that eviction would interfere with their rights and that any such interference would not be proportionate. The defendant contended that the court would have to determine what a reasonable period would be to allow them to vacate the land suggesting a number of months, but the claimant contended that if the order for possession was to be made, the court did not have jurisdiction to extend the normal time for possession orders to take effect; an argument made pursuant to the rule in *McPhail* earlier discussed. It was found by the court of first instance that the defendant was a trespasser although the land was used as a home for some of them. The court held that 'as the court is a public authority and the land is occupied as a home, Article 8 is capable of application even though the land owner is a private individual and the occupiers are trespassers'[46]. The court held that:

> while Article 8 can apply to private landlords, it does not in the circumstances of this matter make an order for possession disproportionate or require the court to stay the order for possession for a period of time to give effect to any Article 8 rights[47].

[46] ibid, para 29.
[47] ibid, para. 33.

The court further held that the provision of section 89 which provides that if an order of possession is to be made, it should not take effect before 6 weeks from the date of the order, did not apply to trespassers and that the court had no jurisdiction to extend time for possession as a result of 'exceptional hardship' with respect to trespassers. The court refused to be persuaded by the use made of the land, or by the argument that the land had greater social advantages than the use to which the claimant was putting, or intended to put the land, and held that:

> ...That may be so, but Mr Malik is the legal owner of this land which has been deliberately occupied by the defendants knowing they had no right to enter. Mr Malik is not to be denied his ownership or right to occupy his own land because others find his use of that land to be less acceptable than the use made of the land by the trespassing defendant.[48]

An appeal to the Court of Appeal failed on the same grounds as held by the court of first instance. The Court of Appeal held, following the decision of the European Court of Justice in *Yordanova v. Bulgaria*[49] that 'Article 8 does not impose on contracting States an obligation to tolerate unlawful land occupation indefinitely...' Consequently, the court's decision laid to rest the law in relation to application of Article 8 of the ECHR in the following words:

> ...the court must approach the claim made by a private landowners against a trespasser in a similar way to that adopted to claims of various sorts made by a local authority as set out in the cases to which [the court] have referred. Thus, the test is whether the eviction is a proportionate means of achieving a legitimate aim. The fact that the landowner has a legal right to possession is a very strong factor in support of proportionality: it speaks for itself and needs no further explanation or justification. Thus, even if the defendants have established a home on the land but where they

---

[48] ibid, para 85.

[49] Application No. 25446/06 dated 24th April 2012.

> have otherwise no legal right to remain there, it is difficult to imagine circumstances which would give the defendant an unlimited and unconditional right to remain. The circumstances would have to be exceptional.[50]

It is therefore clear from the standpoint of judicial authorities that English law would uphold and protect the property right of a land owner whether as individual or as local authority under Article 1 Protocol 1 of the ECHR as against the occupation of a trespasser, and this property right of the land owner is a strong factor in support of proportionality required for eviction of the trespasser and defeats his defence under Article 8. This position holds in England and Wales.

9.6 The Doctrine of Adverse Possession and Squatters' Right

Paradoxically, English law recognises adverse possession and therefore takes cognisance of the right of a squatter in adverse possession of land exercised openly without the use of force or violence against the real owner, and without the consent of the owner.[51] Consequently, adverse possession by a squatter beyond the period of time prescribed by the English Statute of Limitation 1980[52] extinguishes the title of the real owner and vests fee simple absolute in the squatter[53] – a title which may be registered under the English Land Registration Act 2002,[54] subject to the fulfilment of certain conditions.[55] Whatever judicial[56] comments there may

---

[50] ibid, para 28.

[51] For the full requirements of the application of the doctrine of adverse possession in English law, see the House of Lords decision in *Pye (Oxford) Ltd v. Graham* [2003] 1 AC 419 HL.

[52] Limitation act 1980, Schedule 1 para 8:1.

[53] See *Asher v. Whitlock* (1865) LR QB 1; *Re Atkinson and Horsell's Contract* [1912] 2 Ch 1 (CA) 9; *Marylebone Property Co. v. Fairweather* [1962] 1 QB 498 (CA) at 513.

[54] Land Registration Act 2002, Schedule 6 para 1.

[55] ibid.

be against the regime of adverse possession in English law, the doctrine has remained an indelible feature of the English land use policy,[57] and the law is settled that the doctrine of adverse possession is not open to human rights challenge.[58]

However, beyond the recognition of adverse possession and despite incessant protests of squatters against the devastating effect of homelessness, government's attitude to squatting and squatters remains negative. Public disapproval of squatting was fuelled not only by successful cases of adverse possession in court, but also by "their perceived proclivities as a social group."[59] In particular, media reports associated squatters with the "popular mythology…that all squatters are parasitic deviants who steal people's houses and constitute a threat to everything decent in society."[60] The position of government was encapsulated in the declaration of the Home Office that:

> There are no valid arguments in defence of squatting. It represents the seizure of another's property without consent…The Government does not accept the claim that is sometimes made that squatting is a reasonable recourse of the homeless resulting from social deprivation. Squatters are generally there by no more than

---

[56] See e.g. Neuberger J. in *Pye (Oxford) Ltd v. Graham* [2000] Ch 676 and Bingham and Hope LJJ in the House of Lords [2003] 1 AC 419.

[57] See the decision of the Grand Chamber of the European Court of Justice in *Pye (Oxford) Ltd & Anor v. The United Kingdom* [2005] 3 EGLR 1 para 75.

[58] See e.g. the English Court of Appeal in *Pye (Oxford) Ltd v. Graham* [2001] Ch 804 para 52; *Family Housing Association v. Donnellan* [2002] 1 P&CR 449; *Ofulue & Anor v. Bossert* (2009) HL 11.

[59] N. Cobb and Fox, L (2007) 'Living outside the System? The (im)morality of urban squatting after the Land Registration Act 2002.'Legal Studies 27(2) 1 at 19.

[60] N. Anning et al. *Squatting: The real story*N. Wates &C. Wolmar ed. at 3 (London Bay Leaf Books, 1980) . Also available online at www.en.squat.net/wp-content/uploads/en/2013/01/wates-wolmar-squatting-real-story.pdf

self gratification or an un-readiness to respect other people's rights.[61]

The defence of some commentators and squatters to the negative responses of government generally bordered on the defence of necessity pointing at the socio-economic injustices in the housing market as justification for squatting.[62] This defence has not worked however, as the courts refused to be sympathetic to the cause of squatters on this ground. The Court of Appeal in *Southwark London Borough Council v. Williams*[63]held that necessity was no defence to trespass by homeless people squatting in empty council house during acute shortage of housing in London in the 1970s.

Parliament responded by enacting the Criminal Law Act, 1977 which makes it an offence under section 7 for a trespasser to refuse to leave residential premises on being required to do so by or on behalf of a 'displaced residential occupier' or a 'protected intending occupier'.[64] Also, the Criminal Justice and Public Order Act 1994 ''enhanced police powers under the Criminal Law Act 1977 by criminalising squatters who displace the occupiers of residential properties from their homes.''[65] Judicial reluctance to support squatting was manifested in many ways through judicial creativity meant to defeat squatter's claim to adverse possession.[66]

The early years of the 21st century in the United Kingdom have witnessed a resurgence of the socio-economic pre-conditions for urban squatting generated by ''spirally housing costs'' and high incidence of

---

[61] Home Office, Squatting: a Home Office Consultation paper (London: HMSO, 1991), paras 5 and 62.

[62] N. Cobb and Fox L, supra (n 59) at 20.

[63] [1971] 1 Ch 734.

[64] This provision enabled property owners made homeless as a result of squatters' occupation of their properties to lodge complaints to the Police.

[65] N. Cobb and Fox, L.supra (n 59) at 20.

[66] ibid. For examples of judicial creativity in this regard, see *Leigh v. Jack* (1879) 5 Ex D 264 (CA); *Wallis's Holiday Camp v. Shell-Max* [1975] 1 QB 94 (CA); *Beaulane Properties Limited v. Palmer* [2005] EWHC 817.

empty homes across the country.[67]The resulting high rate of squatting raised public concerns especially against the backdrop of the difficulty encountered by owners of residential property in securing the assistance of the police in evicting squatters there from.

Government responded in July 2011 by issuing a consultation paper[68] to criminalise squatting in cases of residential accommodation. In its Response to Consultation, Government through its Parliamentary Under–Secretary of State for Justice, explained the basis for its proposal to introduce the criminal offence of squatting in residential premises. Explaining its proposal to introduce what consequently became section 144 of the Legal Aid, Sentencing and Punishment of Offenders Act 2012 (LASPOA), Government notes the physical and financial distress caused to victims of squatting including "private homeowners who could not move into properties that had been occupied, local authorities who have been unable to refurbish social houses to make them available for priority categories, [and] landlords who had been unable to let their property," It also notes disruption to normal business activity resulting in aggravated damage and huge cost of repairs as a result of squatting.[69]

Whilst Government recognises the availability of civil remedies to landowners and occupiers under Part 55 of the Civil Procedure rules, it appreciates the inadequacy of this remedy and the urgent need for intervention of the criminal law, to offer a greater degree of protection to victims.[70]

---

[67] N. Cobb and Fox, L. (n 59) at 21. It is said that average house prices in England and Wales rose by almost 12% from 2003-2004, following a rise of 16% from 2002 to 2003; and statistics published by the office of Deputy Prime Minister revealed that 3.8 million new households will be in need of accommodation by 2016: See Social Trends 36, (London: Office for National Statistics, 2006 at 158; Statistics from *Housing Statistics: Projections of Households in England 2021* (London: DETR, 1999. It is also said that properties lying empty are available to accommodate about 600,000 new homes: See Social Trends 36, supra.

[68] *Options for Dealing with Squatting* (Consultation Paper CP12/2011).

[69] ibid.

[70] ibid.

The first step taken in this regard by Government deals with squatting in residential properties; a step necessitated by the urgent need to protect the landowners' home. Consequently, the Legal Aid Sentencing and Punishment of Offenders Act (LASPOA) passed by Parliament entered into force on September 1, 2012. The provision of section 144 of the Legal Aid, Sentencing and Punishment of Offenders Act (LASPOA) criminalises squatting in residential buildings.[71] A person commits this offence where he "is in residential building as a trespasser" and having entered as such, "knows or ought to know that conduct amounts to trespassing and "is living in the building or intends to live there for any period."

Section 144 of LASPOA "does not criminalise all residential squatting;"[72] the squatter must have entered into the premises as a trespasser for the purposes of living there. The offence is not committed by a person who was a licensee or tenant upon initial entry and who subsequently holds over.[73] The trespass must have been committed in a "residential building" and not on bare land; and the said squatter must be living in the residential building or "intends to live there for any period."[74]

The effect of section 144 of LASPOA is the limitation of the application of the doctrine of adverse possession under English law in the case of squatting by living in a residential building or intending to live in it for any period of time. It is an extension of the offence of criminal trespass to adverse possession under English law such that a squatter in

---

[71] This Law does not exempt persons already squatting on that date. According to literature premised on official records, "[t]he first person was arrested on 2nd September 2012, convicted, and sentenced to 12 weeks imprisonment," and "[u]p to September 2013, in the London Metropolitan Police area, 247 people had been arrested, 112 charged, 101 convicted and 22 imprisoned." See M. Dixon, "Criminal Squatting and Adverse Possession: The Best Solution?" (2014) Journal of Housing Law vol. 17 at 94. Available online at www.repository.cam.ac.uk/handle/1810/246191.

[72] M. Dixon, supra (n 71) at 94.

[73] LASPOA 2012, s. 144(1)(a).

[74] ibid, s.144(1)(c).

adverse possession of a residential building with the requisite intention of living in it, commits an offence without regard to social consequences such as homelessness, or government responsibility towards provision of housing for the homeless in accordance with international standards.

9.7 Proliferation of Informal Settlements and Forced Evictions in the Developing Countries

Although the strict application of the common law position against trespassers is tempered by the doctrine of adverse possession under the statute of limitations[75] in many common law countries, it paved way for human desperation for a place of abode. In the developed world, illegal occupation of vacant accommodation owned by the State or individuals became rampant and called for legislative intervention in the form of criminalisation of trespass such as in England and Wales.[76]

In many developing countries, there has been a proliferation of informal urban settlements over time resulting in state intervention through forcible evictions.[77] Such informal settlements are often justified

[75] The Limitation Act 1980 applicable in England and Wales for example, legitimises an illegal possession by the trespasser or squatter and extinguishes the title of the owner after twelve years (or twenty years in the case of state land) of uninterrupted possession without violence, devoid of secrecy and without permission of the owner. This concept applies in many common law jurisdictions, although period of limitation may vary.

[76] Parliament responded by enacting the Criminal Law Act 1977 section 7 of which makes it an offence for a trespasser to refuse to leave residential premises on being required to do so by or on behalf of a 'displaced residential occupier' or a 'protected intending occupier.' The Criminal Justice Public Order Act 1994 'enhanced Police powers under the Criminal Act 1977 by criminalising squatters who displace the occupiers of residential properties from their homes.'

[77] See United Nations Human Settlements Programme (UN Habitat) *Forced Eviction-Towards Solution?* (2005) Advisory Group on Forced Evictions; See also,*Nigeria: Deadly mass forced evictions made life misery for water front communities*: Report of Amnesty International.' (Nov 2017). Available online at https://www.amnesty.org/en/latestnews/2017/11/nigeria-deadly-mass-forced-

based on necessity arising from lack of affordable private accommodation and access to land, and failure of the state to provide affordable housing. The development control in these countries is significantly discriminatory and anti-poor.[78] Unlike the situation in many developed countries where development control is seen 'as the tool for assisting lawful development to take place at the right time and in the right place,' it is seen in the developing countries as the 'weapon to attack and demolish development that has occurred in the wrong place'[79] and therefore considered unlawful.

Amongst the various factors responsible for forced eviction of squatters is the idea that squatters without formal titles are trespassing on vested or acquired state land and obstructing an orderly and progressive development by the state or the private sector.[80] Planning laws and regulations allow government to remove illegal structures and there cannot be compensation for the commission of a wrong or for 'taking back' property over which the squatter has no title. Consequently, incessant forced evictions were carried out without compensation or provision of alternative shelter.[81] Many evictions resulted in absolute destruction of property, rendering evictees homeless and inflicting physical injury, mental torture and emotional distress.[82] Deaths were recorded in certain cases involving high handedness of the state apparatus.[83]

---

evictions-make-life-misery. Accessed Nov 19, 2020. Also 'Nigeria: Left with nowhere to go: Stories of Survivors of forced evictions in Nigeria's megacity. Report of Amnesty International (9 Nov. 2018). Available online at http://www.amnesty.org/en/documents/afr44/9290/2018/en/. Accessed Nov 19 2020.

[78] Report of Amnesty International, supra (n 77).

[79] ibid.

[80] ibid.

[81] ibid.

[82] ibid.

[83] ibid.

Incidentally forced evictions often result in gross violation of basic human rights guaranteed under domestic and international law and run counter to the idea of social function of property as earlier discussed.[84]

9.8. The Movement from the Trespass Paradigm to the Human Rights Paradigm

The treatment of squatters as trespassers at common law justifies the need for forced eviction without consequences and without regard to the right of the evictee to life, to the dignity of his/her person, to private and family life and to freedom from discrimination.[85] It is a fallout from the classical theory of absoluteness of property right.[86]

However, this attitude of the common law is not in line with the resonating global idea that the right to housing cannot be viewed in isolation from other human rights such as the rights to life, to respect for private and family life, and to property - rights which have gained popular approval of the international community.[87]While the right to

[84] See n 77 above.

[85] For example, the United Nations' Special Rapporteur on housing noted that 'the right to life cannot be separated from the right to a secure place to live, and the right to a secure place to live only has meaning in the context of a right to live in dignity and security, free of violence.': See UN Special Rapporteur on adequate housing (2016), 'Adequate housing as a component of the right to an adequate standard of living.' available at http://ap.ohchr.org/documents/dpage_e.aspx?si=A/71/310 [accessed 27 November 2020.

[86] For the theoretical basis of the absoluteness of property right, see Pollock, Jurisprudence and Legal Essays, London 1961. See also Tobi JCA (as he then was) in the Nigerian case of *Abraham v. Olorunfunmi* (1990) 1 NWLR (Pt 165) 53. This absoluteness of property right has been criticised as failing the relativity test in determining its functional utility. In the words of Smith, '...the rights conferred by [absolute] ownership of land have been eroded both at common law and by an increasing regime of statutory provisions...': See IO Smith, supra (n 5) at 43.

[87] See A. Kucs et al, 'The Right to Housing: International, European and National Perspectives.' University of Latvia Riga 101 available online at www.corteidh.or.cr accessed on 25 November 2020; P. Kenna, 'Globalization and Housing Rights.' Indiana Journal of Global Legal Studies, vol. 15, No.2 (2008) 436.

housing has not been incorporated into English law and thereby depriving the English and the Welsh the locus to bring an action in court against the government for violation of the right, it is said that such right cannot be taken in isolation from other related rights.[88] Consequently, 'in assessing whether public authorities have violated the right to housing, their actions or lack of actions to protect related rights under the…law will have to be considered by the courts.'[89] It is also said that while it is the duty of government and public bodies generally to protect peoples' right to housing and guarantee their access to justice, it is also incumbent on private landlords and management companies to respect those rights.[90]

In many jurisdictions where constitutional regimes prevail to balance the right of property against the state obligation to make housing provision for the homeless, forcible eviction is discouraged. At alllevels of state engagement therefore, the state's duty towards the land owner has to be reconciled with the state's international obligation and/or constitutional duty towards the homeless. In this regard, the domestic jurisprudence of South Africa and Nigeria provide the requisite window for appreciating the legal protection of squatters.`

9.8.1 The Constitution of the Republic of South Africa 1996

Whilst protecting private right to property within the human rights regime of the Constitution of the Republic of South Africa 1996,[91] section 26 of the Constitution addresses the issue of forceful eviction against the backdrop of the right to adequate housing. It provides:

(1) Everyone has the right to have access to adequate housing

---

[88] Kucs et al, (n 87) at 4-5.

[89] ibid, at 5.

[90] See UN Guiding Principles on Business and Human Rights, Pillar 2, available at https//www.ohchr.org/Documents/Publications/GuidingPrinciplesBusinessHR_EN.pdf accessed on 25 November 2020.

[91] ibid, s. 25.

(2) The state must take reasonable legislative and other measures within its available resources to achieve the progressive realisation of this right.

(3) No one may be evicted from their home or have their home demolished without an order of court made after considering all the relevant circumstances. No legislation may permit arbitrary evictions.

These provisions guarantee access to adequate housing, and prohibit arbitrary evictions, and consequently provide a platform for the enactment and application of the *Prevention of Illegal Eviction from and Unlawful Occupation of Land Act*[92] which makes evictions subject to the requirements of justice and equity and conducted with due process in a fair and equitable manner.

The ensuing conflict between the right to property guaranteed by section 25 of the Constitution and the squatter's right to housing is best illustrated by two decisions of the South African constitutional court. In *Port Elizabeth Municipality v. Various Occupiers,*[93] the Municipality, in response to a neighbourhood petition against 68 adults and children occupying shacks erected on privately owned land, filed an eviction application. The squatters who had been living on this undeveloped land for upward of eight years were willing to vacate the property subject to reasonable notice and suitable alternative land. The High Court granted the eviction order, but on appeal, the Supreme Court of Appeal (SCA)

---

[92] Act No.19, 1998. This Act followed the repeal of the Prevention of Illegal Squatting Act 52, 1951 (PISA) and the Group Areas Act 36 1966 – Apartheid legislation giving landowners the absolute entitlement to evict squatters and thus enabling both the state and the white land owners to take effective control of land and bolster possession by the exercise of regular evictions. In the words of Walt, ' PISA promoted apartheid by granting extensive and arbitrary powers of eviction to state organs and the police…it also obliged white land owners to evict 'unlawful squatters' from their land and provided…with wide-ranging powers for that purpose.' See A.V.Walt, *Property in the Margins* (Portland: Hart Publishing 2009), at 63

[93] 2004 (12) BCLR 1268 (CC).

held that the eviction order should not be granted without an assurance that the occupiers would have some measure of security of tenure. On appeal to the constitutional court, it was held that considering the lengthy period during which the occupiers have lived on the land and that eviction was not necessary for the land to be put to productive use, the Municipality's failure to consider the housing challenges of these occupiers who were homeless and in need, makes it unjust and inequitable to order the eviction.

The ratio of this case was applied by the SCA in the *Modderklip case.*[94] In that case, SCA reasoned that '[t]he state's constitutional duty towards the land owner has to be reconciled with the state's constitutional duty towards the homeless.'[95] The development of squatter's right as human right is a turning point in the evolution of human rights to housing as enshrined in a number of international instruments globally,[96] but it is yet to be accorded recognition under English law.

9.8.2 Homelessness and Squatters' Right in Nigeria

Guarantee of the right to respect for private and family life of the citizen[97], and general prohibition of compulsory acquisition of private property[98] are specific human rights provisions in the Constitution of the Federal

---

[94] *Modder East Squatters v. Modderklip Boerdery (Pty) Ltd; President of the Republic of South Africa v. Modderklip Boerdery (Pty) Ltd* 2004 (8) BCLR 821 (SCA).

[95] AJ Walt, 'The State duty to protect property owners v. The State's duty to provide housing: Thoughts on the Modderklip case.' (2005) 21 SAJHR 144 at 150.It is noteworthy however, that although the constitutional court in this case arrived at the same conclusion as the SCA to the extent that the state had certain obligations to protect fundamental rights arising from the constitution, it did not embark on resolving the conflict between sections 25 and 26 of the constitution.

[96] See International Covenant on Civil and Political Rights (ICCPR), Art. 6 with a corresponding provision on Right to adequate standard of living including Housing as contained in the International Covenant on Social, Cultural and Economic Rights (ICSCER), Art. 11.

[97] The Nigerian Constitution 1999, s. 37.

[98] ibid, s. 44 subject to a number of exceptions.

Republic of Nigeria 1999 (the Nigerian Constitution) as amended, and the African Charter on Human and Peoples' Rights[99] (ACHPR). This is in addition to certain international instruments on the right to housing to which Nigeria is a signatory,[100] albeit non-domesticated.[101]

Whilst the right to housing is a socio-economic right which is non-justiciable under the Nigerian Constitution,[102] the idea that Section 22 of the African Charter on Human and Peoples' Rights (ACHPR) imposes obligations on member states to provide for socio-economic rights and also vests in the courts the power to ensure state compliance with the Charter, give comfort to the application of the right as human right. This is confirmed by Article 9(4) of the ECOWAS Supplementary Protocol which provides that states have a duty to honour any human rights treaty entered into, and incorporated as part of municipal law. Consequently, the domestication of the ACHPR appears to have filled the gap created by the non-justiciability of socio-economic rights under Chapter 2 of the Nigerian Constitution. This reasoning is corroborated by the African Commission Recommendations given in *Social and Economic Rights Action Centre (SERAC) and Centre for Economic and Social Rights (CESR) v. Nigeria*[103] that forcible eviction by Nigeria was a violation of the African Charter.

Since forced evictions are carried out without notice to, or consultation with the communities, and accomplished with 'inadequate or no compensation and/or resettlement resulting in homelessness or further

---

[99] Cap A9 Laws of the Federation of Nigeria, 2010, ss. 14, 18.

[100] See amongst other international instruments, Art 25 of the Universal Declaration of Human Rights (UDHR) 1948; Art 11 of the International Covenant on Economic, Social and Cultural Rights (ICESCR) 1966; Art 14(2) of the United Nations Covenant on the Elimination of All Forms of Discrimination Against Women (CEDAW) 1979; Art 27 of the Convention on the Rights of the Child, 1989 – to mention a few.

[101] An international treaty does not apply in Nigeria unless such treaty is domesticated as part of Nigerian Law by an Act of the National Assembly: See the Constitution of the Federal Republic of Nigeria 1999 (as amended), s. 12(1).

[102] ibid s. 16(2)(d) read along with s. 6(6) (c).

[103] Communication 155/96 para 63.

impoverishment' of the evictees, they constitute serious infraction of basic human rights. Such evictions violate the provisions of the Nigerian constitution and the African Charter on Human and Peoples' Rights on the right to housing and shelter, equal treatment by the law, the right to property and freedom from discrimination.[104] Forced evictions also violate a number of international conventions[105] and contradict the United Nations Basic Principles and Guidelines on Development based Evictions and Displacements, 2007.

In carrying out these evictions, no regard is given to any claim of right on the land based on adverse possession beyond the limitation period. Surprisingly, the High Court of the Federal Capital Territory, in erroneously holding the right to housing unenforceable in Nigeria,[106] held that:

> ...even if the people of Tudun Wada had an enforceable fundamental human right to property under chapter 4 of the constitution, they had failed to prove that they had legally acquired their land and homes in Tudun Wada with the approval of the FCDA...[and] merely *possessing the land in Tudun Wada for over twenty years* [as prescribed by the limitation statute] *did not entitle them to the land...'* [107]

[104] See the Constitution of the Federal Republic of Nigeria 199 (as amended) ss. 16 (2)(d) (interpreted in line with the African Charter), 42, 43, 44 and the ACHPR Cap 10 LFN 2004, Art. 3, 14, 19, 28.

[105] See the International Covenant on Economic, Social and Cultural Rights (ICECSR) Art 11(1); Convention on the Rights of Persons with Disabilities (CRPD) Art 28 (1); Convention on the Elimination of All Forms of Discrimination against women (CEDAW) Art 12(2)(h); Convention on the rights of the Child (CRC) Art 27(3); and the International Convention on the Elimination of All Forms of Racial Discrimination (CERD) Art 5(e)(iii).

[106] See *Residents of Tundun Wada Community v. FCT Minister & Anor* (Citation unavailable but case cited and discussed by IHRDA online at www.ihrda.org/2011/03/tundun-wada-high-court-decision-mar2011/

[107] Supra (n 106).

The reasoning of the court in that case not only runs counter to the African Commission's recommendations given previously in *Social and Economic Rights Action Centre (SERAC) and Centre for Economic and Social Rights (CESR) v. Nigeria*[108] that forcible eviction by Nigeria was a violation of the African Charter, latest judicial decision has concluded that forced eviction is unconstitutional. For example, in a more recent decision of the High Court of Lagos State in *Akakpo Agemo & Ors v. Attorney General of Lagos State & Ors*,[109] the court held that:

> …the eviction/threat of forcible eviction of any citizen from his home at short notice and without any immediate alternative accommodation or sufficient opportunity to arrange for such alternative accommodation before being evicted from his current abode [is] totally undignifying and certainly inhuman, cruel and degrading.

It is said that '[t]his ruling is in line with international human rights law established by the UN Committee against Torture, the UN Human Rights Committee, and the European Court of Human Rights, among others.'[110]

9.9 Regularisation and Integration of Informal Settlements: Lessons from Latin America

Informal settlements are generally characterised by lack of formal legal titles and 'may exhibit irregular development patterns' with 'lack of essential public services such as sanitation, and occur on environmentally vulnerable or public land.'[111] The development may be sporadic or progressive depending on the level of homelessness within the locality.

---

[108] Communication 155/96 para 63.

[109] Suit No. LD/4232MFHR/16.

[110] Joint Public statement of Amnesty International, Justice and Empowerment Initiatives and Nigerian Slum/Informal Settlement Federation of 3 February 2017 (AI Index: AFR 44/5618/2017.

[111] E. Fernandes, 'Regularisation of Informal Settlements in Latin America: Policy Focus Report (2011) Lincoln Institute of Land Policy available online at

The idea of regularisation and integration of informal settlements is the focus of many Latin American countries following the global trend against forceful evictions. It resonates the human rights agenda in the area of housing and reflects the theory of the social context of property in modern times. The pace setters in this regard are Peru and Brazil.

Influenced by the idea of Peruvian economist Hernado de Soto,[112] Peru undertook a 'narrow legalisation of tenure through titling,'[113] and over a period of ten years, it issued a total of 1.6 million freehold titles at an average of $64 per household without charging fees to the households.[114] The success of this land titling process has influenced other countries such as El-Salvador, Cambodia and Vietnam in their regularisation of informal settlements with positive but modest impact on access to credit and investment, while exhibiting great potentials in poverty reduction.[115]

The Brazilian approach is an all-inclusive integration of the various communities into the socio-economic opportunities and benefits of the formal settlements of the urban centres. It is said that while 'titling per se provides legal security of tenure to the residents…it is not sufficient to promote socio-spatial integration and may undermine the permanence of the legalised communities.'[116] The process of integration therefore 'involves the right of all to live in dignified conditions and to participate fairly in the opportunities and benefits created by urban development.'[117] Consequently, there were improved infrastructure and enhancement of

---

www.lincolninst.edu/sites/default/files/pubfiles/regularisation-of-informal-settlements-in-latin-america-full_0.pdf at 2, accessed on 16th January 2021.

[112] E. Fernandes, 'The Influence of de Soto's *The Mystery of Capital.* Available online at www.lincolninst.edu/publications/articles/influence-sotos-mystery-capital, accessed on 16/1/21.

[113] E. Fernandes, supra (n 111) at 5.

[114] ibid at 35.

[115] ibid.

[116] ibid.

[117] ibid, at 31.

the living environment at a cost of between $3,500 to $5000 per household although without charging fees to the households.

Whilst the regularisation and integration processes have not been full-proof,[118] both provide a veritable panacea to the problem of homelessness from the human rights perspective and fulfil the reasonable expectation of the individual right to decent accommodation. The models represent a departure from the common law notion of trespass with the attendant painful consequence of eviction at short notice and without provision of alternative accommodation. The two models embrace instead, the global standard engendered by respect for the right to decent accommodation and the assurance of a home.

9.10 Conclusion

The concept of 'property right' in the globalised world goes beyond the narrow confines of the common law of trespass and the absoluteness or exclusivity of property right. 'Property' essentially serves a social function and the broad lesson taught by regulatory instruments at the local and international levels and the resonating judicial activism is the need to strike a balance between the individual ownership right on the one hand and the protection of the inalienable human rights of occupiers towards attainment of the common good, on the other hand. This social function is assured by a number of international instruments and fulfilled within the constitutional regime of many countries.

The movement from the common law trespass to the human right concept of productive land use, protection of basic rights of occupiers and accommodation of informal settlements within the threshold of social realities, is a unique illustration of the dynamics of the concept of

[118] The two models have been criticised. Among other criticisms, both are said to encourage proliferation of informal settlements hoping for government regularisation of titles or upgrading of the living standards of residents. Abuse by land speculators and developers hoping to make huge profits from purchase of large expanse of land off residents at rock-bottom prices, is another pitfall identified: See E. Fernandes, supra (n 111) at 35-37.

property in the globalised world. It evinces a functional approach to land holding and land use, and engenders economic growth and development in the overall interests of modern societies. Whilst promoting land re-distribution on collective social grounds, it enhances the fulfilment of basic human rights and in turn, the discharge of State obligations in upholding these rights.

CHAPTER 10
CRIMINALISATION OF UNLAWFUL OCCUPATION WITHIN THE REGIME OF ADVERSE POSSESSION.

10.1 Introduction

There is ample evidence in literature[1] to suggest that criminalisation of human conduct should take cognisance of societal moral and cultural values, and reflect the aspirations of the community in which it operates. In particular, the social construct inherent in land use, control and titling in contemporary societies determines the criminalisation process regarding same.[2] In the Consultative Document and Report issued jointly

---

[1] See e.g.C.K Allen, Law in the Making, 6th ed. Oxford Paperback, (1961) at 336; M. Ginsberg, *On Justice in Society* (1965) at 218, 236, 237; H. Demsetz, Toward a Theory of Property Rights, in The Economics of Property Rights 31 (Eirik G. Furubotn & Svetozar Pejovich eds. 1974; A.A. Adeyemi, "The Criminal Process as a Selection Instrument for the Administration of Criminal Justice." *Nigerian Criminal Process*, A.A Adeyemi ed. (1977) 26 at 30-32, 48-51.

[2] For example, one of the objectives of the Nigerian Land Use Act1978 is to forestall acquisition of possession through violence, a factor underlying the criminalisation of false claims to land: See Land Use Act 1978, Cap L5 Laws of the Federation of Nigeria 2004, s.37. Also in the U.K, forceful entry into vacant houses by trespassers resulted in the enactment of the Criminal Act 1977, section 7 of which provides that "it is an offencefor a trespasser to refuse to leave residential premises on being required to do so by or on behalf of a 'displaced residential occupier' or a 'protected intending occupier.' Also, the Criminal Justice and Public Order Act 1994 "enhanced police powers under the Criminal Law Act 1977 by criminalising squatters who displace the occupiers of residential properties from their homes.

by the Law Commission of England and Wales and the Land Registry,[3] land is described as "a valuable commodity...[which] provides space for homes, offices and agriculture...[and] in addition to that, land can be used to raise money to create new businesses and help the economy,"[4] hence there is the need to protect land rights and secure tenure in land against encroachments and illegal occupations. However, social circumstances may breed social necessities resulting in squatting.

Squatting is a social phenomenon necessitated by geometrical increase in population and shortage of housing in many societies.[5] These social circumstances became aggravated as a result of incessant industrialisation and the agrarian revolution of the 18th and 19th centuries. The evolvement of the utilitarian concept of property[6] and the old Labour theory[7] gave impetus to the development of economic importance of private property and necessitated the development of the doctrine of adverse possession as a social policy of the State.

The rapid development of urbanisation resulted in mass rural-urban movement with the associated rise in the cost of accommodation, and the need for legislative intervention to address social challenges brought about by the imbalances between population explosion and the

---

[3] *Land Registration for the Twenty-first Century: A Consultative Document* (Law Com. No. 254) and the subsequent Report, *Land Registration for the Twenty-first Century: A Conveyancing Revolution* (Law Com. 271).

[4] ibid.

[5] In the words of Abrams, "Human history has been an endless struggle for control of the earth surface; and conquest, or the acquisition of property by force has been one of its more ruthless expedients. With the surge of population from the rural lands to the cities, a new type of conquest has been manifesting itself in the cities of the developing world. Its form is squatting, and it is evidencing itself in the forcible pre-emption of land by the landless and homeless people in search of a haven." C. Abrams, *Man's Struggle for Shelter in an Urbanizing World* 12 (1964), *reprinted* in C.J Berger, *Land Ownership and Use* (3rd ed. 1983) 513.

[6] See Chapter 3 ante.

[7] ibid.

limited accommodation available.[8] The proliferation of abandoned public properties in some jurisdictions[9] provided justification for social movements in support of squatting as a socio-economic necessity,[10] and called for legislative and judicial intervention.[11]

In the midst of the prominent social malaise caused by squatting and trespass to abandoned properties, there was the need to protect the right of property owners and secure their tenure. This has been achieved to a large extent by legislative intervention through the instrumentality of title registration as in the United Kingdom[12] and to some extent, in Nigeria,[13] and by streamlining the mode of landholding, as in Nigeria.[14] However, in the case of title registration, there are loose ends enabling the squatter to retain possession due either to the operation of laches and acquiescence to his advantage,[15] or as a result of the skillful conduct of the

---

[8] See generally, Taher et. al, "Transformation of Slum and Squatter Settlements: A way of sustainable living in the context of 21st Century Cities." American Journal of Civil Engineering and Architecture 2.2 (2014), 70-76.

[9] For example, the Department of the Environment in the U.K reported that in 1995, there were an estimated 864,000 empty homes in Britain, out of which 17,000 were reported by the 'Advisory Services for Squatters,' to contain squatters: See I. Hunter, *Streetwise Moves to Outsmart Squatters*, Guardian (London) March 26, 1995, available in 1995WL 7590927.

[10] It is said that following World War II, there was a massive squatting movement in London after the government promised "homes for heroes" but housing was lacking: G. Neale, 50 years on a Squat Fit for Heroes, Sunday Telegraph (London) April 28, 1996.

[11] See for example, Criminal Justice and Public Order Act 1994; *R v. London Borough of Ealing Ex Parte Denny*, CO/390/93 (Q.B. 1993).

[12] See the Land Registration Act 2002.

[13] See the Lagos State Land Registration Law 2015.

[14] See Land Use Act Cap L5 Laws of the Federation of Nigeria 2010, ss. 1, 5, 6, 12, 14, 21, 22, 28, 29.

[15] See for example, LRA 2002, Schedule 6 paras 4, 6.

squatter in holding on to possession outside the registration regime by refraining from applying for registration.[16]

The intervention of the human rights regime locally and at the international level[17] was an attempt to rationalise the legal protection of the right to property against the requirement of land use and control in the larger public interest. As found in the last chapter, the application of the doctrine of adverse possession may not necessarily be a violation of the right to property, and the assurance of efficacy of the doctrine holds as a potent instrument at the disposal of the squatter.

Whilst the legal regime of the tort of trespass brought about by forcible entry into land provides a civil remedy for encroachment or unlawful occupation of land by a squatter, adverse peaceable possession for a period of time stipulated by the statute of limitations, not only extinguishes the title of the real owner, it also makes lawful the initial entry of the squatter which was hitherto unlawful. However, the regime of adverse possession notwithstanding, the high wave of squatting (especially on residential premises) in the United Kingdom, and the nefarious activities of 'land grabbers' in many parts of Nigeria resulted in the criminalisation of acts of trespass in both jurisdictions.

Where the acts of adverse possession amount to an offence under an Act of Parliament, does this fact defeat the right of the adverse possessor in law? And where such an adverse possessor applies to the Lands Registry for registration as a proprietor premised on adverse possession, can the Land Registrar refuse the application for registration on the ground that title cannot be acquired by virtue of a criminal act? The incompatibility between the squatter's right in adverse possession and the criminalisation of the latter's acts of possession sought to be resolved through the legal principle enshrined in the legal maxim *ex turpi causa non*

---

[16] See M. Pawlowski and J. Brown, "Adverse Possession and the Transmissibility of Possessory Rights – The Dark side of Land Registration?" [2017] (2) Conv. 116-131. Also available online at www.http//research.aston.ac.uk at 14

[17] See Chapters 8 and 9 *ante.*

oritur actio has been the subject of purposive construction by the courts over the years.[18]

This Chapter examines the background to the criminalisation of unlawful occupation by squatters; the parameters of the Laws; and the effect of the Laws on the efficacy of the doctrine of adverse possession both in England and Nigeria.

10.2 Criminalisation of Residential Squatting in England and Wales

10.2.1 Background to the English Position

The geometrical rise in the world population has been responsible for scarcity and competition for vital resources including shelter and land.[19]

It is said that "no less than 150 million people or about 2% of the world population are homeless," while "about 1.6 billion (more than 20%) of the world population may lack adequate housing."[20]

The shortage of housing and the deplorable condition of the homeless in both developed and the least developed countries precipitated the establishment of right to housing as an international human right.[21] This has helped to douse the social stigma associated with

---

[18] The incompatibility theory alluded to in chapter 3 of this work is an attempt at resolution of this scenario.

[19] B. Gardiner, "Squatters Rights and Adverse Possession: A search for Equitable Application of Property Laws." [1997] Ind. International & Comparative Law Review, vol. 8:1, 119.

[20] J Chamie, "As Cities Grow so Do the Numbers of Homeless." July 13 2017 Yale University online at yaleglobal.yale.edu/content/cities-grow-so-do-numbers-homeless.

[21] See the Universal Declaration of Human Rights (Art. 25); the International Covenant on Economic, Social and Cultural Rights (Art. 11); the International Convention on the Elimination of All Forms of Racial Discrimination (Art. 5); the

squatting while dispelling the notion that "squatters are criminals."[22]Locally, the acquisition of title through adverse possession translated into a social policy in many jurisdictions across the globe, promoting efficient and economic use of land and "thereby serving important economic and social ends."[23]

In England and Wales, squatting became proliferated from the 1960s as a result of many vacant buildings at the time consequent upon hike in property taxes and urban renewal projects.[24] Social movements with political flavour rose to protest the devastating effect of homelessness and putting pressure on government to effect "changes in existing property policies."[25] But this went too far as "some squatters shifted from urban squatting to residential squatting," with squatters deliberately taking over the apartments of home owners on holidays.[26]

From the perspectives of the media and government, "urban squatting has typically been regarded as a serious social problem."[27] Public disapproval of squatting was fuelled not only by successful cases of adverse possession in court, but also by "their perceived proclivities as a social group."[28] In particular, media reports associated squatters with the "popular mythology...that all squatters are parasitic deviants who steal people's houses and constitute a threat to everything decent in society."[29] The position of government was encapsulated in the declaration of the Home Office that:

Convention on the Elimination of All Forms of Discrimination against Women (Art. 14); and the Convention on the Rights of the Child (Art. 27).

[22] R Sachar, *Working Paper on Promoting the Realisation of the Rights to adequate Housing,* at 4-11, U.N Doc. E/CN.4/sub.2/1992/15.

[23] B. Gardiner, supra (n 19) at 122.

[24] ibid, at 133.

[25] ibid.

[26] ibid.

[27] N. Wates & C. Wolmar, *Squatting: The Real Story* (London: Bay Leaf Books, 1980).

[28] N. Cobb and Fox, L (2007) 'Living outside the System? The (im)morality of urban squatting after the Land Registration Act 2002.'Legal Studies 27(2) 1 at 19.

[29] N. Wates & Wolmar, supra (n 27) at 3.

> "There are no valid arguments in defence of squatting. It represents the seizure of another's property without consent...The Government does not accept the claim that is sometimes made that squatting is a reasonable recourse of the homeless resulting from social deprivation. Squatters are generally there by no more than self gratification or an un-readiness to respect other people's rights."[30]

The defence of some commentators and squatters to the negative responses of government generally bordered on the defence of necessity pointing at the socio-economic injustices in the housing market as justification for squatting.[31] This defence has not worked however, as the courts refused to be sympathetic to the cause of squatters on this ground. The Court of Appeal in *Southwark London Borough Council v. Williams*[32] held that necessity was no defence to trespass by homeless people squatting in empty council house during acute shortage of housing in London in the 1970s.

Parliament responded by enacting the Criminal Law Act, 1977 which provides that: "the person who comes back from holiday may use or threaten to use violence to oust squatters found in his home; but the squatters will commit the offence [of threatening violence without lawful authority] if they retaliate."[33] In particular, it is an offence under section 7 of the Act for a trespasser to refuse to leave residential premises on being required to do so by or on behalf of a 'displaced residential occupier' or a 'protected intending occupier'.[34] Also, the Criminal Justice and Public Order Act 1994 "enhanced police powers under the Criminal Law Act 1977 by criminalising squatters who displace the occupiers of residential

---

[30] Home Office, Squatting: a Home Office Consultation paper (London: HMSO, 1991), paras 5 and 62.

[31] N. Cobb and Fox L, supra (n 28) at 20.

[32] [1971] 1 Ch 734.

[33] P. James, Introduction to English law 420 (12th ed. 1989) at 474.

[34] This provision enabled property owners made homeless as a result of squatters' occupation of their properties to lodge complaints to the Police.

properties from their homes."[35] Judicial reluctance to support squatting was manifested in many ways through judicial creativity meant to defeat squatter's claim to adverse possession.[36]

However, the legislative and judicial intervention notwithstanding, commercial squatting sprang up through agencies set up to "provide information on vacant properties,"[37] enabling squatters to engage in retail commercial property transactions for profit making.[38] Consequently, government "had to differentiate between the squatter who inhabits because of necessity and the squatter who simply is out for profit,"[39] allowing greater latitude for basic humanitarian reasons.[40] This policy was complemented by the possibility of a civil action in the courts "at considerable expense to the homeowner, and the enactment of criminal legislation aimed at checking the encroachment of squatters.

The early years of the 21st century in the U.K have witnessed a resurgence of the socio-economic preconditions for urban squatting generated by "spirally housing costs" and high incidence of empty homes across the country.[41] The resulting high rate of squatting raised public concerns especially against the backdrop of the difficulty encountered by

---

[35] N. Cobb and Fox, L.supra (n 28) at 20.

[36] ibid. For examples of judicial creativity in this regard, see *Leigh v. Jack* (1879) 5 Ex D 264 (CA); *Wallis's Holiday Camp v. Shell-Max* [1975] 1 QB 94 (CA); *Beaulane Properties Limited v. Palmer* [2005] EWHC 817.

[37] B. Gardiner, supra (n 19) at 133.

[38] ibid, at 134.

[39] ibid.

[40] ibid.

[41] N. Cobb and Fox, L, supra (n 28) at 21. It is said that average house prices in England and Wales rose by almost 12% from 2003-2004, following a rise of 16% from 2002 to 2003; and statistics published by the office of Deputy Prime Minister revealed that 3.8 million new households will be in need of accommodation by 2016: See Social Trends 36, (London: Office for National Statistics, 2006 at 158; Statistics from *Housing Statistics: Projections of Households in England 2021* (London: DETR, 1999). It is also said that properties lying empty are available to accommodate about 600,000 new homes: See Social Trends 36, supra.

owners of residential property in securing the assistance of the police in evicting squatters there from.

Government responded in July 2011 by issuing a consultation paper[42] to criminalise squatting in cases of residential accommodation. In its Response to Consultation, Government through its Parliamentary Under–Secretary of State for Justice, explained the basis for its proposal to introduce the criminal offence of squatting in residential premises as follows:[43]

> "Ministerial colleagues and I are very concerned about the harm that squatters can cause. I have been contacted time and time again by MPs and constituents about the appalling impact that squatting can have on their homes, businesses and local communities. This is not media hype. It does really happen; and when it does it can be highly stressful for the owner or lawful occupier of the property concerned. It is not only the cost and length of time it takes to evict squatters that angers property owners; it is also the cost of the cleaning and repair bill which follows eviction. While the property owner might literally be left picking up the pieces, the squatters have gone on their way, possibly to squat in someone else's property. I accept that the law already provides a degree of protection for both commercial and residential property owners as offences such as criminal damage and burglary may apply in certain circumstances. There is also an offence under section 7 of the Criminal Law Act 1977...But there are many residential property owners, including landlords, local authorities and second home owners who cannot be classified as 'displaced residential occupier' or a 'protected intending occupiers.' There are also many commercial property owners, whose businesses may be seriously affected by squatters, who report that they generally have to rely on civil procedures to get squatters to leave. Given the level of public

[42] *Options for Dealing with Squatting* (Consultation Paper CP12/2011).

[43] *Government Response to Consultation* published on 26 October 2011

concern about the issue, the Government has decided as a first step to introduce a new offence of squatting in residential buildings..."

Explaining its proposal to introduce what consequently became section 144 of the Legal Aid, Sentencing and Punishment of Offenders Act 2012 (LASPOA), Government notes the physical and financial distress caused to victims of squatting including "private homeowners who could not move into properties that had been occupied, local authorities who have been unable to refurbish social houses to make them available for priority categories, [and] landlords who had been unable to let their property," It also notes disruption to normal business activity resulting in aggravated damage and huge cost of repairs as a result of squatting.[44] Whilst Government recognises the availability of civil remedies to landowners and occupiers under Part 55 of the Civil Procedure rules, it appreciates the inadequacy of this remedy and the urgent need for intervention of the criminal law, to offer a greater degree of protection to victims.[45]

The first step taken in this regard by Government deals with squatting in residential properties; a step necessitated by the urgent need to protect the landowners' home. Consequently, the Legal Aid Sentencing and Punishment of Offenders Act (LASPOA) passed by Parliament entered into force on September 1, 2012.

10.2.2 Section 144 of the Legal Aid Sentencing and Punishment of Offenders Act 2012, U.K

The provision of section 144 of the Legal Aid, Sentencing and Punishment of Offenders Act (LASPOA) which came into force on September 1, 2012 criminalises squatting in residential buildings.[46] A person commits this

[44] ibid.

[45] ibid.

[46] This Law does not exempt persons already squatting on that date. According to literature premised on official records, "[t]he first person was arrested on 2nd September 2012, convicted, and sentenced to 12 weeks imprisonment," and "[u]p to September 2013, in the London Metropolitan Police area, 247 people had been

offence where he "is in residential building as a trespasser" and having entered as such, "knows or ought to know that conduct amounts to trespassing and "is living in the building or intends to live there for any period."

Section 144 "does not criminalise all residential squatting;"[47] the squatter must have entered into the premises as a trespasser for the purpose of living there. The offence is not committed by a person who was a licensee or tenant upon initial entry and who subsequently holds over.[48]

The trespass must have been committed in a "residential building" and not on bare land; and the said squatter must be living in the residential building or "intends to live there for any period."[49]

10.2.3 Section 144 of LASPOA and the Regime of Adverse Possession

While the provision of section 144 of LASPOA appears to be a straight translation of the government's policy on certain residential squatting into law (especially against the backdrop of the need to enhance the protection given to homeowners when faced with the social malaise of squatting), it does not resolve the apparent conflict with the law of adverse possession. For example, where a person who satisfies all the legal requirements of adverse possession commits a criminal offence under the provision of section 144 of LASPOA in the course of being in possession, does this provision of the law prevent the acquisition of title by adverse possession? In the case of registered land, can such squatter who has committed a criminal offence apply to be registered as a proprietor under

arrested, 112 charged, 101 convicted and 22 imprisoned." See M. Dixon, "Criminal Squatting and Adverse Possession: The Best Solution? (2014) Journal of Housing Law vol. 17 at 94. Available online at https//www.repository.cam.ac.uk/handle/1810/246191.

[47] M. Dixon, supra (n 46) at 94.

[48] LASPOA 2012, s. 144(1)(a).

[49] ibid, s.144(1)(c).

Schedule 6 of the Land Registration Act (LRA) 2002? These questions are very pertinent in view of the deeply rooted old principle of *ex turpi causa non oritur actio* which states that "no court will lend its aid to a man who found his cause of action upon an immoral or illegal act."[50]

Section 144 of LASPOA does not expressly criminalise the act of taking adverse possession of a residential building, and it is said that that was not contemplated by Parliament,[51] and the comment of the Lands Registry as to the impact of the provision on adverse possession raised in response to the Government consultation[52] was practically ignored[53] as a result of this.

The difference between the provision of section 144 and the act of adverse possession lies in the fact that whereas an adverse possessor may be "in possession of property and build up a period of possession asserting his right against the whole world without *living or intending to live in the property*,"[54] an offence is committed under section 144 only where the squatter *actually enters into a residential building and lives in it or exhibit the intention to do so*. To constitute a crime, the squatting must take place in a residential building; squatting in the cartilage of a building such as the garden or garage, or securing possession of the residential building without going to live there is not a criminal offence, although it may, upon the fulfilment of conditions prescribed by law, amount to exclusive possession by the squatter.

However, while the distinction between adverse possession and the squatter occupation of property may appear clear cut, circumstances may arise where adverse possession may constitute an offence under section 144 of LASPOA from the following example:

---

[50] *Holman v. Johnson* [1775] 1 Cow at 341, 343 per Lord Mansfield CJ; *Tinsley v. Milligan* [1994] 1 AC 340, 376 per Lord Brown-Wilkinson.

[51] The Court of Appeal in *Best v. Chief Land Registrar and Secretary of State for Justice* [2015] EWCA Civ 17 at para 37.

[52] ibid, at paras 38, 41.

[53] ibid, para 72.

[54] ibid, para 77. For example, "erection and maintenance of a fence around a property might be sufficient to constitute taking possession."

> Suppose a squatter, has been in exclusive possession of a residential building with the intention to possess by way of adverse possession and remains in occupation for the requisite period of time which would entitle him to title over the property, does his criminal conduct preclude a claim in adverse possession in the case of unregistered land under sections 15 and 17 of the Limitation Act 1980, or registration of his interest in the property as a new proprietor of the property under paragraph 1 of Schedule 6 to the Land Registration Act 2002, in the case of registered land?

This question is pertinent in view of the law of illegality expressed in the old maxim: *ex turpi causa non oritur actio* (a claim cannot be founded on a wrong committed by the claimant).[55] What would be the attitude of the court to an infraction of this old maxim by an adverse possessor? Would such adverse possessor be allowed to benefit from a crime committed by him? How would the court resolve the issue of incompatibility between a claim in the civil law of adverse possession but amounting to a crime under the criminal law, as in section 144 of LASPOA?

In *Best v. Chief Land Registrar and Secretary of State for Justice*[56] *(Best),* the High Court was asked through an application for judicial review, to review the decision of the Chief Land Registrar cancelling the Application for registration by the Applicant on the ground that section 144 of LASPOA prevented a reliance on a period of adverse possession which involved the commission of an offence. In that case, Mr Best had, in 1997, taken possession of an empty semi detached house which he believed to be abandoned although it was actually registered in the name of one Mrs Curtis who had died. Whilst the said property had passed to Mrs Curtis' son upon her death, he did abandon possession and Mr Best moved in and undertook construction work with the intention of moving into possession. From 2001 onward, he had treated the house as his own and moved in towards end of January 2012. Section 144 of the LASPOA came into force in September of that year from which date Mr Best's

[55] See *Les Laboratoires Servier v. Apotex Inc* [2014]UKSC 55; [2014] 3 WLR 1257.
[56] [2015] EWCA Civ 17.

occupation became a criminal offence. Having met the requirement for registration under the LRA 2002, Mr Best applied to the Land Registry to be registered as a new proprietor, but his application was cancelled by the Chief Land Registrar (CLR) on the ground that the LASPOA prevented a reliance on a period of adverse possession which involved the commission of an offence. The decision of the CLR was informed by a decision of HHJ, Judge Pelling sitting as a High Court Judge in *R (on the application of Smith) v. Land Registry*[57]which indicated that an unlawful act (i.e. obstruction of the highway) could not support a claim to adverse possession of a highway. The CLR invoked rule 16(3) of the Land Registration Rules 2003 which provides that if an application seeking registration as a proprietor of land appears to the Registrar "to be substantially defective" he may reject it on delivery or cancel it at any time thereafter. Consequently, Mr Best's application for registration was rejected on the ground that it is "substantially defective" because it revealed that his claim to acquire title by adverse possession was premised on conduct in contravention of section 144 of LASPOA.

Mr Best brought an application for judicial review of the Registrar's decision to cancel his application for registration before the High Court. It was held that the claimant's application should be allowed on the basis that Parliament had not intended that adverse possession be prevented because it was based on a criminal trespass. The decision was upheld by the Court of Appeal. The court held that the effect on the enactment of section 144, and the commission of an offence under it have no material effect on the operation of the law of adverse possession.

In arriving at its decision in support of the lower court, the Court of Appeal was faced with a number of legal and policy issues. First, there was the argument that the claim of the applicant for registration should have failed on the ground that no court will lend its aid to a man who found his cause of action upon an immoral or illegal act. The basis for this argument was found in *R.(on the application of Smith) v. Land Registry*[58] a case concerning a rejection of an application by a squatter to be registered

[57] [2009] EWHC 328 (Admin).

[58] supra, n.54.

as owner of land forming a part of public highway on the grounds that it amounted to the criminal obstruction of the highway.[59] Although the decision was upheld on appeal on different grounds (that is, that a highway was incapable of adverse possession), it was argued that the case was meant to show that like *Best*, criminal activity was collateral to the acts of adverse possession that was relied upon by the claimant to qualify for registration, and could therefore not be divorced from his criminal conduct.[60] The Court of Appeal rejected this argument on the grounds that *R (Smith) v. Land Registry* on Appeal did not apply as a ratio, the principle that an unlawful act could not support a claim to adverse possession but was rather based on the fact that a highway was incapable of adverse possession. Instead, the court relied on *Bakewell Land Management Ltd v. Brandwood*[61]and *Hounga v. Allen*[62] that in some circumstances, an unlawful act was no bar to establishing a proprietary right; a principle endorsed by a long line of authorities.[63]

The attitude of the Court of Appeal to the application of the common law maxim, *ex turpi causa non oritur actio* is that of purposive interpretation depending on varying circumstances. Relying on a number of judicial authorities,[64] the court reasoned that the application of the *ex turpi causa* policy is based on various reasons as between different

---

[59] ibid, at para 14-15; section 137 Highway Act 1980.

[60] I. Okeoma, "The Future of Adverse Possession of Registered Land:In light of the recent decision of the court in Best v. Chief Land Registrar, does section 144 of the Legal Aid, Sentencing and Punishment of Offenders Act 2012 clarify the rationale for the operation of adverse possession in registered land under the new scheme or was Best wrongly decided?" Available online at https://www.academic.edu, at 14. Accessed on 5/5/2020.

[61] [2004] UKHL 14.

[62] [2014] UKSC 47; [2014] 1 WLR 2889.

[63] See among others, *Tinsley v. Milligan* [1994] 1 AC 340; *Gray v. Thames Trains Ltd* [2009] UKHL 33; *Stone & Rolls Ltd v. Moore Stephen* [2009] UKHL 39; *Les Laboratoires Servier v. Apotex Inc* [2014] UKSC 55.

[64] See e.g.*Bakewell Land Management Ltd v. Brandwood* supra (n 62); *Hounga v. Allen* supra (n 62); *Lewisham LBC v. Malcolm* [2008] UKHL 43.

situations and as between rules applicable in different contexts.[65] The court followed the "amalgamated approach" of balancing the policy considerations underlying the provisions of the LRA 2002 relating to acquisition of title by adverse possession against the public policy consideration underlying the provision of section 144 of LASPOA. On this, the court held that "preserving the way in which adverse possession operates outweighs the fact that criminal trespassers would be profiting from their wrongdoing, i.e. by adversely possessing another's land."[66] A strict application of the *ex turpi causa* policy may eventually do more harm than good in this case, "since priority would not be given to the public policy that serves the more useful purpose."[67]

The court reasoned that the mischief intended to be addressed and the objective to be met with section 144 "had nothing to do with the operation of the law of adverse possession."[68] The court found the main object of the section from its clear terms which "make no reference to adverse possession regimes for either registered land or unregistered land,"[69] and from the reasons stated by Government "for seeking its enactment in Parliament."[70] Section 144 was meant to "provide deterrence" to squatters while providing "assistance to homeowners in removing squatters from the property."[71] It was not meant to "re-balance the rights of property owners as against those of adverse possessors."[72]

Also, there is the argument that "trespass is an intrinsic factor in adverse possession,"[73] suggesting therefore that "the claimant necessarily has to commit the criminal offence that would later enable him to apply

---

[65] *Best v. Chief Land Registrar* [2015] EWCA Civ 17, para 52.

[66] I. Okeoma, (n 60) at 15.

[67] ibid.

[68] *Best v. Chief Land Registrar*, supra (n 56), para 70.

[69] ibid, para 73.

[70] *Best v. Chief Land Registrar*, supra (n 56) para 71. See para 40 for extract of these reasons.

[71] ibid, para 71.

[72] ibid.

[73] ibid.

for registration."[74] On this, Sales L.J reasoned that what was required in this case was the balancing of the public policies that underlie both the *ex turpi causa* test and that of acquisition of title by adverse possession in registered land.[75] Consequently there was the need to weigh the objectives both policies were aimed to serve[76] and in doing this, the court held that "preserving the way in which adverse possession operates outweighs the fact that criminal trespassers would be profiting from their wrongdoing, by adversely possessing another's land."[77] This approach was found reasonable in view of the fact that a mechanical application of the maxim could lead to "more harm being done than good since priority would not be given to the public policy that serves the more useful purpose.'[78]

The court further reasoned that Parliament could not have designed section 144 LASPOA "to have any impact on the doctrine of adverse possession in view of the public policy concerns underlying adverse possession in registered and especially unregistered land"[79]

It was also contended that the enactment of section 144 of LASPOA was due to the public concern over the challenge of securing police assistance in evicting squatters from occupied buildings.[80] The need for a more efficient way of combating incessant encroachments on property by squatters under the criminal law as opposed to the slow and dull prospect of deterrence of civil procedure was one of the bases for the response by Parliament through criminalisation of illegal occupation of residential accommodation, to protect homeowners. This reasoning is however flawed by the fact that the law before LASPOA had procedures in place to deal with squatters; the provision of section 144 of that Law "only adds more force to the argument that Parliament intended the

---

[74] Ikeoma, supra (n 60) at 14.

[75] ibid (n 71).
[76] ibid.
[77] ibid.
[78] Ibid, at 15.
[79] ibid.
[80] ibid.

provision of that section to go beyond the function of simply evicting squatters."[81]

Whilst the decision of the Court of Appeal in *Best* is an assurance that applicants would be able to proceed to the next stage of the procedure for registration under the LRA 2002, "it does not guarantee registration"[82] and the applicant would still incur liability under LASPOA, successful registration under the LRA 2012 notwithstanding. The fact that squatters could still be prosecuted and sentenced by the court after successfully bringing an adverse possession claim is disadvantageous them, and may make acquisition of property through adverse possession unattractive.

The Court of Appeal's decision in *Best* has been criticised[83] on two main grounds namely: a misapplication of the decision in *Hounga* and *Bakewell* to the facts in *Best*; and failure of the court to place sufficient weight on the question of parliament's intentions for section 144 in light of adverse possession. On the misapplication of the law, Ikeoma[84] argues that the field of law in which *Hounga* applies is materially different from adverse possession[85] and should not have formed the basis for the court's decision in *Best.* Illegality is a long standing strong policy requirement and therefore makes a significant difference to the balancing of competing

---

[81] ibid.

[82] ibid, at 16. Registration of the squatter under the LRA 2012 is not automatic and may fail where the registered proprietor counters the notice of the squatter's intention to register his interest in the property or indeed, where steps are taken by the landowner to evict the squatter.

[83] ibid, at 17.

[84] ibid.

[85] In *Hounga,* an employee who had been brought to the UK from Nigeria by her employer in breach of the immigration control, to take up employment illegally, was later dismissed by the employer. The claim of the employee for unlawful race discrimination in relation to her dismissal succeeded in the employment tribunal, but the Court of Appeal set the order of the tribunal aside on the ground that the illegality of the contract of employment formed a material part of the claimant's complaint and upholding it would amount to condoning illegality. The Supreme Court however allowed the employee's appeal.

public interests and as such, the public policy interests in ensuring that a trespasser-offender does not benefit from his criminal conduct contrary to section 144 of LASPOA should now outweigh the public policy interests in preserving the operation of adverse possession detailed in Schedule 6 of the LRA 2002. In the case of *Bakewell,* she argues that the court erred in law in applying the reasoning in that case to the facts in *Best* on the grounds that, the illegality principle cannot have the same effect when applied to the case of prescription which is acquired as of right, and the case of adverse possession acquired based on wrong; that the underlying reason for criminalisation of illegal occupation and the Land Registration Act 2002 point to the fact that squatters should not be allowed to acquire rights in other peoples land, "as it is the only means through which a person can claim title to land by way of adverse possession."[86]

10.3 Criminalisation of Illegal Occupation of Land in Nigeria

10.3.1 Background to the Position in Nigeria

Squatting and other illegal occupation of land in Nigeria exhibit certain peculiar characteristics which might be unknown to a more advanced country such as England. This may be due to the peculiarities of the prevailing social structure and the varying policies of government on housing at the federal and state levels.[87] The inadequacy of housing in Nigeria as a result of the mounting population pressure especially in the cities, the high cost of renting accommodation, the inadequate provision of housing by government generally at the federal and state levels and the general neglect of the populace by successive governments in Nigeria

[86] I. Ikeoma, (n 60) at 20.

[87] See generally, A. Bello, "Review of the Housing Policies and Programmes in Nigeria." (2019) International Journal of Contemporary Research and Review." at 20; B.N. Obidadi et al, "Housing Inadequacy in Nigeria: The Case of Failed Housing Policies." Tropical Built Environment Journal (TBE) vol. 1 No. 6, 2017 at 52.

since independence, have been responsible for the staggering number of squatters many of whom exist in urban areas.[88]

In urban centres, squatters perch in and around built up areas and developing sites, constituting nuisance to property owners, and subjecting them to the rigours and expense of eviction exercise. The situation is well captured by the editorial opinion of This Day Newspapers[89] as follows:

> "Thriving communities exist in most partially completed buildings and in some completed structures that have remained in the property market for a long time. Owners are sometimes pushed to the threshold of using violence to remove illegal occupants from their property...Only owners of uncompleted buildings or properties put up for let/lease know how difficult it is to keep squatters at bay...Recently, the owner of a storey building at Airways area of Apapa, Lagos had to remove the roof and windows to evict a thriving colony of stragglers occupying the building that was put in the property market by an estate surveyor."

The foregoing information shows the incessant encroachment on property by squatters and the difficulty encountered by owners in evicting them.

The proliferation of urban slums due to the discriminatory planning policies of government at the state and federal levels encouraged squatting by the unfortunate poor who live in shanties and

---

[88] See generally, B.N Obiadi et al, (n 87); P.K Makinwa-Adebusoye (1988) "Upgrading an Urban Squatter Settlement in Nigeria: The Experiment in Olaleye-Iponri in: *Urban Services in Developing Countries,* D.A Rondinelli et. al (eds) Palgrave, London.

[89] Nigeria: The Agony of Repossessing Buildings from Squatters. This Day Newspapers of 28 September 2013, distributed by All Africa Global Media (Nigeria).

dumping sites.[90] These poor settlements have been allowed to thrive to 'ease' government worries over housing needs of the squatters.

One significant feature of squatting in the Nigerian cities generally and in the Lagos metropolis in particular, is the activities of land grabbers and land speculators.[91] This category of squatters use force and/or violence to 'rob' land owners of their possessions[92] and, in most cases, without consequences as a result of the impecuniousness of the landowners to ventilate their right in court.[93] Sometimes, unoccupied or uncompleted building, or undeveloped parcels of land are the main targets, and peaceable entry in such cases may become adverse possession and the landowner's title subsequently extinguished by law at the expiration of the limitation period. Where violence is applied, the landowner may be forced to abandon possession.[94]

However, while the Nigerian courts may found adverse possession in favour of a squatter in cases where possession by him was acquired unchallenged over the limitation period, *nec vi, nec clam, nec precario*,[95] no such finding may be held where the initial occupation amounted to naked trespass without any claim of right.[96]

---

[90] B.N Obiadi et al, (n 87)

[91] See L. Akintola, "Why Land Grabbers Are On The Prowl." *Independent Newspapers Nigeria,* 15th December 2018 available online at www.independent.ng/why-land-grabbers-are-on-the-prawl. Accessed on 11/6/2020.

[92] ibid.

[93] ibid.

[94] There were reported cases of killings and maiming by land grabbers in different parts of Nigeria including the Federal Capital Territory, Abuja. See C.J Musa, "Effects of Activities of Land Speculators on Women Farmers'Crop Output and Income in Kuje Area Council, FCT Abuja Nov. 2015. Available online at www.kubanni.abu.edu.ng/jspui/btstream/ at 11.

[95] Latin phrase meaning: 'without violence', 'without secrecy', and 'without permission'.

[96] For example, under section 342 of the Penal Code applicable in the Northern Nigeria, whoever enters into or upon property in the possession of another with intent to commit an offence or to intimidate, insult or annoy any person in

The nefarious activities of the land grabbers/the land speculators coupled with the terror usually unleashed on landowners by them,[97] the threat to public peace, and the embarrassment caused to government when land meant for public use is taken over by squatters,[98] consequently resulted in passing Laws at the Federal and State levels criminalising the nefarious activities of land grabbers and speculators to keep them in check.[99] Provisions in this regard are available in statutes on criminal offences such as the Criminal and Penal Codes[100] applicable in the Southern and Northern Nigeria respectively, as well as specific provisions in the Criminal Law of Lagos State[101] and the Property Protection Law[102] of the State. Also, the specific provisions of the Land Use Act 1978[103] earlier discussed[104] and the State Lands Law of the various States in Nigeria,[105] contain provisions criminalising false claims to land and thereby affecting the efficacy of the regime of adverse possession, as known to law.

---

possession of such property, or having lawfully entered into or upon such property, unlawfully remains there with the intent to commit an offence, or to intimidate, insult or annoy any person in possession of such property, commits an offence.

[97] See C.J Musa, supra (n 94).

[98] Their activities tend to defeat one of the objectives of the Land Use Act 1978, Cap L5 Laws of the Federation of Nigeria 2004 as contained in its long title, and renders ineffectual the purpose of revocation under section 28 of the Act.

[99] There are provisions in these laws criminalising forcible entry and illegal occupation of land in possession of another.

[100] Criminal Code Act Cap 38 Laws of the Federation of Nigeria 2010 enacted as an Act to establish a code of Criminal law, and re-enacted in the various States of Southern Nigeria as State Law: See e.g. the Lagos State Criminal Law 2011. The Penal Code Cap 89 Laws of Northern Nigeria 1963 is a Code of criminal law applicable in the States of Northern Nigeria including Kwara State, and in the Federal Capital Territory of Nigeria, Abuja.

[101] Criminal Law of Lagos State, No.11 2011.

[102] Lagos State Property Protection Law 2016.

[103] Cap L5 Laws of the Federation of Nigeria 2010.

[104] See Chapter 6 *ante*.

[105] See e.g. State Lands Law of Lagos State, Law No.8 2015.

10.3.2 The Nigerian Criminal and Penal Codes

Both the Criminal Code Act or Law,[106] and the Penal Code[107] contain provisions protecting possession of land, to forestall a breach of the peace. Consequently, forcible entry into, or detainer of land in actual and peaceable possession of another, or against a person entitled by law to the possession of the land respectively, is an offence punishable with terms of imprisonment.

Section 81 of the Criminal Code for example, provides:

> "Any person who, in a manner likely to cause a breach of the peace or reasonable apprehension of a breach of the peace enters on land which is in actual and a peaceable possession of another, is guilty of a misdemeanour, and is liable to imprisonment for one year."[108]

This is a situation of forcible entry often involving violence such as breaking of doors or locks to access land (including building) in peaceable possession of another. This situation does not fit into the legal regime of adverse possession which requires the squatter to take possession without violence, and an encroachment premised on force simply amounts to criminal trespass punishable under that provision. A criminal trespasser not being an adverse possessor, time does not run in his favour under the statute of limitation,[109] and he could be evicted at any time.

The provision of section 82 complements the provision of section 81. It provides that:

---

[106] Supra (n 100).

[107] ibid.

[108] This is replicated in section 52 of the Criminal Law of Lagos State No. 11 2011, although the term of imprisonment prescribed is "two (2) years."

[109] For time to run in under the Limitation Act, there must be definite acts of adverse possession cognisable in law.

> "Any person who, being in actual possession of land without a claim of right, holds possession of it, in a manner likely to cause a breach of the peace or reasonable apprehension of a breach of the peace, against a person entitled by law to the possession of the land is guilty of a misdemeanour, and is liable to imprisonment for one year."[110]

This provision is an extension of section 81. Adverse and continuous possession for the purpose of the running of the limitation period must not be actualised by violence, and the person entitled to possession, upon discovery of the presence of an adverse possessor, is allowed by law to set the necessary legal process in motion to recover possession.[111]

Except in the two instances covered by the fore-going provisions to forestall breach of the peace, neither the Criminal Code nor the Penal Code contains provisions directly affecting the regime of adverse possession. For example, land as an immovable, is not a 'thing capable of being stolen'[112] and therefore the assertion of "a right which is inconsistent with that of the true owner," as in the case of adverse possession is feasible. This lacunae which has festered the regime of adverse possession in Nigeria, has been identified as the reason for the

---

[110] This is replicated in section 53 of the Criminal Law of Lagos State No. 11 2011, although the term of imprisonment prescribed is "two (2) years."

[111] Both provisions of sections 81 and 82 must be read together with sections 292 and 293 of the Criminal Code, which lay down the degree of force which may lawfully be used by a person in peaceable possession of any land against a trespasser or, if he is in possession with a claim of right, even against a person entitled by law to possession.

[112] The definition of 'things capable of being stolen' in section 382 of the Criminal Code for example, covers only movables to the exclusion of immovables such as land. See also s. 286 of the Penal Code.

failure of the Nigerian criminal law "[113] to give adequate protection to the true legal and beneficial owners" of land. In the words of Adeyemi:[114]

> "...It is not unusual for a bold and clever intruder to divest them, for all practical purposes, of their interests in the land. Once the intruder can gain a peaceful entry on to the land and is in "actual and peaceable possession" of it, then the right of the owner forcibly to eject the intruder will seem to end as otherwise, he may find himself charged with and convicted for forcible entry. This situation is now encouraging a number of problems which are now undermining confidence in dealings in land, and also disorderly behaviour particularly in the Lagos area."

The concerns of commentators such as this persuaded the Lagos State House of Assembly to introduce certain reforms in the area of criminal justice bordering on 'land theft,' and the nefarious activities of the land owning families in the Lagos metropolis.

10.3.3 The Criminal Law of Lagos State, 2011 and 'Land Theft'

One of the innovative features of the Law[115] is the criminalisation of conversion of real property thereby making theft of land possible as an offence in law. Section 278(1)(b), and (2) provides:

> "278 (1) Any person who dishonestly:
>
> (a) ...
>
> (b) converts the property of another person for his own use or to the use of any other person, is guilty of the offence of stealing."

[113] A. A Adeyemi, "The Criminal Process as a Selection Instrument for the Administration of Criminal Justice." in the *Nigerian Criminal Process* , A.A Adeyemi ed. (1977) University of Lagos Press, 26.

[114] A. A Adeyemi, supra (n 113) at 48.

[115] The criminal Law of Lagos State, 2011.

(2) A person is deemed to dishonestly...convert the property of another if he does so with:

(a) intent to permanently deprive the owner of the property;"

...

Also, section 279 of the Law provides that:

"279 (1) Anything which is the property of any person or a body corporate is capable of being stolen.

(2) 'Property' includes money and all other properties, *real* or personal, including things in action and other intangible properties which is the property of another."

While section 278(1)(b) of the Law makes dishonest conversion of the property of another an offence of stealing, section 279(2) of the Law defines the nature of property capable of being stolen to include real property amongst other properties. A person is said to dishonestly convert the property of another if he does so, inter alia, "with intent to permanently deprive the owner of the property;"[116] it does not matter that the conversion is effected without secrecy, or an attempt at concealment.[117]

The combined effect of these provisions of the Law is the introduction of 'land theft' as a feature of the criminal law applicable in Lagos State, departing from the general law of stealing known to the English and the Nigerian criminal law jurisprudence.[118] 'Asportation,' which is generally an element of the offence of stealing under both Criminal and Penal Codes,[119] is no longer a consideration in Lagos State, and the legal concept of conversion has been tailored to accommodate the

---

[116] ibid, s. 278(2)(a)

[117] ibid, s.278(4).

[118] See s. 382 of the Nigerian Criminal Code; s.286 of the Penal Code and s. 4 of the English Theft Act 1968

[119] ibid. Both the Criminal and Penal Codes in Nigeria make movability of the thing stolen an *actus reus* requirement. See *Ojiko v. Police* (1956) 1 F.S.C 62

subject matter of land. Thus, conversion of land by the squatter, intruder or trespasser for his own use and benefit, may constitute an offence of stealing for which an adverse possessor may be prosecuted, convicted and sentenced by a court of competent jurisdiction.[120] The offence is committed notwithstanding that the land "is at the time of the conversion in the possession of the person who converts it."[121] This provision of the law obviously has some implications for the doctrine of adverse possession.[122]

10.4 Effect of the Nigerian Criminal Law on the Regime of Adverse Possession

As suggested earlier, the provisions of sections 81 and 82 of the Criminal Code protect possessions of land from forcible entry and against forcible detainer, and therefore, makes inapplicable the running of time under the Statute of Limitation. A trespasser who enters into possession or remains in possession through violence is not an adverse possessor and time does not run in his favour. Such trespasser may be evicted at any time and may be prosecuted and convicted under those provisions.

The situation is different under the provisions of section 382 of the Criminal Code and its counterpart provision under the Penal Code[123] which restricts 'things capable of being stolen' to movables and thereby excluding immovables such as land from the object of stealing under the Codes[124]. Thus, the exercise of right over land which is inconsistent with that of the true owner and *ipso facto* tantamount to adverse possession, does not amount to conversion of land as it were. Consequently, the regime of adverse possession is not affected in any way under the main criminal code legislation in Nigeria.

---

[120] Criminal Law of Lagos State 2011, s. 285(1).

[121] ibid, s. 278 (5)(a).

[122] See below.

[123] Penal Code, s. 286.

[124] s. 383 of the Criminal Code. See also s. 286 of the Penal Code.

However, conversion of land by a squatter or an encroacher is criminalised under section 278(1)(b) of the Criminal Law of Lagos State as an offence of stealing for which such an adverse possessor may be prosecuted, convicted and sentenced by a court of competent jurisdiction. This position is obvious from the specific provision of 278(5)(a) which provides that, "in the case of conversion, it is immaterial whether...[the land] is at the time of the conversion in the possession of the person who converts it..." suggesting that peaceable possession which is germane to acquisition of title by adverse possession is negated. Also, section 278(4) of the Law provides that "...conversion may be dishonest, although it is effected *without secrecy or attempt at concealment,*" suggesting that acts of possession exercised openly and without concealment-characteristic of adverse possession, do not negate the mental element required for the commission of the offence of stealing.

The provisions of the Criminal Law of Lagos State contain phrases directly negativing the operation of the doctrine of adverse possession, unlike the provisions of section 144 LASPOA which are quiet over this; a position taken by the Court of Appeal in *Best v. R (on the application of Smith) v. Land Registry.*[125] While there is no judicial authority in Nigeria on this point, Nigerian courts are not likely to be persuaded by the Court of Appeal decision in *Best* in the face of very strong indication to the contrary in the relevant provisions of the Criminal Law of Lagos State discussed earlier. Thus, in the Lagos State of Nigeria, the criminal law in force is meant to affect the efficacy of the doctrine of adverse possession unlike section 144 of LASPOA which does not affect the operation of adverse possession as decided by the Court of Appeal of England and Wales, in *Best.*

However, in other parts of Nigeria outside Lagos State, both the Criminal Code Law applicable in the Southern States of Nigeria, and the

[125] [2010] EWCA Civ 200. On this, the Court of Appeal said "[i]t is not plausible to suppose that Parliament would have been silent about the impact of a provision like section 144 on the delicate and comprehensive balance of interests set out in the Limitation Act 1980 and in Schedule 6 to the LRA, had it truly intended that section 144 should have any impact at all on those regimes." ibid, at para 73.

Penal Code Law applicable in the Northern States of Nigeria and the Federal Capital Territory, have no equivalent provisions on land theft, and land is not capable of being stolen. Consequently, in other parts of Nigeria outside Lagos State, peaceful possession of land by a person which fulfils other conditions in law over the limitation period qualifies as adverse possession.

10.5 Land Grabbers and the Lagos State Property Protection Law, 2016

This Law was enacted against the backdrop of the menace of land grabbers exhibited in acts of forceful entry and illegal possession of land, and the need to protect the proprietary interest of land owners in Lagos State. The main object of the Law as contained in its long title is "to prohibit forceful entry and illegal occupation of landed properties, violent and fraudulent conducts in relation to landed properties in Lagos State and for connected purposes."[126] As noted by a commentator, the Law is meant to "frontally address the problems of *Omo-Onile* [land grabbers] which is engendered by the skewed national land policy and practice as exemplified in the provisions of the Land Use Act…"[127] The law is meant "to deter potential offenders and curb the scourge of illegalities pervading the sector."[128]

Section 2 of the Law prohibits the use of force or self-help by any person or group of persons, to take over any landed property, or to *engage in any act inconsistent with the proprietary right of the owner*. This offence applies by extension to persons who have used force to take over the

[126] Long title to the Lagos State Property Protection Law 2016.

[127] A.K. Otubu, "Land Use Act and Land Administration in the 21st Century Nigeria: Need for Reforms." Journal of Sustainable Development Law and Policy (2018) vol. 9(1) 80-108.

[128] This is exemplified by "its strict penal sanctions of long prison sentences ranging between six (6) months to twenty one (21) years, and high premium on fines, ranging between 500,000 Naira and 5,000,000 Naira." A.K Otubu, "Statute Review: Lagos State Property Protection Law 2016". *SSRN Electronic Journal, DOI: 10.2139/ssrn.3505638,* accessed on 20/5/2020.

property of another before the commencement of the law and remain in possession 3 months after the commencement of the Law.[129] The penalty for the offence is ten years imprisonment.

Section 3 compliments the provision of section 2 by criminalising the use of violence or threat of violence by any person without lawful authority, for the purpose of securing entry into land, notwithstanding that the person using or threatening force has a right over the property. It is immaterial that the violence is directed against the person or against the property and/or that the violence is intended to secure entry for the purpose of acquiring possession of the property or for any other purpose. The penalty for the offence is ten years imprisonment.[130]

Where a person encroaching on land or any person deriving title from him fails to vacate the property on being required to do so by or on behalf of the owner of the property, he commits an offence and on conviction shall be liable to a fine not exceeding five million naira or five years imprisonment or both.[131]

The foregoing provisions frown against any form of force or self help to takeover any landed property,[132] and prohibits exercise of *any act inconsistent with the proprietary right of the owner*. An 'act inconsistent with the proprietary right of the owner' suggests adverse possession which may have been actualised through dispossession of the owner or takeover

[129] It has been argued that "[t]o the extent that this provision is retroactive in nature, it will be contrary to the provision of the Constitution [citing section 36(8)] and therefore a nullity." See A.K Otubu, Statute Review (n 127) at 7.

[130] Four (4) years imprisonment where the forceful entry is accompanied with offensive weapons.

[131] Lagos State Property Protection Law 2016, s.4.

[132] This is particularly directed at the owner of land whose land is wrongfully possessed by a squatter or trespasser and who intends to evict such person. The only permitted method of eviction in law is through a court order. This is buttressed by the provision of section 3(2) of the law which provides that "a person's right of possession or occupation of any property shall not for the purpose of subsection (1) of this section constitute lawful authority for the use or threat of violence by him...for the purpose of securing entry into that property."

of land abandoned by the owner without the use of force, but with the intention of continuously exercising acts of possession for the period of the limitation prescribed by law. Consequently, adverse possession of land in Lagos State after the commencement of that law is an offence punishable under section 2(3) of the law. The irresistible conclusion therefore is that any form of use of force in taking possession of land, or the exercise of peaceable possession of land in Lagos State is a criminal offence punishable by law.

In view of criminalisation of adverse possession under the criminal law of Lagos State and the Lagos State Property Protection law, section 100 of the Lagos State Land Registration Law[133] has been rendered otiose. That section provides that "where the court is satisfied that the title of the registered holder of any land or mortgage has been extinguished under the Limitation Law, the court may order the register to be rectified accordingly, and the person aggrieved by such rectification shall not receive any compensation." The incongruity in establishing a right of adverse possession in civil law before the court when the claimant's act amounts to an offence in law is incomprehensible. This is more so in view of the clear provisions of the various provisions of the law in Lagos State criminalising adverse possession. Such a situation would trigger the operation of the rule of illegality encapsulated in the legal maxim: *ex turpi causa non oritur actio* (meaning: 'a person shall not benefit from his illegality'). Express or implicit admission of adverse possession by the claimant in his pleading before the court is sufficient for the court to invoke this rule of public policy and to refuse the relief sought.

Whilst this situation does not suggest that the rule of illegality applies mechanically in all situations where a civil claim is based on a criminal act,[134] it is a good example of situations where the rule would apply without exceptions; a situation where, unlike the situation in *Best v.*

[133] Law No.1 2015.

[134] See *Hounga v. Allen* [2014] UKSC 47; *Tinsley v. Milligan* [1994] 1 AC 340; *Gray v. Thames Trains Ltd* [2009] UKHL 33; *Stone & Rolls Ltd v. Moore Stephens* [2009] UKHL 39; *Les Laboratoires Servier v. Apotex Inc* [2014] UKSC 55.

R (on the application of Smith) v. Land Registry,[135] Parliament has specifically criminalised adverse possession and has therefore, left no discretion to the courts in applying the *ex turpi causa* principle.[136]

10.6 Conclusion

The decision of the Court of Appeal for England and Wales in *Best* has resolved the ambiguity left by section 144 of LASPOA 2012 regarding its applicability to adverse possession cases, and has preserved its efficacy as a mode of acquiring title to land. Also, there is no doubt that the commission of an offence under LASPOA is not a bar to registration of the offender as a proprietor of registered land after fulfilling the conditions prescribed by the LRA 2002. This is the position generally in Nigeria except in Lagos State where the Laws have criminalised acts of adverse possession thereby obviating the application of the regime of adverse possession.

However, in view of the criminalisation of adverse possession under the Criminal Law of Lagos State and the Lagos State Property Protection Law, section 100 of the Lagos State Land Registration Law[137] has been rendered otiose. Section 100 provides that "where the court is satisfied that the title of the registered holder of any land or mortgage has been extinguished under the Limitation Law, the court may order the register to be rectified accordingly..." Going by the criminalisation of all acts of adverse possession in Lagos State, it is not likely that the title of the existing registered owner of land would be extinguished under the Limitation Law, and the possibility of admitting such title on the register is remote. It is also yet to be seen how the Nigerian courts would construe the doctrine of adverse possession against the backdrop of the legal maxim, '*ex turpi causa non oritur actio.*'

---

[135] supra (n 56).

[136] See in contrast, the position in the cases cited in (n 64).

[137] Law No.1 2015.

CHAPTER 11
JUXTAPOSING APPLICATION OF THE DOCTRINE OF ADVERSE POSSESSION UNDER THE ENGLISH AND NIGERIAN LAW

11.1 Introduction

The efficacy of the doctrine of adverse possession under the English and Nigerian law may be determined by juxtaposing its application under the different legal systems prevailing in England and Wales on the one hand, and in Nigeria on the other hand. This chapter is meant to show that the application of the doctrine is relative depending on the country's legal structures generally, and the nature, content and application of the operating land tenure systems in particular, and other relevant laws in general.

A comparative study of the application of the doctrine of adverse possession in England and Nigeria engaged in this chapter will proceed in the following chronological order of inquiry:

i. What are the effects of the prevailing social circumstances and the extant legal systems applicable in England and Nigeria on the application of the doctrine of adverse possession?

ii. To what extent is the Nigerian legal system receptive of the common law doctrine of adverse possession applicable in England Nigeria?

iii. What is the comparative effect of adverse possession on unregistered title in England and Nigeria?

iv. What is the comparative effect of adverse possession on registered title in England and Nigeria?

v. From a comparative perspective, to what extent is the application of the doctrine of adverse possession open to human rights challenge?

vi. How efficacious is the doctrine of adverse possession in England and Nigeria in light of various pieces of legislation on criminal trespass?

11.2 Effect of the Prevailing Social Circumstances and the Extant Legal Systems on the Application of the Doctrine of Adverse Possession.

The common law system applicable in England and Wales is a monolithic system encapsulating a uniform land tenure system evolving originally from a feudal system of land tenure which promoted heredity and limited access to land, to a system that emphasised protection of individual property rights and free alienation"[1]. The development of the middle class and an economy based upon wages as opposed to rendering services led to the emergence of individual property rights in real property[2].

Whilst the Crown technically holds land by way of absolute ownership, in practical terms, an individual is referred to as the 'owner' of the land[3]. However, what the individual owns is not the land, but an estate in it, which is the right to *seisin* "or possession, of the land for a period of time"; certain or uncertain[4]. Since the Law of Property Act 1925, the estates that can exist at common law are limited to fee simple absolute in possession, and term of years absolute,[5] although "this did not change the nature of land ownership or of the doctrine of estate"[6]. Thus in English law, ownership of land is premised on the doctrine of estate

---

1 B. Gardiner, Squatters' "Rights and Adverse Possession." [1997] IND. International and Comparative Law Review, vol. 8:1 at 125.

2 J.Dukeminier & J. Krier, Property 112 (1981) cited in B. Gardiner supra (n 1) at 126.

3 Burn & Cartright, *Modern Law of Real Property*, 18th ed. Oxford at 12-13.

4 ibid, at 13.

5 LPA 1925, s.1(1).

6 Burn & Cartright, supra (n 3) at 13.

"which itself is inextricably linked to the notion of right to possession of the land[7].

Possession is the root of title and the possessor is a title holder from the day he enters into possession or from the day he dispossesses another, although the title is relative to the extent that a person who could show a better title could recover the land[8]. Consequently, the concept of possession as root of title is the foundation of adverse possession at common law applicable in England and Wales and entitles the adverse possessor to fee simple absolute upon extinguishment of the owner's title.

The social circumstances and the legal position in Nigeria before colonisation by the British in 1861[9] and consequently the reception of English law, were different. Contrary to the position at common law which recognises individual ownership through the concept of possession as root of title, the idea of individual ownership before colonisation was foreign to the indigenous system of land tenure applicable within the geographical entity.

It is said regarding ownership under the indigenous land tenure system that "land belongs to the community, the village or the family, never to the individual"[10]. The head of the village, family or community is said to hold the land in trust with the power to allocate to members of the village, family or community[11]. When a member of the family or the community is allocated portion of land, he acquires a usufructuary right – a right to occupy and use the land mainly, devoid of any form of proprietary right unlike the holder of a fee simple under English law. Thus, unlike the freeholder at common law, the holder of customary land right cannot alienate or encumber the land in any way without the consent of the family, and cannot devise the land by Will. These social circumstances form the background to the Nigerian customary law, and

---

[7] ibid, at 13

[8] ibid.

[9] See generally, Chapter 6 ante, and, in particular, pp 122-130.

[10] Per Lord Heldane in *Amody Tijani v. Secretary of Southern Nigeria* (1921) A.C 399 at 404.

[11] *Lewis v. Bankole* (1908) 1 N.L.R 82.

impacts on the application of the doctrine of adverse possession. Encroachment by third parties is prohibited at customary law but customary tenancy on the land may be created in favour of third party individual, family or community for occupation and use mainly, subject to exhibition of good behaviour such as acknowledgement of the overlord's title and payment of tribute.[12]

The customary tenancy is a parallel concept to the English leasehold in terms of creation, incidents and determination[13]. It lacks the certainty of duration which characterises the English lease, and the incident of the tenure is payment of tribute not rent by the customary tenant to the overlord[14]. The interest of a customary tenant, unlike the English lease with certainty of duration, enures in perpetuity subject to good behaviour[15]; its character is said to be akin to an *emphyteusis;* a perpetual right in the land of another[16].

The position of Islamic law is also reminiscent of the social circumstances prevalent in Northern Nigeria before the advent of British rule. As discussed earlier on in Chapter 6, the jihad of Uhman dan Fodio in 1804 revolutionised the land tenure system in that region. Upon conquest, ownership of the whole land acquired was said to belong to Allah represented by the Emirs who held the land in trust for the people. Land allocated to the individual by the Emir was to be occupied and used mainly subject to the payment of tribute; alienation in any form was prohibited, and encroachments by outsiders frowned upon.

---

[12] *Aghenghen v. Waghoreghor & Ors* (1974) 1 SC 1; *Abioye v. Yakubu* (1991) 5 N.W.L.R (Pt.190) 130.

[13] *Aghenghen v. Waghoreghor & Ors* supra (n 12).

[14] The difference between rent at common law and tribute under the Nigerian customary law lies in the fact that rent represents the economic value of the leasehold in the property market and quantifiable in monetary terms, tribute under customary law represents a mere acknowledgment of the overlord's title without reference to the economic considerations and paid in kind (as opposed to cash) such as presentation of some portions of farm produce, alcoholic drinks, etc. See *Lasisi & Anor v. Oladapo Tubi & Anor* (1974) 1 All N.L.R (Pt II) 438.

[15] *Abioye v. Yakubu* (1991) 5 NWLR (Pt 190) 130.

[16] Per Elias C.J.N in *Aghenghen v. Waghoreghor* supra (n 12) at 6.

The social circumstances under customary law prevalent in the Southern Nigeria and Islamic law predominant in the Northern Nigeria underline the exclusion of these indigenous land tenures from the ambit of the various statutes of limitation in Nigeria - statutes copied from English law, but disguised as local legislation[17]. It constitutes, in effect, a significant exception to the universality of the doctrine of adverse possession and demonstrates the relativity of its application as a foreign concept to indigenous circumstances.

The reception statutes in Nigeria received English common law subject to local circumstances and local legislation. It was in response to this that the various limitation laws in Nigeria excluded customary land tenure, and by extension, Islamic land tenure[18] from the ambit of its application, and makes the application of the common law of land tenure subject to the provisions of the Land Use Act, 1978.

There are implications flowing from the prevailing social circumstances and the extant legal systems in the jurisdictions under enquiry vis-a-vis the application of the doctrine of adverse possession. In the first place, the ownership structure differs as between the common law of England on the one hand and the customary and Islamic law on the other hand. Whilst possession characterised by proprietary interests is the root of title under English law, occupation and user rights with no proprietary interest characterise individual holdings under customary and Islamic law; right of ownership lies with the family or community represented by the head chief, Oba or head of the family in the case of customary land tenure, and with the Emir who is the representative of Allah in the universe in the case of Islamic law.

Secondly, from the result of the foregoing inquiry into the position of both the customary and Islamic law of land tenure, it is clear

---

[17] The provisions of the various statutes of limitation in Nigeria pertaining to adverse possession are substantially the same in England and Wales, and Nigeria.

[18] Both the District Court Laws and the High Court Laws in Northern Nigeria treat Islamic Law as part of Customary Law. See e,g. the District Courts Law of Niger State Cap 37 Laws of Niger state of Nigeria 1992, s.2 ; and the High Court Law of Katsina States Cap 52 Laws of Katsina state of Nigeria 1991, s.2.

that both indigenous land tenures have in-built mechanisms for tackling stale claims outside the statute of limitation and, *ipso facto*, present an alternative approach as against the common law doctrine of adverse possession. As discussed in Chapter 6, customary law is subject to certain rules of validity imposed by local legislation in both the Northern and Southern Nigeria. For example, the various High Court Laws in Nigeria empowers the High court to observe and enforce the observance of customary law that is not repugnant to natural, justice, equity and good conscience nor incompatible with the local legislation for the time being in force[19]. It was on that basis that the court in *Akpan Awo v. Cookey Gam*[20] preferred to enforce the equitable principle of proprietary estoppel against stale claims than the exception made for customary law under the statutes of limitation:

> ...on the ground that the court will not allow a party to call in aid principles of native law, and least of all principles, which, as in this case, were developed in and are applicable to a state of society vastly different from that now existing merely for the purpose of bolstering up a stale claim[21].

The court found a fair and just principle in proprietary estoppel rather than in the common law doctrine of adverse possession. As the court made clear in that case: "We do not decide this point in accordance with any provision of English law as to the limitation of actions, but simply on the grounds of equity..."[22]

In the case of Islamic law, the principle of *hauzi* which is the equivalent of the right of prescription under Roman Law as opposed to English law is rooted in Islamic jurisprudence to protect long possession and ensure that land is put to productive use. It is said that the effect of prescription known as *usucapio* in Roman law is:

---

[19] See e.g. the High Court Law of Lagos State Cap H3 2003, s.26.
[20] (1913) 2 N.L.R. 445.
[21] ibid.
[22] ibid.

> to confer a positive title to the land upon a person who had remained in possession for a certain time…[it] exemplified what is sometimes called acquisitive prescription in the sense that possession of another's land for a given period conferred a positive title upon the occupier, but English law has never adopted this theory in its treatment of corporeal hereditaments and chattels though it has done so in the case of easements and profits[23]

In the *Hadith* (one of the sources of Islamic law) however, the principle of *hauzi* as interpreted by scholars of Islamic Law[24] is as follows:

> He who sees somebody in possession of his (claimant's) property and claiming and using the same as his own over a long period [10 years] without any objection from him, the person in possession becomes the owner. If the original owner later brings an action to recover it neither the complaint nor evidence in support thereof will be listened to. But there are exceptions to this principle: 1. cogent reason for not complaining in time e.g. blood relationship or fear of harm from authority; 2. minorship; 3. the person in possession is put there by the claimant either as a free or paying tenant; 4. the person in possession is put in there as a trustee; 5. the claimant is a partner or co-proprietor to the person in possession.[25]

The essence of bringing the principle of *hauzi* and its exceptions to the fore is to appreciate the fact that its rule of prescription and the exceptions to it keep the concept of prescription strictly within the ambit of Islamic law, thereby constituting an in-built machinery for dealing with stale claims in Islamic law outside English law.

---

[23] See Burn and Cartwright, supra n.3 at 1127-1128.

[24] Ashalul Madarik vol. 3 at 236.

[25] Mayyarah Vol. II 164; Maliki Law (Summary Translation of Mukhtasha Khalil by Ruxton) 309 para 1698

11.2.1 Summary

The English common law applicable in England and Wales on the one hand, and the Nigerian Customary and Islamic law of land tenure on the other hand exhibit parallel social circumstances with implications for the application of the doctrine of adverse possession. Whilst the evolution of possession as root of title under English law facilitates the application of the doctrine of adverse possession in England and Wales, the peculiar social circumstances in Nigeria which does not permit possessory right as root of title to land but communal ownership and right of occupation and user right mainly, inhibit the application of the doctrine.

11.3 How are the Land Tenure Systems in England and Nigeria Receptive of the Doctrine of Adverse Possession?

In Nigeria, the period of limitation regarding State land is 20 years as opposed to 30 years applicable to the Crown land in England and Wales. Whereas actions to recover possession of the foreshore by the Crown in England is 60 years, the statutes of limitations in Nigeria contain no limitation period in this regard.

Whilst the English Limitation Act in relation to land applies to successive and future interests which are features of the English land tenure, the Nigerian Land Use Act allows only "a plain transfer of the whole of the rights of occupation over the whole of the land"[26] thereby jettisoning the common law tenure of successive and future interests.[27] This obviously obviates the possibility of creating interests in succession or future interests in Nigeria sequel to the enactment of the Land Use Act. It would therefore be out of context in Nigeria to consider the implications of the running of time under the limitation statutes on future interests such as entailed interest, settlement made by person out of

[26] See s. 25 of the Act.

[27] G. Ezejiofor, 'The Land Use Decree: A critique.' Paper presented at an International Conference in New York, September 1980.

possession, entitlement to successive interests; settled land and land held on trust. The basis for non recognition of lesser estates and beneficial, successive and future interests by the Act lies in the distinction between proprietary freehold interests which is tantamount to absolute ownership at common law applicable in England and Wales, and a non proprietary interest in the form of a right of occupancy created by grant.

The common law concept of *seisin* is the bedrock of adverse possession as required by the statute of limitation. The Limitation Act of 1980 applicable in England and Wales states that:[28]

> Where the person bringing an action to recover land, or some person through whom he claims, has been in possession of the land, and has while entitled to the land been dispossessed or discontinued his possession the right of action shall be treated as having accrued on the date of the dispossession or discontinuance.

The provision is the same in the limitation statutes of the thirty six states of the federation of Nigeria and the Federal Capital Territory.

A significant factor common to dispossession and discontinuance of possession is the *act of possession* taken upon the *entry* of a squatter.[29] Possession must be singular, exclusive, adverse, open, and continuous for the period of limitation. At the expiration of the limitation period, the title of the owner is extinguished and the squatter becomes a title holder in fee simple by virtue of his possession.

Before the advent of the Land Use Act 1978 in Nigeria, this common law position was applied by the Nigerian courts in a plethora of cases. However, the extant regimes of the Land Use Act and the State land Laws appear not to be receptive of the doctrine of adverse possession as known to the common law of England and Wales, considering the various

---

[28] Limitation Act 1980, s. 15(6) Sch 1, para 1.

[29] *J.A Pye (Oxford) Ltd v. Graham* [2003] A.C 419 at para. 38 per Lord Brown Wilkinson; *Powell v. Mc Farlane* (1977) 38 P& CR 452 per Slade J at 470.

derogatory provisions and apparent exclusions of the doctrine respectively.

In Nigeria, a right of occupancy which is the only right cognisable under the Land Use Act, is not a fee simple estate and is far from being a lease. The fact that the Act allows sub-leases and sub-underleases to be created from a right of occupancy is of no moment. As Okuniga[30] warned:

> ...one must be wary: First against rashly inferring that a statutory right of occupancy is a leasehold interest simply because there are references to the grant of sub-lease or sub-underleases. The Act is no doubt sufficiently confusing in its provisions in this regard, but that does not entitle one to adopt the Humpty-Dumpty type of definition. The lease is a concept of English law and has its own characteristics and incidents unknown to our own indigenous system of landholding. The statutory right of occupancy does share with the English leasehold the quality of certainty of duration but that is about all that is invariably common to both.

Also, the anomalous situation created by the use of the nomenclature such as sub-lease or sub-underlease when the person creating it has no estate in the property but a mere license, is not unusual. For example, the House of Lords in *Brunton v. London and Quadrant Housing Trust*[31] held that a Trust that had no estate out of which it could create a tenancy was held liable under a tenancy created by it in favour of Brunton, although Brunton himself had no estate binding on third parties[32].

---

30 A.O Okuniga, 'The Land Use Act 1978 and Private Ownership of land in Nigeria' being text of a paper delivered at the Law Teachers Conference at the University of Ife-Nigeria, 1979.

31 [2000] 1 AC 406

32 In arriving at that decision, the House of Lords relied on the criteria for determining a valid tenancy as laid down earlier in *Street v. Mountford* [1985] A.C 809 namely: that exclusive possession, tenure and payment of rent would create a valid tenancy.

Every right to land in Nigeria lies in, or is traceable to an actual or deemed grant by the Governor. A right of occupancy is not the equivalent of a free simple estate absolute in possession which forms the bedrock of title of an adverse possessor in England and Wales. It is consequently bereft of the incidents which characterise a fee simple estate including relativity of title. In the words of Ezejiofor[33]:

> Since in Nigeria, the fee simple is equivalent to absolute ownership under customary law, that interest cannot also now be held in land. Since an estate tail can be created only out of a fee simple or its equivalent it cannot also now exist in the country. A series of beneficial interests or trusts in land in favour of a succession of persons can only be created out of the fee simple or its equivalent which has been withdrawn from individuals and groups. Besides, where it possible to create such interest, that cannot be validly done unless the required consent is obtained. Nor is it likely that such consent will be given if sought. Consequently settlements including future interests and the rule against remoteness under the received English law will henceforth have no place in our law...Also to be laid to rest is the conceptual argument about the applicability of the fee simple in Nigeria.

The holder of a right of occupancy lacks the form of proprietary rights associated with a holder of a fee simple estate absolute in possession in English law. It is said that a right of occupancy is less than ownership and cannot therefore amount to a proprietary right; it is essentially and inextricably the right to occupy and use land.[34]

A squatter cannot enter any land in purported exercise of any right in relation to possession necessary to acquire title by adverse possession at common law, under the Land Use Act regime. Section 37 of the Act prohibits and makes it unlawful for any person other than the

---

[33] G. Ezejiofor, supra (n 27).

[34] I.A Umezulike, *ABC of Contemporary Land Law in Nigeria,* First ed. (2013) Snaap Press Nig. Ltd at 81.

holder of a right of occupancy from entering, or from making false claim in relation thereto. Consequently, no action of dispossession of the holder of a right of occupancy required by the statute of limitation is cognisable under the Act nor is it of moment that the holder has discontinued possession. Any purported exercise of right of possession including right of alienation which is inchoate without the consent of the Governor[35] or the Local Government[36] depending on the status of the land[37], is tantamount to making false claim punishable under the provision[38].

One of the critical requirements of adverse possession at common law is the act or series of acts of physical possession which is prohibited of any person who is not a holder of a right of occupancy.[39] Thus, it is illegal to build or farm on the land, erect fences, make unexhausted improvements of any kind etc.[40]

Acquisition of title by adverse possession at common law requires exercise of exclusive possession which is not possible under the Land Use Act for, not only is the Governor exempted from such exclusive possession[41], the Governor or any officer duly authorised by him is statutorily empowered to enter into and inspect the land or any improvement thereon at any reasonable hours of the day ''and the occupier shall give free access to the Governor or any such officer to enter and inspect''[42].

However, since the Land Use Act is not applicable in the Federal Capital Territory (FCT), all the derogatory provisions against the application of the doctrine of adverse possession do not apply therein. It

---

[35] The Land Use Act Cap L5 Laws of the Federation of Nigeria 2010, s.22

[36] ibid, s.21

[37] Alienation of right to land the subject of a statutory right of occupancy is subject to Governor's consent, while land right the subject of a customary right of occupancy is subject to consent of the Local Government.

[38] The Land Use Act, s.37.

[39] ibid, s.43.

[40] ibid, s.43(3).

[41] ibid, s.14.

[42] ibid, s.11.

is therefore most probable that time would run in favour of an adverse possessor of allocated land in the FCT under the Limitation Act.

As discussed in Chapter 6, the whole land comprised in the FCT is acquired land with all pre-existing rights abolished. Barring land allotted by the Minister on behalf of the President of the Federal Republic of Nigeria therefore, vacant land qualifies as State land and susceptible to the application of the State Lands Act[43]. The State Lands Act in the FCT and the State Land Laws applicable in the various states of the federation excludes all state Lands from the ambit of the statute of limitation; an exception unknown to English law.

11.3.1 Summary

The foregoing analysis suggests that whereas England and Nigeria have similar provisions in their statutes of limitation on adverse possession, and whereas Nigeria received the common law of England including the common law requirements for acquisition of title by adverse possession, the prevailing land tenure system is largely not receptive of the application of the doctrine. Not only are the derogatory provisions of the Land Use Act contradictory of the common law requirements for acquisition of land by adverse possession, the provisions of the State Lands Law applicable in the various states within the federation prevent the application of the doctrine to state lands. Also, with the exception of allocated land in the FCT, the doctrine does not apply to state land, that is, the unallocated acquired land, by virtue of the State Lands Act applicable there.

11.4 Adverse Possession of Unregistered Land

The position at common law is that a squatter on unregistered land is not regarded as the successor or transferee of the person barred by the statute

[43] See Cap 22 Laws of the Federal Capital Territory 2007, s.13.

of limitation[44]. It is said that ''the squatter enters and acquires a title by virtue of his possession''[45]. The title acquired is a fee simple absolute in possession, and this is so ''notwithstanding the possibility of determination by ejection by title paramount''[46]. However, the time-barred owner's title is extinguished as against the squatter but not as against interested third parties such as a lessor when time has run against the lessee.[47] This position would ordinarily apply in Nigeria under the received English law and it is buttressed by the Statutes of Limitation applicable in the federating states and the Federal Capital Territory[48].

However, in the case of customary law and by extension Islamic Law[49], the running out of the limitation period by an adverse possessor does not extinguish customary or Islamic title on land. However, it is said that ''where the claimant relies solely on documents couched in English form and it is not suggested that any reliance is placed on customary law, such claimant has excluded the application of customary law and cannot be heard to say that there cannot be adverse possession of the land''[50]. This position is explicated in the words of Graham Paul J. in the Nigerian case of *Green v. Owo*[51] as follows:

> Now what is the plaintiff's position in this case? He has in his possession documents in English Conveyancers' jargon, and Plans attached to them. He has nothing but these documents. There is no

[44] M.S. Dockray: 'Adverse Possession and the Limitation of Actions to Recover land.' Thesis submitted for the degree of Ph.D in Laws of the University of London, 1984 at 414. Available online at https://kclpure.kcl.ac.uk/portal/ visited on 11/8/2020

[45] ibid.

[46] ibid.

[47] *Fairweather v, St Marylebone Property Co. Ltd* [1963] A.C 510.

[48] See e.g. Limitation Act 1966, s. 30.

[49] See s.2 of both the various District Court Laws and the various High Court Laws of Northern Nigeria which define customary law to include Islamic law.

[50] J. A Omotola: 'The Adverse Possessor of Registered Land'. Nig Law Journal vol. 7, 38 at 39.

[51] (1936) 13 N.L.R 43 at 45.

> evidence except the documents as to the title of the grantees to grant them. There is no evidence of possession under them. These documents profess to give to the plaintiff a right to the land in dispute which the defendant and his predecessors have occupied without interference for over twenty years and which so far as the evidence before me goes-none of the plaintiff's predecessors has ever occupied...The Statute of Limitations in such circumstances in England would certainly bar the plaintiff's present claim. Where is the existing native custom to the contrary? There is, so far as I know, no native custom as regards the effect of documentary titles in English Conveyancer form. How would there be?

In such cases the statute of limitation extinguishes the title of the claimant at the expiration of the limitation period under the general law. This position of the law has been replicated by the courts in subsequent cases.[52]

11.4.1 Summary

The effect of adverse possession on unregistered land in England and Nigeria is the same. It extinguishes the title of the owner at the end of the limitation period and entitles the adverse possessor to title in respect thereof. But where the title is one existing under customary or Islamic land tenure, time generally does not run against the holder of such title except the matter falls within the exceptions discussed in Chapter 6.

---

[52] See Coker Ag. C.J in *Agboola v. Abimbola* (Unreported) SC.336/67 OF 4/7/69; *Oyedele v. Ogun* (Unreported) LD/40A/69 of 14/8/71.

11.5 Effect of Adverse Possession on Registered Land.

11.5.1 The System of Land Registration

Unlike the situation in England where there is a single and uniform system of land registration namely, the Land Registration Act 2002 (LRA) which deals with title registration, Nigeria has two types of land registration system namely, land instrument registration and title registration. The system of title registration in Nigeria comparable to the LRA 2002 applicable in England and Wales, are the Registration of Titles Act 1935 (RTA) applicable in the Federal Capital Territory Abuja[53] (FCT), and the Land Registration Law (LRL) of Lagos state 2015.

11.5.2 The Land Instrument Registration Law and the Statute of Limitation

In Nigeria, the Land Instrument Registration Law applies throughout the thirty six states of the federation and in the FCT, unlike the situation in England and Wales where this is not applicable. Consequently in Nigeria, registration of Instrument without possession could be defeated by the statute of limitation in favour of adverse possession. The futility of land instrument without possession was described by the English court as follows:

> Title deeds come to little without evidence of actual enjoyment, for otherwise anyone might pretend to give away the lands of anybody

[53] This Law which was formerly in force in the former Federal Territory of Lagos but which was later repealed in 2015 by the Land Registration Law was made applicable in the Federal Capital Territory, Abuja by the Federal Capital Territory Act 1976: See s.13 of the Act and Schedule 2 thereto.

> else. Parchment, of itself, comes to little; the real question is as to actual enjoyment.[54]

It follows therefore that adverse possession of land by a party for the duration of the limitation period without eviction by the owner extinguishes the title of the latter against the adverse possessor [55].

11.5.3 Title Registration and the Limitation Period

One significant feature of the LRA 2002 applicable in England and Wales is that no period of limitation runs against a registered proprietor[56] and consequently, a squatter's exercise of adverse possession for the limitation period does not extinguish the title of the registered proprietor[57]. However, such adverse possessor may apply to be registered after ten years of adverse possession through a procedure set out in Schedule 6 to the Act. The procedure for registration is administrative through the Lands Registry involving service of Notice, engagement of due process and fulfilment of certain statutory conditions by the applicant[58] before alteration of the register. Where the adverse possessor becomes registered consequently, he becomes the new registered proprietor of the estate after taking a Parliamentary transfer of the existing proprietor's title[59], and his former title based on possession is extinguished. The emphasis therefore shifted from a consideration of possession to the register as root of title. This is not the case under both the Registration of Titles Act 1935 (RTA)

---

[54] *Lord St Leonards v. Ashburner* (1870) 21 LT , 595 at 596 per Bramwell B. See also *Malcolmson v. O'Dea* (1863) 10 HLC 593 at 614; *Bristow v. Cormican* (1878) 3 App Cas 641 at 668; *Johnston v. O'Neill* (1911) AC 552.

[55] *Green v. Owo* supra (n 51); *Agboola v. Abimbola* supra (n 52).

[56] LRA 2002, s.96(1).

[57] ibid, s.96(2).

[58] See Schedule 6 to the LRA 2002.

[59] This new title does not affect the priority of any interest affecting the estate: See LRA 2002, Sch 6, para 9(2), and is subject to the estates and interests that bound the original paper owner except for any registered charge affecting the estate immediately before his registration: ibid, para 6(3).

made applicable in the FCT pursuant to section 13 of the FCT Act 1976 and the Second Schedule to the Act.

Under the RTA applicable in the FCT, the register of title may be rectified only upon an order made to that effect by the court where it is shown to the satisfaction of the court that the title of the registered owner has been extinguished under the provisions of the Limitation Law[60]. Contrary to the position of the LRA 2002, the period of limitation under the RTA and the running of time against a registered proprietor and consequently, a squatter's exercise of adverse possession for the limitation period, extinguish the title of the registered proprietor. In this case, the adverse possessor shall not only bring an action in court for declaration of title based on adverse possession and seek an order of court for rectification of the register, but must necessarily do so only upon the expiration of the limitation period. The implication of this provision is to make the basis of title to registered land possession as opposed to registration.

This position which makes the court the only arbiter on the question whether or not the register shall be rectified so as to give effect to the title gained by the adverse possessor is reminiscent of the old position in England under the Land Transfer Act 1897[61]. But this position has changed since the enactment of the Land Registration Act 1925[62] which made the Registrar the arbiter in this regard. This new position which is adopted by the LRA 2002 is a better approach considering the enormous delay experienced in the Nigerian courts and the adverse effect on ''the right of the adverse possessor which remains inchoate and contingent on the court's willingness to exercise this discretion in his favour''[63]. Thus, the position under the LRA 2002 appears to be better.

---

[60] Registration of Titles Act Cap 181 Laws of the Federation of Nigeria 1958 (made applicable in the FCT by virtue of section 13 of the FCT Act 1976 and the Second Schedule thereto), s.62.

[61] Land Transfer Act 1897, s.12.

[62] Land Registration Act 1925, s.75(2) and (3).

[63] J.A Omotola, supra (n 50) at 44.

The effect of the Limitation Law on the provisions of the Lagos State Land Registration Law 2015 is contained in section 112 (1) and (2) as follows:

(1) The holding of land may be acquired by uninterrupted adverse possession:

a. against the State after a period of twenty (20) years, and

b. in any other case after a period of twelve (12) years

(2) Any person claiming to have acquired land by virtue of the provisions of sub section (1) of this section shall, having advertised or given notice in such manner as the Registrar may require, apply to the court for an order directing him to be registered as the holder of such land.

Section 100 of the Law provides that:

> Where the court is satisfied that the title of the registered holder of any land or mortgage has been extinguished under the Limitation Law, the court may order the register to be rectified accordingly, and the person aggrieved by such a rectification shall not receive any compensation.

The above provision of section 112(2) of the Land Registration Law (LRL) of Lagos state on registration of an adverse possessor as a registered proprietor is vague[64] and do not, unlike the LRA 2002, afford the registered proprietor adequate notice and time within which to respond. Also, unlike the LRA 2002 which "disapplies the Limitation Act 1980 in relation to registered land" by placing emphasis on registration as opposed to possession,[65] the basis of section 100 of the LRL is clearly

---

[64] For example, there is no clue as to whom to serve a notice on unlike the LRA, or what form the advertisement should take.

[65] See s. 96(1) of the LRA 2002. Thus, for example, Sch 6 Para. 1(1) of the LRA 2002 allows the squatter to apply for registration if he has been in adverse possession

shown to be the limitation statute with emphasis on possession. It is said with regards to the LRA 2002 that "...the mere fact that the squatter has been in possession of the land for a period of time does not give him a right to the land; merely a right to apply to be registered – a right which the registered proprietor can resist"[66].

Whereas the LRA 2002 contains inbuilt processes superintended by the Registrar of titles for registration of an adverse possessor in deserving cases while generally protective of the registered proprietor, the LRL like the RTA "is not that protective of the existing registered proprietor"[67]. Aside from isolating the existing registered proprietor in the process and denying him of an early response to the claim of the squatter through a counter notice, there is no indication in the provision of section 112(2) of the LRL as to whom the notice shall be served on or whether a response is required.

A spontaneous application to court by the squatter after advertisement or notice without a response from the existing proprietor cannot be a satisfactory compliance with the condition precedent before the action is brought[68]. While the court may likely request that the squatter put the existing proprietor on notice of the application for registration, "it may be difficult to see through the fraudulent designs of a squatter in bye-passing the existing proprietor since, in most cases, the intention of the adverse possessor is in bad faith"[69].

11.5.4 *Registration and overriding interests*

---

for a period of ten years as opposed to a longer period set by the Limitation Act 1980.

[66] E.H Burn, J. Cartwright, Maudsley & Burn's Land Law: Cases and Materials, 9th ed. Oxford University Press 2009, 280.

[67] I.O.Smith, *The Relevance of Adverse Possession as a Registrable Interest under the Lagos State Land Registration Law.* Essays on Lagos State Land Registration Law (A publication of the Department of Private and Property Law, University of Lagos-Nigeria 2017) 1 at 18, 19.

[68] ibid, at 18.

[69] ibid.

The concept of overriding interests is recognised under the LRA 2002 as it is under the RTA and the LRL. Overriding interests are interests which do not appear on the register but which are binding on both the registered proprietor and any person who acquires an interest in the property[70]. These interests "detract from the principle that the register should be a mirror of title"[71] and contradicts the theory of indefeasibility of registered title.

The provision of Schedule 1 paragraph 2 of the LRA 2002 lists as one of the interests that will override first registration, "an interest belonging to a person in actual occupation...except for an interest under a settlement under the Settled Land Act 1925", while the Act listed in Schedule 3 paragraph 2 with reference to a registered disposition, "an interest belonging at the time of the disposition to a person in actual occupation,...except for an interest which belongs to a person whose occupation would not have been obvious on a reasonably careful inspection of the land at the time of the disposition, and of which the person to whom the disposition is made does not have actual knowledge at that time".

The rationale behind these provisions appears to be the "protection against purchasers where needed but it is either not reasonable to expect nor sensible to require any entry on the register"[72]. It does not necessarily protect the interest of the adverse possessor, the basic policy of the Act being the creation of a complete register of land as much as possible[73]. Does this underlying rationale behind the provisions of Schedules 1 and 3 of the LRA 2002 referred to above, the same as the provisions of section 52(h) of the RTA and section 66(f) of the LRL?

The provisions of section 52(h) of the RTA and section 66(f) of the LRL make all registered land subject to certain overriding interests

---

[70] This definition captures the meaning ascribed to it by the LRA 1925 replaced by the LRA 2002, as well as the RTA and LRL.

[71] Burn & Cartright supra (n 3) at 1100.

[72] ibid, at 1101, relying on the Consultative Document on Land Registration for the Twenty First Century (1998), para 4.17: See Law Com No.254.

[73] ibid.

including "rights acquired or in the process of being acquired by virtue of *any enactment relating to the limitation of actions* or by prescription." The right of an adverse possessor as an overriding interest is preposterous and obviously confronting the existing proprietor with a *fait accompli.* This common provision in both statutes which recognises such overriding interest without a legal obligation to register same clearly defeats the notion of indefeasibility of title often associated with registration. It blurs the distinction between registered and unregistered land in determining the status of a registered owner vis-à-vis the squatter in adverse possession and appears to put the adverse possessor in a stronger position as regards registered land than unregistered land.

It is said that "[t]he simple lesson from a juxtaposition of the position in England and Wales, and the position in Nigeria...is that in Nigeria, the register of title has practically ceased to be a mirror of title and no longer serves as notice to the existing registered proprietor to beware". Thus, "the same measure of supervision expected of the owner of unregistered land is expected of the registered proprietor with respect to registered land"[74].

11.5.5 Summary

The effect of adverse possession on registered land varies as between England and Nigeria. Whilst the LRA 2002 applicable in Englanddis-applies the Limitation Act 1980 in relation to registered land by placing emphasis on registration as opposed to possession, the basis of both the RTA and the LRL is clearly shown to be the limitation statutes with emphasis on possession.

The LRA 2002 contains in-built mechanism for registration of an adverse possessor in deserving cases whilst generally protective of the registered proprietor and making his title more secure. It significantly reduces the ability of a squatter to obtain title to the land and brightens the chances of the existing registered proprietor to resist the claim of the

[74] ibid.

adverse possessor and to take steps to recover possession. On the contrary, both the RTA and LRL in Nigeria are not protective of the registered proprietor. Whereas the main objective of the LRA 2002 is to balance the interest of the registered proprietor against public interest, make land available for the market, and make the register a true mirror of title, in Nigeria, the register of title has practically ceased to be a mirror of title and does not serve as notice to the registered proprietor to beware; the same measure of supervision expected of the owner of unregistered land is expected of the registered proprietor with respect to registered land.

11.6 Adverse Possession and Human Rights Challenge

One striking difference as between England and Nigeria before 1998 is that whilst successive Nigerian Constitutions had always guaranteed and protected property rights including possessions along with the right to compensation[75], there was no such specific protection offered under any codified domestic law with regards to England. With no bill of rights in place, it was difficult to subject any law on deprivation of possession to human rights scrutiny and consequently, there was no basis for the courts to hold whether or not statutory provisions relating to adverse possession violated any rule of human right contained in any instrument.

The extant Constitution of the Federal Republic of Nigeria 1999 like the earlier constitutions, not only guarantees and protects property right, but also provides circumstances under which such right may be derogated from to include "any general law relating to limitation of actions"[76]. The consequence of that constitutional provision is that any deprivation of property right including possession resulting from the

[75] The Nigerian Republican Constitution, 1963, s.31; The Constitution of the Federal Republic of Nigeria 1979, s. 40; The Constitution of the Federal Republic of Nigeria 1999 as amended, s. 44. See the Constitution of the Federal Republic of Nigeria, 1999 as amended, s. 44(1).
[76] ibid, s.44(2)(i).

operation of a ''general law'' relating to the statute of limitation shall not amount to deprivation of property right under section 44(1).

The Land Registration Act 1925, the precursor of the Land Registration Act 2002 applicable in England, had certain features which exposed it to human rights challenge. It is said of registered and unregistered land where the period of limitation is completed under the LRA 1925 that:

> ...the paper owner could lose his title in favour of an adverse possessor. There is no requirement for the adverse possessor to give him any formal notice of his possession, or that he is approaching the completion of the limitation period; nor is there any provision for the paper owner to be compensated for his loss of title[77].

This dilemma was confronted by the human rights regime with the advent of the European Convention on Human Rights and its domestication under the Human Rights Act 1998 (HRA) and in particular, its provisions on property rights as contained in Article 1 of the First Protocol to the Convention which provides:

> Every natural or legal person is entitled to the peaceful enjoyment of his possessions. No one shall be deprived of his possessions except in the public interest and subject to the conditions provided for by law and by the general principles of international law.
>
> The preceding provisions shall not, however, in any way impair the right of a State to enforce such laws as it deems necessary to control the use of property in accordance with the general interest or to secure the payment of taxes or other contributions or penalties.

Both the Human Rights Act of 1998 and the Nigerian Constitution protect the interest of the property owner from encroachment or acquisition except in prescribed circumstances. However, derogation from

[77] Burn & Cartwright, Modern Law of Real Property, supra (n.3) at 1164.

such protection by the State depends on varying circumstances as between the two jurisdictions: whereas in England, derogation from protection shall be *in the public interest and subject to the conditions provided for by law and by the general principles of international law*; in Nigeria, the constitutional provisions on protection of property right may be derogated from *in the manner and for purposes prescribed by a law that provides for prompt payment of compensation and access to court by the property owner, to determine the extent of interest and quantum of compensation*. Thus, the scope of appreciation left to the State for the purpose of striking a fair balance between the individual property right and public interest in both jurisdictions differs. Also, whilst the requirement of prompt payment of compensation is a *sine qua non* for taking control or for acquiring such interest compulsorily under the Nigerian Constitution, this is not so provided under the HRA 1998 applicable in England.

However, both the HRA 1998 applicable in England and the Nigerian Constitution contain common exceptions from their provisions on guarantee and protection of possessions. In the case of Nigeria, any deprivation of property right including possession resulting from the operation of a "general law relating to the statute of limitation" shall not amount to deprivation of property right under section 44(1)[78], whilst in the case of England, the second paragraph of Article 1 of the First Protocol of the HRA which provides that "the right of a state to enforce such laws as it deems necessary to control the use of property in accordance with the general interest..." is an exception to the general protection of property right under the general rule.

It follows also that the provisions as to the manner and conditions for such acquisition including payment of compensation are inapplicable. With regard to compensation, the Grand Chamber of the European Court of Human rights held in *UK v. Pye*[79] that:

> A requirement of compensation for the situation brought about by a party failing to observe a limitation period would sit uneasily

[78] ibid, s.44(2)(i).

[79] (2008) 46 EHRR 45.

alongside the very concept of limitation periods, whose aim was to further legal certainty by preventing a party from pursuing an action after a certain date.

This position applies in Nigeria consequent upon the provision of section 44(2)(*i*) which makes the provisions of section 44(1) on guarantee and protection of property and provision on compensation in section 44(1) (a) and (b) inapplicable to *the general law relating to the statute of limitation.*

Also, under the provisions of the Land Registration Act 2002, no compensation is payable by a person who is registered as a new owner of registered land after the fulfilment of the conditions in Schedule 6 of the Act[80]. Same applies in Nigeria under the RTA applicable in the Federal Capital Territory[81], and under the Land Registration Law of Lagos State[82].

The African Charter on Human and Peoples' Rights domesticated in Nigeria as part of the Nigerian domestic law[83] has a similar provision on property rights with implications for the statute of limitation and adverse possession. Article 14 of the Charter guarantees property right which may be encroached upon "in the interest of public need or in the general interest of the community and in accordance with the provisions of appropriate laws".

In terms of content, the provision of Article 14 is vague compared to either section 44 of the Nigerian Constitution which it is meant to complement as a human right instrument, or the provision of Article 1 of the First Protocol of the HRA with which it shares international flavour. It therefore requires judicial interpretation which may be given but not yet, by the domestic court pursuant to Article 26, or by the African Court on Human and Peoples' Rights in respect of which no declaration

---

[80] This case falls outside the provision of Schedule 8 Paragraph 1 of the LRA, 2002.

[81] Registration of Titles Act Cap 181 Laws of Nigeria 1958, s. 62.

[82] Land Registration Law, Lagos State 2015, s. 100.

[83] See the African Charter on Human and Peoples' Rights (Ratification and Enforcement) Act Cap A9 Laws of the Federation of Nigeria 2010.

recognising its jurisdiction is yet to be deposited by Nigeria pursuant to Article 36(4) of the Charter[84].

Article 1 of the First Protocol of the HRA contain a better and much more detailed provisions on circumstances under which the right may be derogated from by the state, than the African Charter. For example, whilst the question whether the derogation clause in Article 14 covers limitation of actions in relation to adverse possession would depend on the court's interpretation of the vague clause on derogation by the state from the property right guaranteed, the second paragraph of Article 1 of the First Protocol of the HRA contains a much more detailed and definitive provision on the subject appropriately interpreted in *Pye* by the Grand Chamber of the ECtHR. Thus, unless the provision of Article 14 of the African Charter is interpreted in light of Section 44(2)(*i*) of the Nigerian Constitution to exempt the "general law relating to statute of limitation" from its ambit, it may be difficult to take a definitive position as the Grand Chamber of the ECtHR did in *Pye.*

Unlike the position in England where *Pye* has shed light on the impact of the human rights regime on the doctrine of adverse possession, there are no judicial decisions in Nigeria on the point, and this may be critical in cases of registered land where, unlike the LRA 2002 which provides some measure of protection for the registered proprietor against the adverse possessor-applicant for registration as a new proprietor of title, both the RTA and the LRL in Nigeria contain no such safeguards. Both statutes entitle the adverse possessor to apply for registration upon showing that the court is satisfied that the title of the registered holder of the land has been extinguished under the limitation law without advance notification of imminent loss of title to the existing proprietor or the opportunity to object to such registration.

The tenacity of the doctrine without some palliatives for loss of title and in circumstances which may appear unfair or unconscionable

---

[84] See Article 36(4) of the Charter which requires a deposit of a Declaration recognising jurisdiction of court to accept cases from individuals and Non Governmental Organisations.

due to absence of good faith, may open doors for human rights challenge in the Nigerian jurisdiction in future. In the case of unregistered title or where only land instrument is registered, enforcement of the limitation law without compensation to the actual owner may work injustice particularly as the law does not take cognisance of the owner's lack of knowledge of the presence or the motive of the adverse possessor.

11.6.1 Summary

The position from a digest of the foregoing analysis is that the law in England and other European countries is that the application of the doctrine of adverse possession is not a violation of the right to property. This is the position of the European Court on Human Rights in *U.K v. Pye* and it is in tandem with the letters and spirit of the extant Land Registration Law 2002. Whatever impression formed by the Land Registry with regards to registered land has to change sequel to that decision.

In Nigeria, the enjoyment of rights in land is subject, among other exceptions, to the law relating to limitation of actions and *ipso facto*, the law of adverse possession. Although there are no judicial decisions unlike the position in England streamlining the parameters of application of the constitutional provisions to the registered or unregistered land, those provisions and the African Charter on Human and Peoples' Rights (ACHPR) would ordinarily apply to unregistered land from the unambiguous provision of section 43(2)(*i*) of the Constitution and, on the face of it, the provision of section 14 of the ACHPR, thereby making it impossible to impugn the application of the doctrine of adverse possession from the human rights perspective. But the same cannot be said of registered land where both the RTA and the LRL do not exude the kind of fairness and equity associated with the reform of the registration procedure under the LRA - a reform which makes vast concessions for registered land owners in England and Wales. Thus, the enforcement of the limitation law against registered proprietors in Nigeria may be subject of human rights challenge in future.

11.7 Adverse Possession and Criminalisation of Squatting

Apart from the local circumstances and the various local statutes making the application of the doctrine of adverse possession by the Nigerian courts questionable, there are statutes criminalising unlawful entry under English and Nigerian law with consequences. First, there is the question whether the acquisition of title by adverse possession which constitutes an offence under a statute criminalising the act of adverse possession is valid. This question is fundamental as the adverse possessor, if found guilty, is not absolved from punishment under the law. The second question is whether the commission of an offence by an adverse possessor may defeat his application for registration under the extant registration laws in England and Nigeria. These questions are examined seriatim from the comparative perspective in this segment.

11.7.1 When Will Acquisition of Title by Adverse Possession Constitute an Offence?

In England and Nigeria, forceful entry into possession is criminalised and does not amount to peaceful possession required to acquire title by adverse possession. In England, both the criminal law statutes[85] and judicial creativity[86] meant to defeat squatter's claim to adverse possession exist. In Nigeria under the Criminal Code (applicable in Southern Nigeria except Lagos State), the Penal Code (applicable in the Northern Nigeria including the Federal Capital Territory), and the Lagos State Property

---

[85] See for example, the Criminal Law Act 1977, s.7; Criminal Justice and Public Order Act 1994

[86] See *Leigh v. Jack* (1879) 5 Exch.D 264; *Wallis's Holiday Camp v. Shell Max* [1975] 1 QB 96; *Beaulane Properties Ltd v. Palmer* [2005] EWHC 817.

Protection Law[87], forceful entry amounting to criminal trespass is also an offence punishable by law[88].

However, different positions prevail between England and Nigeria regarding peaceful entry and acquisition of possession in relation to residential building. A distinction was drawn by the Court of Appeal for England and Wales in *Best v. Chief Land Registrar and Secretary of State for Justice*[89]*(Best)* between a peaceful entry into a residential building and consequent exercise of exclusive possession against the whole world *without living or intending to live there* over a period of limitation on the one hand, and peaceful entry into a residential building by a squatter who *actually lives in it or intend to do so,* which may constitute an offence under section 144 of the Legal Aid Sentencing and Punishment of Offenders Act 2012 (LASPOA). The distinction which is fine but significant is that as between a squatter who took possession of a residential building technically through the exercise of physical possession[90]*with no intention of living therein* on the one hand, and a squatter who actually enters the building *to live there, or having the intention to do so*. Whilst the first scenario may lead to acquisition of title by adverse possession at the expiration of the limitation period and is not caught by section 144 of LASPOA, the second scenario which may also constitute adverse possession, amounts to criminal trespass which constitutes an offence there under.

It is instructive to note that this distinction applies only in respect of residential buildings mainly in England and does not apply to commercial properties. Also, the position under LASPOA does not apply across the federation of Nigeria due to disparity in social circumstances.

Over the decades, the English government has been battling with challenges arising from illegitimate occupation of residential

---

[87] Lagos State Property Protection Law 2016, s. 2.

[88] See the Criminal Code Law applicable in the Sothern states of Nigeria, ss.81 and 82; and the Penal Code Law of the various Northern states of Nigeria including the Federal Capital Territory, s.342.

[89] [2015] EWCA Civ 17.

[90] These may include among others, fencing, renovation of the premises and warding off trespassers.

accommodation by squatters at the slightest opportunity with serious consequences for the home owners and the local councils. The concerns of the public heightened over the difficulty encountered by home owners of residential property in securing the assistance of the Police in evicting squatters there from[91]. In response to consultation published on 26 October 2011, the Parliamentary Under-Secretary of State articulated the position of government as follows[92]:

> …I have been contacted time and time again by MPs and constituents about the appalling impact that squatting can have on their homes, businesses and local communities. This is not media hype. It does really happen; and when it does it can be highly stressful for the owner or lawful occupier of the property concerned. It is not only the cost and length of time it takes to evict squatters that angers property owners; it is also the cost of the cleaning and repair bill which follows eviction. While the property owner might literally be left picking up the pieces, the squatters have gone on their way, possibly to squat in someone else's property.

This was the position in England and Wales in spite of the enactment of the Criminal Law Act 1977 meant to frustrate the illegitimate occupation of squatters on residential premises[93], and the Criminal Justice and Public Order Act 1994 which enhanced Police powers under the Act. Both legislative efforts and judicial creativity[94] meant to defeat squatters' claim to adverse possession on residential premises failed to yield fruitful results. It was against this backdrop that the provision of section 144 of LASPOA was conceived.

---

[91] *Options for Dealing with squatting* (Consultation Paper CP12/2011).

[92] *Government Response to Consultation Paper,* published on 26 October 2011.

[93] Criminal Law Act, s.7. This section enables property owners made homeless as a result of squatters' occupation of their properties to lodge complaints to the Police.

[94] For examples of judicial creativity in this regard, see *Leigh v. Jack* (1879) 5 Ex D 264 (CA); *Wallis's Holiday Camp v. Shell-Max* [1975] 1 QB 94 (CA); *Beaulane Properties Limited v. Palmer* [2005] EWHC.

The social circumstances in Nigeria are different. What is prevalent in Nigeria is land grabbing and land speculation tantamount to acquisition of land by forcible entry. The relevant provisions of both the Criminal Code[95] and the Penal Code[96] were meant to criminalise such forcible entry and penalise the trespasser, and the same situation obtains under the Lagos State Property Protection Law[97]. These laws prohibit forcible entry and illegal occupation mainly; none of these laws prohibits peaceful entry and possession of land whether in respect of residential accommodation or any other. Also, the kind of distinction drawn by the England and Wales Court of Appeal in *Best* between *peaceful possession* by a squatter living or having the intention to live in the residential accommodation and another not living in or having such intention, does not obtain in Nigeria.

Sections 81 and 82 of the Criminal Code and section 342 of the Penal Code contain no provisions directly affecting the regime of adverse possession and the reason is not farfetched. For example, under both Laws, an immovable property such as land is not capable of being stolen; asportation is required. Hence, any other interference with the land by peacefully taking possession of it, or having taken peaceful possession, by peacefully remaining in possession of it and exercising a right inconsistent with that of the land owner, may lead to a claim of adverse possession after the period of limitation, without constituting an offence. On the contrary, the land owner may commit an offence by interfering with the peaceful possession of the squatter through forceful entry[98]. Section 81 of the Criminal Code provides:

> Any person who, in a manner likely to cause a breach of the peace or reasonable apprehension of a breach of the peace enters on land

[95] Criminal Code Act Cap C38 Laws of the Federation of Nigeria 2010, s. 382, 383.

[96] See Penal Code Cap 89 Laws of Northern Nigeria 1963, s. 286.

[97] Lagos State Property Protection Law 2016.

[98] However, recovery of possession may be possible through an action for recovery of possession in court.

> which is in actual and a peaceable possession of another, is guilty of a misdemeanour, and is liable to imprisonment for one year.[99]

This provision which has festered the regime of adverse possession in many parts of Southern Nigeria, has been identified as the reason for the failure of the Nigerian criminal law "[100] to give adequate protection to the true legal and beneficial owners" of land. In the words of Adeyemi:[101]

> ...Once the intruder can gain a peaceful entry on to the land and is in "actual and peaceable possession" of it, then the right of the owner forcibly to eject the intruder will seem to end as otherwise, he may find himself charged with and convicted for forcible entry. This situation is now encouraging a number of problems which are now undermining confidence in dealings in land, and also disorderly behaviour particularly in the Lagos area."

The Lagos State Criminal Law is the only criminal legislation which criminalises peaceful possession which could amount to adverse possession at the expiration of the limitation period. Unlike the position under the Criminal and Penal Codes, conversion of land by a squatter or an encroacher is criminalised under section 278(1)(b) of the Criminal Law of Lagos State as an offence of stealing for which such an adverse possessor may be prosecuted, convicted and sentenced by a court of competent jurisdiction. This position is made clearer from the specific provision of 278(5)(a) which provides that, "in the case of conversion, it is immaterial whether...[the land] is at the time of the conversion in the possession of the person who converts it..." suggesting that peaceable

---

[99] This is replicated in section 52 of the Criminal Law of Lagos State No. 11 2011, although the term of imprisonment prescribed is "two (2) years." See also s. 16 of the Lagos State Property Protection Law 2016 for similar provision.

[100] A. A Adeyemi, "The Criminal Process as a Selection Instrument for the Administration of Criminal Justice." in the *Nigerian Criminal Process,* A.A Adeyemi ed. (1977) University of Lagos Press, 26.

[101] A. A Adeyemi, supra (n 100) at 48.

physical possession which is germane to acquisition of title by adverse possession is an offence under this Law.

Also, section 278(4) of the Law provides that "...conversion may be dishonest, although it is effected *without secrecy or attempt at concealment,*" suggesting that acts of possession exercised openly and without concealment-characteristic of adverse possession, do not negate the mental element of *dishonesty* required for the commission of the offence of stealing.

These provisions, apply to any type of property including residential and commercial property in Lagos State, deviates from the position of criminal law in relation to adverse possession in other parts of the country, and runs counter to the criminal legislation on adverse possession and criminalisation of trespass in England and Wales. Also, unlike the decision of the Court of Appeal for England and Wales in *Best* that section 144 LASPOA does not affect the application of the doctrine of adverse possession, the provisions of the Criminal Law of Lagos State is meant to affect the efficacy of the doctrine and make it inapplicable.

11.7.2 Is the Commission of Criminal Trespass by an Adverse Possessor a Bar to Registration?

The legal doctrine which states that a person will be unable to pursue legal remedy arising out of illegality (*ex turpi causa non oritur actio*) is an age long common law doctrine applicable in all cases where it would be against public policy to entertain a claim which would be unconscionable or repulsive to public morality[102]. A typical example of a situation such as this is where a person seeks to benefit from his own wrongdoing or crime. However, while the doctrine remains a matter of public policy, it is lacking in consistent legal principles, and "that policy is not based upon a single justification but on a group of reasons which vary in different situations"[103]. This was demonstrated by the England and Wales Court of

---

[102] See *Gray v. Thames Trains* [2009] 4 All ER 81.

[103] Per Lord Hoffman in *Gray v. Thames Trains,* supra (n 102) at 91 para.'b'

Appeal in *Best v. The Chief Land Registrar & Secretary of State for Justice*[104] (CLR) (*Best*).

The question which the Court of Appeal had to resolve in *Best* was whether an application for registration under the LRA 2002 by reason of a period of adverse possession is valid where part of the relevant period of possession consisted of the occupation of a residential building in circumstances constituting an offence under section 144 of LASPOA. Whilst the provision of section 144 of LASPOA is silent on its effect on adverse possession, rule 16(3) of the Land Registration Rules 2003 vests the Registrar with the power to reject an application for registration on delivery or cancel it at any time thereafter, if it appears to be substantially defective. The Registrar rejected Mr Best's application for registration on this ground because the application revealed that he was relying on conduct in contravention of section 144 of LASPOA. This reasoning could be said to be in consonance with the principle *ex turpi causa no oritur actio.* However, the England and Wales Court of Appeal, like the lower court, for the various reasons discussed in the last chapter, held that the commission of an offence under LASPOA is not a bar to registration of the offender as a proprietor of registered land after fulfilling the conditions prescribed by the LRA 2002.

There is no judicial decision in Nigeria akin to that in *Best* and various reasons could be responsible for this. First, under both the Registration of Titles Act (RTA) applicable in the Federal Capital Territory (FCT), and the Lagos State Land Registration Law (LRL), the Registrar has no role to play in determining whether or not the title of the adverse possessor is registrable; the Registrar merely acts on the court order for rectification of the register in favour of the adverse possessor as his responsibility is administrative in that regard. The question whether or not adverse possession was acquired in circumstances constituting the commission of a criminal offence ought to have been raised and dealt with (if raised at all) by the court before making an order for rectification of the register. Second, there is no replica of rule 16(3) of the Land

[104] [2015] EWCA Civ 17.

Registration Rules of the LRA regarding the rejection or cancellation of a defective application for registration on the ground contemplated by the Registrar. Third, there is no replica of section 144 in the criminal laws applicable in Nigeria as discussed earlier on.[105]

However, where the Nigerian court is requested to determine the validity of the adverse possession on the same ground as in *Best*, the court will have to construe the existing criminal statutes accordingly to determine the appropriate approach in applying the *ex turpi causa* rule within the parameters of the prevailing circumstances, as it was done in *Best*. Thus, whilst *Best* may not be a binding authority in Nigeria, it could be a valuable compass showing the way to go.

11.7.3 Construing the Nigerian Criminal Law in Relation to Adverse Possession

As discussed in the last chapter, the provisions of the Criminal Code[106] and the Penal Code[107] applicable in the Southern states (except Lagos State) and the Northern states (including the FCT) respectively, criminalise only forceful entry; peaceful entry and exercise of adverse possession for a period limited by the statutes of limitation is not an offence. It follows therefore that the title of such adverse possessor is registrable under the RTA and may be registered upon an order for rectification made by a court of competent jurisdiction.

On the contrary, in Lagos State, the unequivocal provisions of the Criminal Law of the State and the Property Protection Law run parallel to the requirements of adverse possession and make it impossible for time to run in favour of the squatter who may have committed an offence under the relevant Law. Thus while both section 144 of LASPOA and section 278(1)(b),(4) and (5)(a) of the Criminal Law of Lagos State criminalise peaceful entry and possession, the effect of their provisions on the

[105] See Chapter 10 *ante*.
[106] ibid, s. 81, 82
[107] ibid, s. 342.

application for registration of the title of the adverse possessor cannot be the same.

Amongst other reasons adduced by the Court of Appeal in *Best* are: "that Parliament could not have intended section 144 to have any impact on the operation of the doctrine specified in the LRA because of the public policy concerns underlying adverse possession in registered and especially unregistered land"[108]; and that "the Act was for the purpose of providing practical assistance to homeowners in removing trespassers from their property in a less cumbersome and more efficient way under the criminal law instead of the procedures that exist at civil law"[109] These two reasons falter when applied to the Nigerian situation.

Whilst there might be no evidence in the provisions of LASPOA that "parliament could not have intended section 144 to have any impact on the operation of the doctrine specified in the LRA" as the provisions of the Act coincides with the requirements for adverse possession through peaceful possession, the provisions of the Criminal Law of Lagos State and the Property Protection Law of the State run parallel to the requirements to be met for adverse possession and make any entry into possession an offence *in limine*. Again, whilst the LASPOA may seek to assist the homeowners in removing trespassers from their property, the main objective from the tenor of the Criminal Law of Lagos State and the Property Protection Law of the State is to forestall and make impossible any act of adverse possession in the first place.

Consequently, while under the LASPOA regime, a squatter may qualify as an adverse possessor in favour of whom time runs under the Limitation Act 1980 albeit his conduct constituting an offence under the LASPOA, a squatter cannot attain the status of an adverse possessor under the Criminal Law of Lagos State and the Property Protection Law of the State, and automatically commits a crime under those Laws.

---

[108] Law Commission and HM Land Registry Report No. 254, *Land Registration for the Twenty-First Century : A Consultative Document* (1998)

[109] I. Ikeoma, 'The Future of Adverse Possession of Registered Land etc.' Accessed online at www.academic.edu at 15.

Thus, where a claimant of adverse possession approaches the court for an order of rectification of the register and registration as a new proprietor under the Land Registration Law of Lagos State on the ground that the limitation period had run out against the land owner who opposes his claim on the ground that the claimant cannot benefit from his crime under the Criminal Law of Lagos State or the Property Protection Law of the State on the ground of illegality (*ex turpi causa non oritur action*), the court would be faced with the issue of correct interpretation to place on the principle of *ex turpi causa.*

In *Best,* the Court of Appeal observed that the principle is susceptible to different interpretations depending on the peculiar circumstances of each case, and consequently bent towards the "amalgamated approach" of balancing the policy consideration underlying the provisions of the LRA 2002 relating to acquisition of title by adverse possession against the public policy consideration underlying the provision of section 144 of the LASPOA. That approach may not be appropriate in a situation posed by the provisions of section 278 of the Criminal Law of Lagos State and the relevant provisions of the Property Protection Law[110] which, unlike the LASPOA, do not recognise adverse possession, but outlaws same so that there are no two policies to balance, one against the other as the Court of Appeal did in *Best.*

The Nigerian Court may instead be influenced by the statutory policy objectives which is one of the main principles guiding the application of the test of *ex turpi causa* in decided cases[111] . The main policy objective from the tenor of the Law is to criminalise any form of entry or possession albeit peaceful, unlike the provision of LASPOA. In this situation, the court may apply the principle of *ex turpi causa* from the standpoint of this statutory policy objective and may refuse to make an order for the rectification of the register in favour of the squatter.

In view of the criminalisation of adverse possession under the Criminal Law of Lagos State and the Lagos State Property Protection Law,

---

[110] ibid, ss. 2 and 3.

[111] See e.g. *Revill v. Newberry* [1996] 2 W.L.R 239.

section 100 of the Lagos State Land Registration Law[112] has been rendered otiose. Section 100 provides:

> where the court is satisfied that the title of the registered holder of any land or mortgage has been extinguished under the Limitation Law, the court may order the register to be rectified accordingly…

Going by the criminalisation of all acts of adverse possession in Lagos State, it is not likely that the title of the existing registered owner of land would be extinguished under the Limitation Law, and the possibility of admitting such title on the register is remote. It is also yet to be seen how the Nigerian courts would construe the doctrine of adverse possession against the backdrop of the legal principle of illegality enshrined in maxim, '*ex turpi causa non oritur actio.*'

11.7.4 Summary

The criminalisation policy underlying section 144 of LASPOA applicable in England and Wales differs from that underlying the various criminal statutes criminalising peaceful possession in Nigeria from the angle of the varying social circumstances and the main objectives of those statutes. While the criminalisation policy against forceful entry in the jurisdictions under inquiry generally coincide, there is disparity between the kind of peaceful entry and possession tolerable by the various jurisdictions. Indeed, the Criminal Law of Lagos State unlike the Criminal Code applicable in other parts of Southern Nigeria, or the Penal Code applicable in the Northern states of Nigeria including the FCT, do not allow peaceful entry or peaceable possession of another person's land thereby foreclosing acquisition of title by adverse possession. Also, the policy behind the Criminal and Penal Codes in Nigeria in adverse possession cases involving peaceful entry and peaceable possession is not the same as in section 144 of LASPOA.

---

[112] Law No.1 2015.

Whilst there is nothing from the tenor of section 144 of LASPOA suggesting that it was meant to jettison the doctrine of adverse possession, the provisions of section 278 of the Criminal Law of Lagos State and the relevant provisions of the Property Protection Law of the State[113] are apparently opposed to the operation of adverse possession. Consequently, the application of the principle of *ex turpi causa* in both cases cannot be the same for, whilst the situation in *Best* may require weighting the public policies that underlie both the *ex turpi causa* test and that of acquisition of title by an adverse possessor in registered land, the provisions of section 278 of the Criminal Law of Lagos State of Nigeria and the relevant provisions of the Property Protection Law of the State are driven by strong statutory policy against adverse possession.

It is therefore difficult to suggest that the Nigerian courts will follow the decision of the Court of Appeal for England and Wales in *Best* when faced with the same situation, and it is unlikely that a Nigerian court will make an order directing the Registrar of titles in the Lagos State of Nigeria to register an applicant who purportedly acquired title by adverse possession in the course of committing an offence punishable under the Criminal Laws of the State.

[113] ibid, ss. 2 and 3.

CHAPTER 12
THE FUTURE OF ADVERSE POSSESSION

12.1 Introduction

A critical overview of the application of the doctrine of adverse possession in England and Nigeria reveals the social realities facing the application of the doctrine in both jurisdictions. It suggests that the peculiarities of every legal system determines to a large extent, the efficacy of the doctrine. It demonstrates that the need to balance the individual interests in land against a larger public interest is also as crucial as recognising and protecting possessions and property rights. Above all, it has driven home the need for governments to discharge their social responsibility by meeting the housing needs of their citizenry not only as a human right obligation but also as a potent mechanism for solving the problem of homelessness endemic in many jurisdictions.

The responses of governments worldwide in arresting homelessness amidst the Covid-19 pandemic is a testimony to the fact that a strong political will by government to deliver on the housing needs of its citizenry will go a long way in getting homeless people off the streets, and may consequently whittle down the spate of adverse possession claims in many jurisdictions. The proliferation of empty houses owned by government and individuals in England[1] and the geometrical increase in the activities of 'land grabbers' and land speculators particularly in Nigeria[2] call for spontaneous responses by the government in both jurisdictions. There is therefore a human right perspective to adverse possession claims to be addressed by government.

The future of adverse possession under the Anglo-Nigerian law would depend on the contextual overview of the doctrine of adverse possession in contemporary world, the lessons learnt from the application of the doctrine in other jurisdictions outside the focus of this book, and the bitter lessons drawn from the world wide pandemic and the responses

---

[1] See Chapter 9 *ante*.

[2] See Chapter 10 *ante*.

of governments around the world and, in particular, within the jurisdictions under study, to the challenges of homelessness.

12.2 Re-Thinking the Doctrine of Adverse Possession

12.2.1 Adverse Possession and Putting Land to Productive Use

Amongst the well known factors of production[3], land occupies a vantage position; it is not only the platform for the operation of the other factors of production such as labour and capital, it is the whole essence of human existence. The control and management of land use in the public interest is therefore a major concern of governments the world over. Whilst the ownership structure may differ from one jurisdiction to another, certain basic necessities of life such as food, shelter and medication cannot be met, major facilities for decent living and major revenue generating activities on land cannot be accomplished without an effective legal framework regulating ownership and use of land. Intrinsically therefore, mass acquisition or preservation of land is not an end in itself, it is the use of it which the law appreciates and protects.

The doctrine of adverse possession from the Roman law to the English legal jurisprudence facilitates land use, quietens title towards ensuring its certainty, and forecloses stale claims in ensuring an end to land litigation. However, the very essence of adverse possession which is putting the land to productive use is not assured by law. Whilst the statute of limitation may extinguish the title of the landowner in favour of the adverse possessor of unregistered land or registers his title upon fulfilment of certain legal conditions, there is no assurance that the land would be put to productive use. There is therefore a need to ascertain not only that the real owner has been dispossessed of land or has discontinued possession over a period stipulated by the statute of limitation, but also, that the land is being put to productive use by the

[3] Adam Smith recognised Land, Labour and Capital as major factors of production. See Adam Smith (1776) *The Wealth of Nations* B.I. Ch.6

adverse possessor. This lacuna in English law ought to be filled, otherwise the doctrine meant to fulfil the reasonable expectations of people may turn out to be an avenue for illegitimate land acquisition and land speculation tantamount to 'robbing Peter to pay Paul.'

12.2.2 The Requirement of Good Faith as a Mental Element

In many parts of Nigeria and particularly in Lagos State, land grabbing or land speculation is rife resulting in the state criminalising even peaceful entry and peaceable possession of another's land exercised without violence, secrecy or permission[4]. Also, in England and Wales, not all squatters take adverse possession due to homelessness or penchant for use[5]. These facts make it imperative to factor some mental element or motive into the doctrine in contemporary times to enhance its utility as a mode of acquisition of title and separate genuine cases of adverse possession in the public interest from naked 'land theft'[6].

In a 2006 Report of the British Institute of International and Comparative Law[7], it was found that good faith had a role to play in the

[4] Criminal Law, 2011, s.278.

[5] It is said that "squatters are not a homogenous group" for, whilst some has a genuine need of the property, some may have political objectives, some may prefer the "lifestyle of squatting and its cheapness" and others may be a disaffected group or individuals who welcome the freedom and anonymity of squatting…": Department of Environment, *Consultation Paper on Squatting* London HMSO 1975.

[6] A phrase first used by P. J Proudhon in his work *What is Property?* (1840).

[7] The British Institute of International and Comparative Law was asked by Her Majesty's Court Service to conduct comparative research in some common law and civil law jurisdictions with respect to the applicable statutes of limitation. The request was made sequel to counsel appearance before the Grand Chamber of the European Court of Human Rights in *J.A. Pye (Oxford) Ltd v. United Kingdom* wherein the United Kingdom was appealing against an earlier decision of the Court at first instance that "a failure to provide compensation for loss of title to land acquired on expiry of a statutory period of limitation violates Article 1 of Protocol 1 of the Human Rights Convention (Application 44302/02)": See Report

application of the statutory period of limitation in some common law and civil jurisdictions. For example, it was found that in jurisdictions such as France and Spain, "good faith on the part of the [adverse] possessor of the land will significantly reduce the limitation period"[8], whilst the limitation period for acquisition of prescriptive title is shorter in Poland and Sweden when possession was in good faith as opposed to a longer period when possession was in bad faith.[9] These findings, when compared with findings in other jurisdictions (such as Hungary, Germany, and Massachusetts in the United States of America) where evidence of good faith is of no consideration[10], demonstrate the relativity of the doctrine of adverse possession in spite of its recognition generally in the civil and common law jurisdictions[11].

There are strong arguments in favour of considering good faith as one of the requirements for acquiring title by adverse possession. Apart from the fact that acquisition of adverse possession in bad faith (such as where the squatter is aware that he is trespassing on another person's land) upsets the market mechanism for the transfer of property right, it often fails to effectively balance the interest of the individual in his property against public interest of putting land to productive use.

In England and Nigeria, there are no assurances that an adverse possessor acting in bad faith is going to put the land into productive use since that is not a requirement for acquiring adverse possession. Also, in many parts of Nigeria and particularly in Lagos State, adverse possessors are known to be land speculators or 'land grabbers', amassing wealth for self aggrandisement rather than putting such land to productive use.[12]

---

by the British Institute of International and Comparative Law for Her Majesty's Court Service, 'Adverse Possession' available online at www.biic.org/files/2350_advposs_sept_ftnsv3.pdf. Accessed on 5/10/20.

[8] ibid, at 3-5.

[9] ibid, at 7-9.

[10] ibid, at 3, 8, 9, 12.

[11] ibid, at 3.

[12] See Chapter 10 of this book for an exposition of the problem.

The dilemma faced by the Court of Appeal for England and Wales in *Best v. Chief Land Registrar*[13](*Best*) in resolving the conflict between the civil right of the adverse possessor and criminalisation of trespass, and the criticisms engendered by its decision[14], would be obviated in future by drawing a distinction between adverse possession premised on honest but mistaken belief as to ownership of land (good faith), or lack of it. Where a person enters a residential building under a mistaken belief that he owns it, and subsequently meets all other common law requirements of adverse possession, he is entitled to apply for registration under Schedule 6 of the Land Registration Act 2002 without breaching section 144 of the Legal Aid Sentencing and Punishment of Offenders Act (LASPOA) 2002. This reasoning removes the paradox in the position of an adverse possessor who was found to have breached section 144 of LASPOA, but was held in *Best* to be eligible to apply for registration under Schedule 6 of the LRA 2002 with the attendant risk that he could still be prosecuted for the offence, thereby making such acquisition of adverse possession as in *Best*, unattractive.

It is suggested with regards to trespassers or squatters acquiring possession in bad faith (in the sense that they are aware that they are trespassing on land that does not belong to them), that the limitation period should be extended far beyond what the law prescribes at the moment to afford the landowner ample opportunity of retaking possession and putting the land to productive use, or enable the squatter to occupy the land lawfully by granting a licence or a lease. The law in some jurisdictions fixes the limitation period at between twenty and thirty years[15].

---

[13] [2015] EWCA Civ 17.

[14] See I. Ikeoma, 'The Future of Adverse Possession of Registered Land in light of the recent decision of the court in Best v. Chief Land Registrar…' available online at https://www.academia.edu accessed on 5/10/19

[15] Such as the position in France and Poland. See the Report by the British Institute of International and Comparative Law for Her Majesty's Court Service, 'Adverse Possession' supra (n 7).

To discourage landowners from going out of possession and encourage them to put the land into productive use (which is one of the main objectives of adverse possession), it has been suggested for England and Wales that government should levy penal Council tax on absentee landowners who are out of possession for more than a year "in an effort to tackle housing crises in Britain"[16].

12.3 Filling the Gaps in the Legal Framework for the Application of Adverse Possession

There are gaps in the legal framework for the application of the doctrine of adverse possession in jurisdictions under study. The position under the Land Registration Act (LRA) 2002 applicable in England and Wales for example, is that the claim of the adverse possessor may be defeated by an objection from the registered proprietor upon service of notice on the latter by the Registrar and may lead to the eviction of the adverse possessor through eviction proceedings in court. The result as discussed earlier in this work[17] is the development over time of a 'black market' for land titles where the adverse possessor goes underground and refuses to apply for registration of his adverse title. This situation may enure indefinitely until the adverse possessor is found out by the registered owner since registration is not compulsory. Consequently, one of the major rationales of adverse possession which is to quiet title and therefore obviate incessant land disputes is defeated.

It is recommended, following the suggestion of Pawlowski and Brown[18] that registration of title by an adverse possessor be made compulsory and time bound so that failure to register the adverse title

[16] I. Ikeoma, 'The Future of Adverse Possession of Registered Land in light of the recent decision of the court in Best v. Chief Land Registrar…' available online at https://www.academia.edu accessed on 5/10/19.

[17] See Chapter 7 of this book.

[18] M. Pawlowski and J. Brown, 'Adverse Possession and the Transmissibility of Possessory Rights – The Dark Side of Land Registration?' [2017] (2) Conv. 116 at 117, discussed in detail in chapter 7 of this book.

within a stipulated period after lapse of the limitation period extinguishes the title of the adverse possessor. Bringing every land owner on the register in England and Wales would work *in tandem* with the doctrine of adverse possession and strengthen its efficacy in actualising one of its main objectives, which is to quiet title.

In Nigeria, the system of land instrument registration applicable across the thirty six states of Nigeria is a major challenge to balancing the interest of the adverse possessor against that of the innocent third party. Under a system of land instrument registration, a registered deed is not protective of the landowner in any way; not only does it fail to cure defect in title of the landowner, the latter title is subject to existing overriding interests such as adverse possession. Whilst possession of a registered deed of transfer without possession is precarious for the landowner but advantageous to the adverse possessor, an innocent third party purchaser may eventually bear the brunt, since such purchaser would be bound by the interest of the adverse possessor. Even in Lagos State-Nigeria, the interest of the first registered proprietor under what appears to be title registration[19], is subject to all overriding interests including the interest of the adverse possessor subsisting at the time of registration[20]. This is so even where neither the transferor nor transferee had knowledge of the existence of the adverse possessor[21]. It is suggested that unless the interest of the adverse possessor is registered, a third party purchaser for value without notice of the interest of the adverse possessor should take free of it.

---

[19] See the Preamble to the Law which indicates that the Law governs registration of title in Lagos State.

[20] See s. 66(f) of the Land Registration Law of Lagos State, 2015.

[21] Under the Anglo-Nigerian law of adverse possession, Knowledge of the presence of the adverse possessor by an absentee owner is not a bar to the interest of the adverse possessor.

12.4 Amending the Nigerian Land Use Act to Accommodate Adverse Possession

In Nigeria, the regime of the Land Use Act 1978 has made the doctrine of adverse possession inefficacious due to the various provisions making the application of the doctrine difficult or impossible[22]. Whilst section 48 of the Act gives the impression that the common law of England is retained under its dispensation and in line with the reception Statute[23], many provisions of the Act frustrate its application in spite of the Statutes of limitation[24]. Thus, whilst the application of the doctrine in appropriate cases by the Nigerian courts before March 29 1978 when the Act came into effect was in order, cases decided after that date without taking cognisance of the various provisions of the Act were decided *per in curiam* and tantamount to bad law. If the Nigerian jurisdiction is desirous of retaining the doctrine of adverse possession with modifications regarding registered land in line with the position of English law as encapsulated in the Land Registration Act 2002 applicable in England and Wales, an amendment to the relevant provisions of the Act such as sections 11, 14, 37, 43 is suggested.[25] It would however take the ingenuity of the draftsman to align the amendment to fit into the concept underlying the Act which is vesting radical title over land within the territory of the state in the federation in the Governor of the state, and radical title over land in

---

[22] See Chapter 6 of this book.

[23] ibid.

[24] The statute does not apply to title to land unless there is adverse possession: See e.g., the Nigerian Limitation Act 1966, s.19.

[25] It would however take the ingenuity of the draftsman to align the amendment to fit into the concept underlying the Act which is vesting radical title over land within the territory of the state in the federation in the Governor of the state, and radical title over land in the Federal Capital Territory in the Minister on behalf of the President of the Federal Republic of Nigeria. Also, an amendment to the Land Use Act is, like an amendment to the Nigerian Constitution, very difficult to accomplish; the Land Use Act is entrenched in the Constitution of the Federal Republic of Nigeria 1999 as amended, and can only be amended in accordance with the provisions of the Constitution for its amendment: See ss. 9 and 315 (5) (d) of the Constitution

the Federal Capital Territory in the Minister on behalf of the President of the Federal Republic of Nigeria.

Also, an amendment to the Land Use Act is, like an amendment to the Nigerian Constitution, very difficult to accomplish. The Act is entrenched in the Constitution of the Federal Republic of Nigeria 1999 as amended, and can only be amended in accordance with the provisions of the Constitution for its amendment. A bold attempt by the regime of President Musa Yar'Adua to amend the Act as part of the suggested Land Reform under a seven point agenda of that administration in 2007, did not see the light of the day. Not only were the relevant provisions of the Act hampering the application of the doctrine of adverse possession, not contemplated by the provisions of the Land Use Amendment Bill 2009, the Bill was not passed by the National Assembly. However, pending such amendment of the relevant sections of the Act, it is suggested that Nigerian courts should only apply the doctrine of adverse possession to cause of action arising before March 28 1978 and hold that time does not run under the limitation statute against a holder of a right of occupancy after that date since the various provisions of the Act earlier mentioned make adverse possession impossible.

The provision of the State Land Law or Act in Nigeria expressly excluding the application of the doctrine from its ambit also needs to be addressed. An Act of the National Assembly or a Law of the State Houses of Assembly in Nigeria undoubtedly overrides the common law and more so, where there is an express provision against its application. Consequently, the State Lands Act applicable in the FCT and the State Lands Law applicable in the various States of the federation of Nigeria, are not susceptible to the application of the Statutes of Limitation since the requirement of adverse possession is a *sine qua non* for the application of the Statute of Limitation. To preserve the doctrine of adverse possession, an amendment removing the provisions of the Law excluding its application under the State Lands Act or Law is suggested.

12.5 Giving Consideration to the Social Function of Property in Resolving Issues and Conflicts in Property Relations

The concept of social function of property deprecates the idea of property as a subjective and absolute right to property. Property serves a social function in the sense that it creates an obligation on the part of the owner of property to put it into the service of the community which is tantamount to putting it into productive use. It underscores the extinction of title over unproductive land at the end of the limitation period and forms the basis for the protection of the right to housing to accommodate the homeless.

Consequently, it is expected that the State would take cognizance of that significant role of property relations in formulating policies and in making laws to regulate these relations and to resolve conflicts which may arise there from. In appreciating this social function of property, the State is able to harmonise the existing major and marginal interests in property and, through the restorative perspective of criminal justice, re-calibrate the conflict between the squatter, the land owner, the community and the State towards understanding and resolving the conflicts.

12.6 Addressing the Problem of Homelessness

The geometrical progression in population and acute shortage of housing worldwide, the increasing disparities in wealth resource between the world's rich and poor and widespread poverty in the less developed countries, have continued to force many of the world's citizens into homelessness resulting in proliferation of squatting and assertion of squatting rights.[26] This assertion is in line with the old but impactful anecdote by Henry George[27]. In his words:

---

[26] B. Gardiner, "Squatters Rights and Adverse Possession: A search for Equitable Application of Property Laws." [1997] Ind. International & Comparative Law Review, vol. 8:1, 119..

[27] H. George,*Progress and Poverty*(1897) at 241.

> The equal right of all men to use land is as clear as their equal right to breathe the air...For we cannot suppose that some men have a right to be in this world and others have no right.

This thought coincides with the contemporary notion of right to life as contained in the Constitution of many common law countries[28] and many international instruments[29], and has been given very liberal interpretation by the international community[30] and the courts[31].

The international community through the United Nations has been responding over time, to "the condition of the homeless and poorly housed"[32]. Apart from the various international instruments containing provisions on housing[33], Constitutions and pieces of domestic legislation support government policy on delivering on the housing need of the people. In England and Wales for example, the provision of Article 8 of the Human Rights Act 1998 contains provisions safeguarding the right to private and family life which includes the right to housing as it were, whilst paragraph 3 of the Article 1 Protocol 1 empowers the State "to enforce such laws as it deems necessary to control the use of property in accordance with the general interest...". Also, section 37 of the Constitution of the Federal Republic of Nigeria 1999 guarantees and

---

[28] See e.g the Constitution of the Federal Republic of Nigeria, 1999; s. 31.

[29] See International Covenant on Civil and Political Rights (ICCPR), Art. 6 with a corresponding provision on Right to adequate standard of living including Housing as contained in the International Covenant on Social, Cultural and Economic Rights (ICSCER), Art. 11

[30] For the indivisibility and interdependence between the right to life and the right to adequate housing, see UNGA Res. A/71/310.

[31] See e.g the Indian case of *U.P.AvasVikas Perishad v. Friend Coop Housing Society Ltd* AIR 1996 SC 114, where the court held that the interpretation of the right to life under Art. 21 of the Indian Constitution included right to shelter.

[32] ibid, at 120.

[33] See the Universal Declaration of Human Rights (Art. 25); the International Covenant on Economic, Social and Cultural Rights (Art. 11); the International Convention on the Elimination of All Forms of Racial Discrimination (Art. 5); the Convention on the Elimination of All Forms of Discrimination against Women (Art. 14); and the Convention on the Rights of the Child (Art. 27).

protects "[t]he privacy of citizens and their homes", whilst section 44 (1) (i) embraces the general law on limitation of actions as an exception to prohibition of compulsory acquisition of property. Social Movements and pressure groups have been instrumental in stimulating positive policies of government towards provision of housing for the homeless and efficient utilisation of scarce resources in the public interest.

Then came the COVID-19 pandemic worldwide with the attendant misery, hopelessness and despair. Governments all over the world went into panic and started putting measures in place to protect the citizenry. Apart from other palliatives, government saw the need to provide accommodation for the homeless and was able to discharge the social responsibility within weeks[34]. Eviction process through the courts was outlawed in the meantime to facilitate government efforts in keeping vulnerable occupants of tenanted premises safe.[35]

The foregoing intervention by governments locally and by States at various international levels suggest that strong political will is what is required to nip the problem of homelessness in the bud thereby reducing the challenges posed by squatters to home owners and local councils with regard to residential accommodation. When that is accomplished, application of the doctrine of adverse possession becomes essentially

---

[34] For the English position, visit: www.england.shelter.org.uk/legal/housingoptions/covid Accessed on 3/7/2020.

[35] In England and Wales, the initial ban on eviction of tenants and vulnerable occupants by government sometime in March 2020 was extended by two months in a Press Release published in June 2020. The ban includes suspension of evictions from rented accommodation. Government became committed to ensuring that no one is evicted from their home in summer due to corona virus. Also, on the request of the Lord Chancellor, the Civil Procedure Rules Committee agreed to extend the ban on eviction proceedings by a further two months with effect from 25 June 2020. A Working Group was put in place to consider and address so far as possible, matters affecting litigants and the courts when the present stay on possession proceedings is lifted. New court rules will ensure vulnerable renters will be protected when the ban on eviction ends. See www.gov.uk/govt/news/ban-on-evictions-extended-by-2-months-to-further-protect-renters. Accessed on 3/7/2020.

useful in the resolution of boundary disputes mainly, and the essence of running of time under the limitation statutes in other cases guided by the good faith of the adverse possessor as the legislature may deem it necessary.

12.7 Exploring Alternatives for Nigeria: Lessons from Other Jurisdictions

There is hardly a jurisdiction globally where stale claim to land title is encouraged.[36] Stale claims are generally discouraged either by encouraging positive acquisition of title through adverse possession, or by way of negative acquisition of property through the equitable doctrine of laches and acquiescence or the rule of proprietary estoppel. In Nigeria in particular, in addition to the common law devices highlighted, the rule of prescription as encapsulated in the decision of the court in *Awo v. Cookey Gam,* [37] and the rule of *Hauzi*[38] in Islamic law, are all geared towards discouraging stale claims. Also, one of the five ways of proving title to land as formulated by the Supreme Court of Nigeria in *Idundun v. Okumagba*[39]is 'acts of long possession and enjoyment of land'[40] suggesting that it could be used as a defence by a defendant in an action for declaration of title to land by the plaintiff.

However, while the common law jurisdictions have generally retained the application of the law of adverse possession to unregistered

---

[36] That generally was the position of the British Institute of International and Comparative Law in a Report submitted consequent upon directive of Her Majesty's Court Service to conduct comparative research in some common law and civil law jurisdictions with respect to the applicable statutes of limitation. For details and source of information, see (n 7).

[37] [1913] 2 NLR 97.

[38] This rule suggests that time runs in favour of the adverse possessor/squatter against the real owner upon fulfillment of certain established conditions. See *Hunare v. Nana* [1996] 1 NWLR (Pt 425) 381; *Gwadanagaji v. Shalele* [2013] All FWLR (Pt 705)353.

[39] [1976] 10 SC 227.

[40] ibid.

land titles including land covered by mere registration of title deeds, there appears to be consensus of many jurisdictions on its non-applicability or its restricted application to registered land. For example, the Singaporean Land Title Act 1993[41] generally bars application of the doctrine of adverse possession to registered land,[42] while there is restricted application of the doctrine of adverse possession to registered land under the Land Registration Act 2002 [43] applicable in England and Wales. The Law Commission in Hong Kong had in 2014, while recommending the retention of the doctrine of adverse possession as a 'practical solution to some of the land title problems,'[44]suggested that 'when a registered regime is in place in Hong Kong,[45] adverse possession should not extinguish title to a registered estate.'[46]

---

[41] Land Title Act No. 27 1993 which came into force on March 1994.

[42] Section 50 of the Act provides that: 'No title to land adverse to or in derogation of the title of a proprietor of registered land shall be acquired by any length of possession by virtue of the Limitation Act (Cap 163) or otherwise, nor shall the title of any proprietor of registered land be extinguished by the operation of that Act.' This provision applies except where an application of an adverse possessor for registration was pending under the repealed Act before the advent of the new Act or where such adverse possessor was entitled to lodge such application for registration before March 1 1994 (See s. 174 (7)(8) of the Act), in which cases the provisions of the repealed Law enabling registration would apply.

[43] Schedule 6 thereof. Therein, a balance has been struck between 'the conclusiveness of the register, protection of private property right and enabling the law on adverse possession to work in very limited range of situations…[on compelling grounds].' See Reference by the Secretary for Justice and Chief Justice to the Law Commission of Hon Kong on review of existing law on adverse possession in the country.

[44] Law Commission in Hong Kong: Report on Adverse Possession (October 2014) 147. Available online at www.hkreform.gov.hk

[45] Presently, Hong Kong operates a deeds registration system. Although legislation establishing a registration system for title to land has been enacted, it has not come into effect.

[46] Report of the Hong Kong Commission on Adverse Possession (n 44). Para 7.26-7.34

Judicial criticism against application of the law of adverse possession is not unknown. In *Pye*,[47] Neuberger J. described the law as 'illogical and disproportionate',[48] which criticism was echoed by some members of the House of Lords.[49]. This was followed by the decision of the European Court of Human Rights on further appeal where the court held that the appellant's right under the European Convention on Human Rights (domesticated as the Human Rights Act 1998) had been violated and that the appellant was entitled to compensation for the loss of the land.[50] This decision was upturned by the Grand Chamber of the Court narrowly on a majority of 10 to 7 on appeal by the government of the United Kingdom[51] There was criticism and reform advocated by the Supreme Court of India in *Waghajijat v. Harijan & Ors*[52] (following Neuberger J. in *Pye*), and in *State v. Kumar*[53] where Bhandari J. described the law of adverse possession as 'archaic' 'and needs a serious relook in the larger interest of the people.'[54] The court reasoned that 'if the law is to be retained according to the wisdom of Parliament, then the law must require those who adversely possess land to pay compensation to the title owner according to the prevalent market rate of the property.'[55]

Whilst its non-applicability to registered land such as it is the case under the Singaporean Land Title Act 1993,[56] and its applicability to registered land under the Land Registration Law of Lagos State of Nigeria

---

[47] *JA Pye (Oxford) Ltd v. Graham* [2000] Ch 676.

[48] ibid.

[49] See Bingham and Hope LJJ in the House of Lords [2003] 1 AC 419.

[50] *JA Pye (Oxford) Ltd v. United Kingdom* [2005] 3 EGLR 1.

[51] *United Kingdom v. JA Pye (Oxford) Ltd* [2007] ECHR 700.

[52] AIR 2009 SC 103. The court observed that 'the law of adverse possession which ousts an owner on the basis of inaction within limitation is irrational, illogical and wholly disproportionate' and that 'there is an urgent need of fresh look regarding the law on adverse possession.'

[53] [2011] 10 SCC 404.

[54] ibid.

[55] ibid.

[56] supra (n 41).

2015[57] remain examples of two extreme thoughts on the application of the doctrine, the question is: whither Nigeria?

It is argued[58] that '[t]he law on adverse possession in Nigeria is obsolete and archaic...a legislative endorsement of trespass on land and land theft.'[59] Abolition of the doctrine of adverse possession is recommended with the suggestion that 'the gap should be filled by the equitable rule of *laches and acquiescence,* or the rule in *Awo v. Cookey Gam,* or *Hauzi* in Islamic jurisprudence, depending on the nature of the adverse possession being pushed forward as the basis of title to land.'[60]

It is necessary to probe the preference for these three rules since the basis of their application lies in adverse possession of some sorts – in all the three cases for example, the person relying on them must have been exercising a right inconsistent with the right of the real owner over a fairly long period of time without challenge by the real owner. However, there are significant areas of divergence: first, in all the three cases, there is no link with the statute of limitation in force and each could stand on its own without it;[61] second, unlike the common law of adverse possession, no reliance could be placed on any of these three concepts where the real owner had no knowledge of the existence or use of the land by the adverse possessor[62] - there is no acquiescence and time does not run against the real owner unless the latter had knowledge of the adverse possession; third, in any event, the three cases can only be used as a shield of defence in the event of an action for declaration of title by the real

---

[57] As pointed out earlier, it defeats the whole essence of registered title. See Chapter 7 *ante.*

[58] G. Ojo, 'Acquisition of title to land by adverse possession: Need to stop endorsement of land theft.' The Gravitas Review of Business and Property Law March 2019 vol.10 No.1, 85.

[59] ibid 98.

[60] ibid.

[61] The three concepts were developed by the courts without reference to any statute of limitation.

[62] See *Ige v. Dobi* [1993] 3 NWLR (Pt 596) 950; *Awo v. Cookey Gam* (supra).

owner and not as a sword of action by the adverse possessor,[63] or as basis for registration of title unlike the common law of adverse possession;[64] fourth, unlike the common law of adverse possession, it is unthinkable that, in the three concepts, a trespasser will claim title based on his own trespass without more. It therefore, admits flexibility and a wide range of exceptions.[65] The three concepts are therefore based on the general equitable principles of what is fair, just and conscionable in the circumstances, rather than hard core law devoid of minimum moral content. On the strength of these considerations, perhaps the three alternative concepts may constitute the Nigerian law of adverse possession and the Nigerian statutes of limitation may be amended accordingly.

However, while obsolete claim by a plaintiff may be defeated by the defendant's plea of any one of the alternative rules as an adverse possessor depending on whether the claim lies in English law, customary law or Islamic law respectively, the impediment created by sections 11, 14, 27 37 and 43 of the Land Use Act remains to defeat any of those defences. It is also clear that none of the three concepts can override the provisions of the State Lands Act/Law on the exclusion of adverse possession from its ambit.

It is recommended therefore that both the provisions of the Land Use Act which are impediments to the application of the doctrine of adverse possession and the relevant provisions of the State Lands Act/Law excluding the application of the law of adverse possession from its ambit be expunged therefrom for effective application of any of the doctrines suggested as alternatives to fill the gap in the event of abolition of the English doctrine of adverse possession.

---

[63] *Mogaji v. Cadbury Nigeria Ltd* [1985] 7 SC 59; *Atunrase v. Sunmola* [1985] 1 SC 349.

[64] See Chapter 4 *infra*.

[65] For these exceptions, see *Umaru v. Bakosi* [1996] 1 NWLR (Pt 425) 381. These very many exception to the Islamic rule of Hauzi have made it difficult for the adverse possessor to sustain title.

12.8 General Conclusion

A study of the application of the Anglo-Nigerian law of adverse possession engaged in this book has revealed the nature, scope and limitations of the doctrine against the backdrop of the diversity in the social, legal and institutional frameworks applicable in the various jurisdictions. The inevitable conclusion is that whereas the doctrine is a universal concept within the common law and civil law jurisdictions, it is not a one cap fits all, and that the doctrine is susceptible to the applicable local statutes and the peculiarities of the land tenure system in existence in each jurisdiction. As the Grand Chamber of the European Court of Human Rights noted in *UK v. Pye*[66]: "it is characteristic of property that different countries regulates its use and transfer in a variety of ways. The relevant rules reflect social policies against the background of the local conception of the importance and role of property..."[67]

One of the lessons drawn from the discourse in this book is that legal transplant such as the reception of the common law doctrine of adverse possession is susceptible to local circumstances including pre-existing laws such as customary and Islamic law, and extant pieces of legislation. The fact that many jurisdictions across the globe have zero tolerance for stale claims as discussed earlier and that the Nigeria's indigenous legal structure has in-built mechanisms to protect adverse possession as opposed to stale claims, suggest that there is need for recognition of the local construction of adverse possession required for the application of the provisions of the statutes of limitation.

Where the common law doctrine of adverse possession is to be applied, recent developments in England and Wales require that the principle of indefeasibility of title be protected and the end of justice met by making it generally inapplicable automatically to defeat registered title. This position which has been adopted by Singapore and recommended by the

[66] [2007] ECHR 700.
[67] ibid, para 74.

Law Commission in Hong-Kong has introduced 'checks and balances on acquisition of title to land by adverse possession.'[68]

In England and Wales with a monolithic system of land tenure, the efficacy of the doctrine is not in doubt as the courts recognise and protect the doctrine within the regime of the statute of limitation and in ensuring the necessary balance between the demands of the public interest and the interests of the individuals. This plays out well in giving effect to the doctrine as against the criminalisation policy of the State.

Although the doctrine was received into the Nigerian legal system consequent upon colonisation, its application is either excluded or frustrated by local circumstances or local laws. Added to these is the peculiar situation in Lagos State which expressly criminalises acts of adverse possession such as peaceful entry or peaceable possession.

The doctrine of adverse possession does not sit well with the plural system of land tenure and runs parallel to certain provisions of the Land Use Act (which is the principal legislation on title to land in Nigeria) and the State Lands Act/Law. For the doctrine of adverse possession to apply in Nigeria, those provisions of the Act or Law referred to need be amended as suggested.

In England and Wales with a monolithic system of land tenure, the efficacy of the doctrine is not in doubt as the courts recognise and protect the doctrine within the regime of the statute of limitation and ensuring the necessary balance between the demands of the public interest and the interests of the individuals. This applies to both unregistered and registered land and plays out well in giving effect to the doctrine as against the criminalisation policy of the State.

[68] G Ojo, supra (n 58) at 94.

BIBLIOGRAPHY

BOOKS/BOOK CHAPTERS

AA Adeyemi, 'The Criminal Process as a Selection Instrument for the Administration of Criminal Justice' in the *Nigerian Criminal Process,* A.A Adeyemi ed. (1977) University of Lagos Press, 26.

AN Allot, *New Essays in African Law,* London, Butterworth 1970.

AN Allot, *The Future of African Law,* London, Butterworth & Co. (Publishers) Ltd 1960

AWB Simpson, *An Introduction to the History of English Law* (1961) Michigan Law Library, University of Michigan.

Adam Smith, *An Inquiry into the Nature and Causes of the Wealth of Nations* B.I (1776) Ch. 6.

B Goldson, 'Taking liberties: Policies and the Punitive Turns' in H Hendrick (ed) *Child Welfare and Social Policy* (Policy Press, 2005).

Blackstone, *Commentaries on the Laws of England.* http://Avalon lwa.yale.edu>blackstone_bk2

C Nwalimu, *Nigerian Legal System* (2005 New York).

C O Olawoye, *Title to Land in Nigeria* 1974 University of Lagos/Evans Brothers

Cheshire, Burn, Cartwright, *Modern Law of Property* 18th ed. O.U.P. at 1127-1128

D Knowles, *PoliticalPhilosophy* Routledge (2001).

DA Rondinelli et al., *Urban Services in Developing Countries.* Palgrave Macmillan London (1994).

DGN Darby, FA Bosanquet, *A Practical Treatise on the Statute of Limitations in England and Ireland* (W Maxwell & Son 1867) 390.

E. Fernandes, 'The Influence of de Soto's The Mystery of Capital at www.lincolinst.edu/publication/articles/influence-soto-mystery-capital

EH Burn, J Cartwright, Maudsley, Burn, *Land Law: Cases and Materials,* 9th ed. Oxford University Press 2009, 280

FH Ruxton, *Maliki Law* (1916) O.U.P 1976

H Grotius, *The Law ofWar and Peace,* Bk 2 (Kesley translation, Oxford Clarendon Press, 1925).

H Hausmaninger & R. Gamauf, *A Case book on Roman Property Law* (O.U.P USA).

Harpumet et al., Megarry & Wade, *The Law of Real Property* 6th ed. (Sweet and Maxwell 2012).

IA Umezulike, *ABC of Contemporary Land Law in Nigeria*. First ed. (2013) Snaap Press Nigeria Ltd.

IM Valderrama, 'Legal Transplants and Comparative Law.' Available online at https//researchgate.net/publication/256014383_Legal_Transplants_and_Comparative_Law (December 2004). Accessed on 16 January 2020.

IO Smith, et. al, (eds) *Essays on Lagos State Land Registration Law,* Department of Private and Property Law, University of Lagos (2012).

IO Smith, *Practical Approach to Law of Real Property in Nigeria* (Revised ed.) 2013 Ecowatch Publications Nigeria Ltd

J Bentham, 'Anarchical Fallacies Nonsense upon stilts' in *Bentham, Burke, and Max on the Right of Man,* Waldron ed., (London, Menthuen, 1987) 53.

JA Bentham, *Fragment of Government and an Introduction to the principles of Morals and Legislation* (1776, Harrison W. Ed 1948) 3 para 2.

J Hiatt and J Hladik, *Adverse to Change: A Modern look at Adverse Possession.* Centre for Rural Affairs. www.cfra.org

J Bentham, *Theory of Legislation* London, Trubner & Co. (1914)

J Bentham, *Fragment of Government and an Introduction to the Principles of Morals and Legislation* (1776, Harrison W. ed 1948)

J Churchill et. al, (eds) *Of the Law of Nature and Nations* (1703)

J Duddington, *Land Law,* second ed. Pearson (2014).

J Dukeminier, J Krier, *Property* 112 (1981).

J Dukeminier & J.E Krier. *Property 131* (4th ed. 1998).

J Locke, *Two Treatises of Government* (1690 Laslet P (ed) 1963 Oxford Blackwall (1966)

J Waldron, *The Right to Private Property,* (Oxford Clarendon Press 1988).

JGN Darby and FA Basanquet, *Practical Treatise on the Statute of Limitationsin England and Ireland* (W Maxwell & Sons 1867).

JO Ogbonaiya & H Chioma, *Legal Transplant:An Appraisal.* Journal of Law, Policy and Globalisation vol 5 (2016).

JS Mill, *Principles of Political Economy* (1902) University of Chicago Press 1993

K Gray, *Elements of Land Law* (1989).

K Gray and SF Gray, *Elements of Land Law* 5th ed. Oxford University Press (2009) 1183.

K Green, 'Citizens and Squatters: Under the Surface of land law' in S. Bright and JK Dewar (eds) *Land Law: Themes and Perspectives* (1998)

L Duguit, *Las Transformaciones Del Derecho Publico Y Privado* (Editorial Italiasta 1975)

L Lomansky, *Persons, Rights and the Moral Community* 111-51 (1987).

LW King, *Code of Hammurabi,* Yale Law School., Lilian Goldman Law Library.

M Rayned, *Adverse Possession of Land.* Encyclopaedia Britannica.

Mayyarah Vol II 164, *Maliki Law* (Summary Translation of Mukhtasha Khalil by Ruxton) 309 para 1698.

MJ Radin, *Reinterpreting Property* (University of Chicago Press, 1993).

N Wates & C Walmar, *Squatting: The Real Story*(London Bay Leaf Books, 1980)

OW Igwe, *Land Instruments Registration Law and Practice in Nigeria* (2014) Lap Lambert Academic Publishing 14

PA Oluyede, *Modern Nigerian Land Law,* Evans Brothers (Nig. Publications) Ltd (1989).

Pollock and Maitland, *History of English Law,* 46

R Posner, *Economic Analysis of Law*(2nd ed. 1977).

RW James, *Modern Land Law of Nigeria* (1973, University of Ife Press).

S Bright & JK Dewar (eds) *Land Law: Themes and Perspectives* (1998) 229

S Jordan and O Radley-Gadner, *Adverse Possession* 2nd ed. Bloomsbury Professional Ltd 2011 West Sussex, England-UK.

S Munzer, *A Theory of Property* (Cambridge University Press, 1990).

S Pufendorf, *Of the Law of Nature and Nation.* J. Churchill et. al, (ed) (1703)

The Doctrine of Adverse Possession Law. Essays, Law Teacher, U.K.' (Nov. 2013).www.lawteacher.net

Thompson on *Real Property*(Davis A Thomas ed. 1994).

Van der Walt, *Property in the Margins,* Oxford: Hart Publishing 2009.

WL Morison, *John Austin,* Stanford: Stanford University Press 1962

W Allan, *Legal Transplants,* 1974 Edinburgh Scottish Academy Press Ltd.

W Hayes, *An Introduction to Conveyancing* (5th ed. Sweet 1840, vol.1).

JOURNAL ARTICLES

A Abdi, Derogation from Constitutional Rights and Implications under the African Charter on Human and People's Rights' (2013) 1 LDD 78.

A Ali, 'Derogation from Constitutional Rights and Its Implications under the African Charter on Human and Peoples' Rights (2013) 1 LDD 78.

A Bello, 'Review of the Housing Policies and Programmes in Nigeria' (2019) International Journal of Contemporary Research and Review at 20603.

A Klass, 'Response Essay: The Personhood Rationale and its Impact on the Durability of private Claims to Public Property.' 103 GEO L.J 41 (2014).

AC Meredith, 'A Paradox of Sugden's' (1918) 34 LQR 253.

AK Otubu, "Land Use Act and Land Administration in the 21st Century Nigeria: Need for Reforms. " Journal of Sustainable Development Law and Policy (2018) vol. 9(1) 80-108.

AK Otubu "Statute Review: Lagos State Property Protection Law 2016". SSRN Electoral Journal, DOI: 10.2139/ssrn.3505638.

B Baruch, 'Adverse Possession and Human Rights', L&T Review (2008), 12(1), 3-5.B Gardiner, 'Squatters' Rights and Adverse Possession.' (1997) IND. International and Comparative Law Review, vol. 8:1 at 125.

BN Obiadi et al, 'House Inadequacy in Nigeria: The Case of Failed House Policies.' Tropical Built Environment Journal (TBE) vol. 1 No. 6, 2017 at 52.

CJ Musa, 'Effects of Activities of Land Speculators on Women Farmers' Crop Output and Income in Kuje Area Council, FCT Abuja Nov. 2015.

CM Merrill, 'Property Rules, Liability Rules and Adverse Possession' (1984-85) 79 Northwestern University Law review, 1122.

CM Rose, "Possession as origin of property." 52 Univ. Chicago L. Review 73 (1985)

D O'Mahony & LF O'Mahony, 'Crime as Property: A restorative perspective on the criminalization of squatting and the 'ownership' of unlawful occupation. University of Essex available online at www.researchgate.net.

DL Rosendorf, 'Homelessness and the Uses of Theory: An Analysis of Economic and Personality Theories of Property in the Context of Voting Rights and Squatting Rights.' 45 U. Miami L. Rev. 701, 772 (1990-1991).

E Fernandes, 'The Influence of de Soto's *The Mystery of Capital.*' www.lincolnist.edu/publication/articles/influece-soto-mystery-capital

EM Panalver & SK Katyal, 'Propert Outlaws' University of Pennsylvania Law Rev. [2007] vol. 155 No. 5. 1095.

ER Claeys, 'Locke Unlocked: Productive Use in Trespass, Adverse Possession, and Labour Theory,' (2012) George Mason University Law and Economics Research Paper Series, 1-70.

E. Ekhator, 'The Impact of the African Charter on Human and Peoples' Rights on domestic law: A case study of Nigeria.' (2015) Commonwealth Law Bulletin vol 41 No. 2 253 at 255.

G Calabresi, AD Melamed, 'Property Rules, Liability Rules, and Inalienability: One view of the Cathedral,' (1972) 85 Harv. L. Rev. 1089, 1093-94.

G Calabresi, AD Melamed, 'Property Rules, Liability Rules, and Inalienability: One view of the Cathedral,' (1972) 85 Harv. L. Rev. 1089, 1093-94.

G Ezejiofor, 'The Land Use Decree: A Critique. 'Paper presented at an International Conference in New York, September 1980.

G Ojo, 'Acquisition of title to land by adverse possession: Need to stop the endorsement of land theft.' The Gravitas Review of Business and Property Law, March 2019 Vol 10 No.1.

H Demsetz, 'Towards a theory of Property Rights' American Economic Review: Proceedings and Papers, 57 at 348 (1967).

HR Helmholz 'Adverse Possession and Subjective Intent', 61 WASH. U.L.Q 331(1983).

HW Ballantine, 'Title by Adverse Possession', Harvard Law Review, vol. 32 No. 2 (Dec 1918) 135.

I Issaias, Property Law and Human Rights (2020)I Okeoma, 'The Future of Adverse Possession of Registered Land in light of the recent decision of the court in *Best v. Chief Land Registrar…*' available online at https://www.academia.edu

I Okeoma, 'The Future Of Adverse Possession of Registered Land: In light of the recent decision of the court in Best v. Chief Land Registrar, does section 144 of the Legal Aid, Sentencing and Punishment of offenders Act 2012 clarify the rationale for the operation of adverse possession in registered land under the new scheme or was Best wrongly decided?' htpps://www.research.aston.ac.uk .

IM Valderrama, 'Legal Transplant and Comparative Law' https//researchgate.net/publication/256014383_Legal_Transplants_and_Comparative_Law(Dec2004)

IO Smith, 'Legal Transplant in a Developing Society: A Critical Appraisal of the Reception of English Law in Nigeria.' Lagos State University (1987) Faculty of Law Seminar Series vol. 1 at 1

IO Smith, 'The Relevance of Adverse Possession as a Registrable Interest under the Lagos State Land Registration Law.' Essays on Lagos State Land Registration Law.' A Publication of the Department of Private and Property Law, University of Lagos-Nigeria. (2017) 1.

I Toukochoriti, 'Comparative Rights Jurisprudence: An Essay on Methodologies.' Special Issues Comparative Law LaM November 2017, DOI: 10.5553/REM/.000030.

J Getzler, 'Theories of Property and Economic Development.' Journal of Interdisciplinary History, XXVI: 4 (1996).

JA Clarke, 'Adverse Possession of Identity: Radical Theory, Conventional Practice' Oregon Law Review (vol. 84, 2005)

JA Omotola, "The Adverse Possessor of Registered Land."Nig. Law Journal vol. 7, 38 at 39

JE Stake, 'The Uneasy Case for Adverse Possession'. 89 Geo. L.J 2419 at 2435

JH Beckstrom, 'Reception of Law in Ethiopia.' American Journal of Comparative Law vol. 21, 557

JW Singer, 'The reliance interest in property.' 40 Stanford Law Review 611 at 666-667 (1988).

JO Ogbonnaya, H Chioma, 'Jurisprudential Issues Arising from Legal Transplant: An Appraisal.'Journal of Law, Policy and Globalisation vol. 50 (2016).

K Green, 'Citizens and Squatters: Under the surfaces of land law' in Bright S. & Dewar J.K. (eds.) Land Law: Themes and Perspectives (1998) 229 at 243.

L Griggs, 'Possession Indefeasibility and Human Rights' (2008) 8(2) QUT Law JJ 286.

LA Fennell, 'Efficient Trespass: The case of bad faith', 100 Northwestern University Law Review (2006).

L Katz, 'The Moral Paradox of Adverse Possession: Sovereignty and Revolution in Property Law' (2010) 5 McGill Law Journal, 47

LA Fennell, 'Efficient Trespass: The Case of bad faith', 100 Northwestern University law Review, (2006) 1037.

M Dixon, 'Adverse Possession and Human Rights (2005) Conv. 160-165.

M Dixon, 'Criminal Squatting and Adverse Possession. The Best Solution? (2014) Journal of Housing Law, vol. 17 at 94.

M Dixon, 'Human Rights and Adverse Possession: the final nail? Conveyancer and Property Lawyer, 2008, 2 160-165.

M Nicole, 'The Fiction of Adverse Possession: An alternative conceptualization of the right to control land.' 2017 (A thesis submitted for the Degree of Doctor of Philosophy) Leicester University.

M Pawlowskiand J Brown, "Adverse Possession and the Transmissibility of Possessory Rights – The Dark Side of Land Registration?" (2017) (2) Conv. 116 at 117; [2017] (2) Conv. 116-131.

M Rayned, 'Adverse Possession of Land'. Encyclopedia Britannica, last updated February 2020.

MJ Radin, 'Time, Possession and Alienation' 64 WASH U L.Q 739, 739-74.

MJ Radin, 'Property and Personhood' (1982) 34 Stanford Law Review 957 at 959

MR Baron, '*Weeks v. Krysa*: Cultivating the Garden of Adverse possession' 62 Me. L. Rev. 289 (2010).

N Cobb, L Fox, 'Living outside the system?' The (im) morality of urban squatting after LRA 2002.' (2007) Legal Studies 27(2).

N Curwen, 'The Squatter's Interest at Common Law' (2000) Conv 528, 532-33

N Ogbu, 'The African Charter on Human and Peoples' Right as Incompatible with despotism: The Nigerian Experience (2005) 8 UBLJ 113

OW Holmes, 'The Path of the Law (1897) 10 Harvard Law Review 457 at 477.

P Kenna, 'Globalisation and Housing Rights.' Indiana Journal of Global Legal Studies vol. 15 No. 2 (2008) 436.

Pollock and Maitland, *History of English Law*, 46

R Lowie, 'Incorporeal Property in Primitive Society' 37 Yale Law Journal at 551 (1928).

RA Posner, 'Savigny Holmes, and the Law and the Economics of Possession' 86 VA.L.Rev. 535, 559-60 (2001)

S Panesar, (2000) Theories of Private Property Denning Law Journal, Vol. 15, 113 at 118.

S Panesar and J Wood (2007), 'Adverse Possession and the European Convention on Human Rights 1950 Protocol 1 art. 1.' Coventry Law Journal, vol. 12(2), 41 at 54.

SL Martin, 'Adverse Possession: Practical Realities and an Unjust Enrichment Standard' Frank G Zarb School of Business, 2008.

SR Foster & D Bonilla, 'The Social Function of Property: A Comparative Law Perspective.' Fordham Law Review [2011] vol. 80 101.

TW Merrill, 'Property Rules, Liability Rules and Adverse Possession (1984-85) 79 Northwestern University Law Review, 1122.

BOOK REVIEW

DC Miller, Book Review on AJ Van der Walt, University of Aberdeen Edinburg Law Review (2010) vol. 14.

ANCIENT CODE

Code of Hammurabi: Translated by LW King, Yale Law School, Lilian Goldman Law Library, The Avalon Project, 2008. Available at Avalon.law'.yale.edu/ancient/hamframe.asp

INTERNATIONAL CONVENTIONS, COMMENTARIES AND GUIDES

African Charter on Human and Peoples' Rights. Convention on the Rights of Persons with Disabilities (CRPD).

Convention on the Elimination of All Forms of Discrimination Against Women (CEDAW).

Convention on the Rights of the Child (CRC).

European Convention on Human Rights (213 U.N.T.S 221, E.T.S).

European Convention on Human Rights, 4th ed. (ICJC 5132.A41 95 V36 2006)

International Covenant on Economic, Social and Cultural Rights (ICECSR)

International Convention on the Elimination of All Forms of Racial Discrimination.

(CERD)

Human Rights Guide on Art. 8 of the European Convention on Human Rights.

Practitioners Guide to the European Convention on Human Rights, 3rd ed. (KJC5132 R45 2008).

Short Guide to the European Convention on Human Rights 3rd ed. (KJ5132.G66 2005)

Theory and Practice of the European Convention on Human Rights 4th ed. (KJC5132.A 4195V36 2006).

Additional Practice Guide LRPG005, Sept14 2007.

GOVERNMENT/LAW COMMISSION/NGO REPORTS AND CONSULTATIONS

Department of Environment, Consultation Paper on Squatting (London, HMSO 1975).

First Report of the Commissioners on the Law of Real Property (1829)

21st Report of the Law Reform Committee 1977.

Report of the British Institute of International and Comparative Law for Her Majesty's Court Service, September 2016.

Report No. 271 of the Law Commission, UK 2002.

Law Commission /HM Land Registry, Land Registration for the Twenty First Century: Consultation Document (1998) No. 254.

The Law Commission Consultation Paper, Updating the Land Registration Act 2002, No. 227 (2016).

Home Office, Squatting: A Home Office Consultation Paper (London HMSO 1991).

Options for dealing with squatting (Consultation Paper CP12/2011).

Government Response to Consultation published 26 October 2011.

Law Commission in Hong Kong: Report on Adverse Possession (October 2014).

Amnesty International Nigeria: The Human Cost of a megacity: Forced Evictions of the Urban Poor in Lagos 2017.

Amnesty International Nigeria: Analysis of the Air Force Raid in Adamawa State 2018.

Joint Public Statement of Amnesty International, Justice and Empowerment Initiative and Nigerian Slum/Informal Settlement Federation, 13 February 2017

MEMORANDA

FD Lugard, *Political Memoranda* No. 10 Lands, para 7.

Ph.D THESES

MS Dockray, *Adverse Possession and the Limitations of Actions to Recover Land*. Thesis submitted for the degree of Ph.D in Laws of the University of London, 1984 at 414.

M Nicole, *The Fiction of Adverse Possession: An alternative conceptualization of the right to control land* 2017. (A thesis for the degree of Doctor of Philosophy), Lancaster University.

CONFERENCE PAPERS

AO Okuniga, 'The Land Use Act 1979 and Private Ownership of Land in Nigeria' Text of a paper delivered at the Law Teachers Conference at the University of Ife, 1979.

G Ezejiofor, 'The Land Use Decree: A critique.' Paper presented at the International Conference in New York, September 1980

NEWSPAPER ARTICLE AND EDITORIAL

L Akintola, 'Why Land Grabbers Are on the Prowl' Independent Newspapers Nigeria, 15th December, 2018.

'Nigeria: The Agony of Repossessing Buildings from Squatters.' This Day Newspapers, 28 September 2013.

INDEX

A

B

C

I

J

L

R

S

T

www.ingramcontent.com/pod-product-compliance
Lightning Source LLC
LaVergne TN
LVHW102009210926
848483LV00010B/237
* 9 7 8 1 8 7 1 8 9 1 4 3 0 *